DEMCO

Special Education:
Research and Practice:
Synthesis of Findings

Other titles of related interest

WANG *et al.*
Handbook of Special Education, Volume 1: Learner Characteristics and
Adaptive Education

WANG *et al.*
Handbook of Special Education, Volume 2: Mildly Handicapped Conditions

WANG *et al.*
Handbook of Special Education, Volume 3: Low Incidence Conditions

McLEOD and CROPLEY
Fostering Academic Excellence

STEPHENS *et al.*
Teaching Mainstreamed Students, 2nd Edition

MORRIS and BLATT
Special Education: Research and Trends

Special Education: Research and Practice: Synthesis of Findings

Edited by

MARGARET C. WANG
Temple University, Philadelphia, USA

MAYNARD C. REYNOLDS
University of Minnesota, Minneapolis, USA

HERBERT J. WALBERG
University of Illinois at Chicago, USA

PERGAMON PRESS
Member of Maxwell Macmillan Pergamon Publishing Corporation
OXFORD · NEW YORK · BEIJING · FRANKFURT
SÃO PAULO · SYDNEY · TOKYO · TORONTO

U.K.	Pergamon Press plc, Headington Hill Hall, Oxford OX3 0BW, England
U.S.A.	Pergamon Press, Inc., Maxwell House, Fairview Park, Elmsford, New York 10523, U.S.A
PEOPLE'S REPUBLIC OF CHINA	Pergamon Press, Room 4037, Qianmen Hotel, Beijing, People's Republic of China
FEDERAL REPUBLIC OF GERMANY	Pergamon Press GmbH, Hammerweg 6, D-6242 Kronberg, Federal Republic of Germany
BRAZIL	Pergamon Editora Ltda, Rua Eça de Queiros, 346, CEP 04011, Paraiso, São Paulo, Brazil
AUSTRALIA	Pergamon Press (Australia) Pty Ltd, PO, Box 544, Potts Point, NSW 2011, Australia
JAPAN	Pergamon Press, 5th Floor, Matsuoka Central Building, 1–7–1 Nishishinjuku, Shinjuku–ku, Tokyo 160, Japan
CANADA	Pergamon Press Canada Ltd, Suite No. 271, 253 College Street, Toronto, Ontario, Canada M5T 1R5

Copyright © 1990 Pergamon Press plc

First edition 1990

Library of Congress Cataloging in Publication Data
Special education: research and practice: synthesis of findings/edited by Margaret C. Wang, Maynard C. Reynolds, Herbert J. Walberg.
1st ed.   p. cm.
Summary volume to: Handbook of special education.
1. Special education.   2. Special education—United States.   3. Handicapped—Education—United States.
I. Wang, Margaret C.   II. Reynolds, Maynard Clinton.
III. Walberg, Herbert J., 1937– .   IV. Handbook of special education.
LC3965.S65 1989   371.9'0973—dc20   89—71366

British Library Cataloguing in Publication Data
Special education: Research and practice: synthesis of findings
1. Special education
I. Wang, Margaret C.   II. Reynolds, Maynard C.   III. Walberg, Herbert J.   371.9

ISBN 0-08-040238-0 Hardcover
ISBN 0-08-040237-2 Flexicover

Printed in Great Britain by BPCC Wheatons Ltd, Exeter

Contents

Contents

Preface

Significant progress has been made, especially in recent decades, in providing equal access to free and appropriate schooling for students. At this point in our history, nearly all school-age children in the United States and other industrialized countries attend school. This effort to achieve universal and effective education is based on a recognition of the rights of children to basic education that enables them to thrive in a complex society, as well as a realization that technological and economic growth is facilitated by increasing the number of students, even those with poor academic prognoses, who are, in fact, successful in school learning. Thus, recent and current efforts to improve schooling serve both private and social interests.

In the United States, as in many other parts of the world, we are engaging in a new wave of education reform efforts, particularly the improvement of schools' capabilities to serve students who have greater-than-usual needs for educational support but were often either left out of earlier reform movements or kept on the sidelines. The students we refer to are those with physical, behavioral, or cognitive disabilities; students from economically, culturally, or language-disadvantaged backgrounds; and students with chronic low achievement or those who otherwise can be considered academically at risk.

Over the past several years 70 scholars have collaborated in making a review of research and practices in the field of special education. The results are now available in a three-volume publication by Pergamon Press titled *Handbook of Special Education: Research and Practice*. Forty-five chapters are included in the three-volume series, and each chapter falls under one of nine subdomains in special education. These subdomains are: (1) Learning Characteristics of Handicapped Students and the Provision of Effective Education, (2) Effectiveness of Differential Programming in Serving Handicapped Students, (3) Noncategorical Programming for Mildly Handicapped Students, (4) Mild Mental Retardation, (5) Behavioral Disorders, (6) Learning Disability, (7) Education of Deaf Children and Youth, (8) Education of Visually Handicapped Children and Youth, and (9) Handicapped Infants. The appendix in this volume contains a complete listing of content and authors for the larger

three-volume publication. By using this appendix, readers will be able
to turn to the more complete reports comprising the three-volume *Handbook* publication.

This book is composed of summary chapters written by nine of the
authors who served as section editors of the subdomains included in the
original three-volume series. Each chapter covers one of the subdomains. A brief tenth chapter has been added as an Epilogue. In the
Epilogue some license is taken in presenting several general observations about research and practice in special education, along with a
'future scenario' that reflects how we would like to see special education
develop. We hope the ideas presented in the Epilogue will help to keep
this book off the shelf and contribute to significant dialogue regarding
the future of special education.

The various authors involved in writing chapters for the three-volume
Handbook were asked, first, to summarize the research in their assigned
field, defining research broadly to include all forms of inquiry which help
to create and confirm knowledge. We refer to this first task as describing
the "state of the art." Authors were then asked to describe the "state
of practice" in the same field and to note where, in their judgments,
practices tend to fall below standards suggested by the "state of the art."
Where significant discrepancies were observed, authors were asked to
propose promising activities to improve practices. They were also asked
to suggest areas of needed research and policy change. Thus, although
a main function was to review or synthesize research, there was also a
call for practical deliberations about the quality of present practices and
suggestions for improvement in each field. That same perspective is
carried through in this summary volume.

A second perspective concerning the entire effort, as summarized
in this book, derives from the movement to provide more inclusive
arrangements for disabled persons and for others who often find themselves at the margins of schools and other institutions. These efforts are
variously described as deinstitutionalization, normalization, and mainstreaming. Even persons with severe impairments are now less often
segregated in special enclaves and more often mainstreamed into ordinary community situations. As a result, it is critical that the findings
from research on persons with special needs be made available to
broader groups than ever before, and that the future research be conducted in new settings and on the specific processes of change involved in
implementing new policies. In a sense, research needs to be "mainstreamed." Accordingly, the reviews reported here are intended to
reach a wide range of readers.

The need to coordinate services across a wide range of caretakers and
agencies provided a third perspective for the research syntheses.
Specifically, special education must be coordinated with services such

as health and welfare, family services, correction, rehabilitation, and employment assistance. Many of the "new morbidities," such as child abuse, drug addiction, and the erosion of "natural" support systems as a consequence of broken family structures and incomplete mother–child attachments, have grave effects on school children. Often, children who are referred to special education programs come from unsupported families and disordered communities. Schools must respond by linking up with other community agencies in order to construct high-quality, broadly coordinated programs for students and families with special needs. At the same time, it is necessary to recognize and delimit the special functions of the schools. The research summaries reported here were designed to be instructionally relevant, while also acknowledging the larger networks of service to which educational processes must be linked.

The dependence of special education on public policy and legal imperatives is yet another perspective that has guided the work summarized here. Several reports, court decisions, and policies have enlarged this perspective in recent years. Examples include Nicholas Hobb's 1975 work entitled, *The Futures of Children* (San Francisco, CA: Jossey-Bass); and the 1982 report by the National Academy of Sciences Panel on Selection and Placement of Students in Programs for the Mentally Retarded, entitled *Placing Children in Special Education: A Strategy for Equity* (K. A. Heller, W. H. Holtzman, and S. Messick, Editors, Washington, DC: National Academy Press). These and other reports by leading scholars cast doubt on some of the long-standing policies and practices of special education.

The courts also have had far-reaching effects on educational policy. For instance, the 1972 decision of *Larry P. v. Riles* (Civil Action N.L.-71-2270, 343 F. Supp. 1306, N.D. Cal., 1972) held that the use of intelligence tests as a prime determiner of the classification and placement of children as educable mentally retarded is unconstitutional. Similar court decisions have been the basis for many program changes. Clearly, the field of special education is held accountable to the procedural standards and practices outlined by binding court decisions. Thus, the research reviews summarized in this work were sensitive to studies of policy and policy related developments.

Finally, the research syntheses took account of the rising public concern over the general quality of schools, as expressed in the widely heralded 1983 report by the National Commission on Excellence in Education entitled, *A Nation at Risk: The Imperative for Educational Reform* (Washington, DC: U.S. Department of Education), as well as at least a dozen other recent and significant national reports. They reflect growing public demand for better instruction and for a greater focus on all forms of school accountability, including a commitment to provide the greater-than-usual educational interventions required by students who are difficult to teach. Because recent developments in special education (e.g., more individualized planning, closer partnerships with parents, better measurements of instructional outcomes) are congruent with the increasing general demands made of schools, it should be possible, as we see it, for special educators to be helpful in the general reform of schools. To this end, the authors of the chapters in this Summary Volume sought to define the knowledge base and extend its application in the field of special education in the broadest and most helpful way. Just as students with special needs are no longer isolated in the schools, research and practices in special education should no longer be treated in isolation.

The schools of the United States are now well into the second decade under the mandates of changed national policy concerning special education and related services for students with special needs. We refer to the very important Public Law 94–142, passed by the Congress in 1975 and made effective in 1977. However, the authors of this Summary Volume have been mindful of the international scope of the research literature and of the similarity in trends and problems surrounding special education throughout the world.

The work leading to this book had its beginning several years ago in a project funded through our response to a "request for proposal" from the Office of Special Education and Rehabilitation (OSER) of the U.S. Department of Education. We are grateful for the opportunity to work with Nancy Safer, Judy Fine and other staff of OSERS in implementing the project. We cannot adequately express the appreciation we feel for the 70 authors of the three-volume *Handbook*, and the more than 100 reviewers who helped by providing sound judgment and advice that were invaluable to our editorial process. Special appreciation goes to the nine section editors of the *Handbook* who also joined with us in preparing this summary volume: Kenneth Kavale, Daniel Reschly, Frank Wood, Barbara Keogh, Joseph Fischgrund, Geraldine Scholl, and Verna Hart. The process of producing these several volumes has been very satisfying not only in technical and professional ways, but in personal ways as well. The cooperation and good spirit shown through literally thousands of contacts have been totally positive and helpful.

Special thanks are due to Kim Tihansky, who shouldered the technical editing responsibility in the preparation of this volume; to Tom Treffinger, whose organizational and editing expertise were invaluable for the timely completion of this volume; and to Veronica Young and Marilyn Johnson for the final typing of the manuscript. We would also like especially to acknowledge our gratitude to Barbara Barrett,

Editorial Director of Social and Behavioral Sciences and Humanities, for her encouragement and assistance from the inception phase through the completion of this manuscript for copy-editing at Pergamon Press.

MARGARET C. WANG
MAYNARD C. REYNOLDS
HERBERT J. WALBERG
Editors

Learning Characteristics of Students with Special Needs and the Provision of Effective Schooling

MARGARET C. WANG

*Temple University Center for Research
in Human Development and Education*

This chapter provides an integrative analysis of the research base on the learning characteristics of students with special needs. It also examines the implications of this research base for providing effective schooling to students with special needs. The chapter is organized into six sections. The first presents a general overview of salient themes that are reflected in the findings from several recent research syntheses in areas related to learner characteristics and instructional interventions. The next four sections summarize synthesis findings in the relevant topic areas: ethno-cultural and social-psychological effects on learning characteristics of children with special learning needs; learner characteristics and current classification practices in special education; the role of the learner as an individual difference variable in school learning and functioning; and educational approaches that are adaptive to individual differences. In the final section of the chapter, recommendations for research, program development, classification system reform, and improved educational delivery systems are summarized.

Salient Themes in the Literature

The commitment to providing greater-than-usual educational and related services that enable students with special needs to experience schooling success has been a guiding force in the design and implementation of special, compensatory, and remedial education programs. The theoretical and technical advances made during the past two decades of research on learning and effective teaching hold important implications for improving current practice, in particular the type of information

1

about the learner characteristics of the individual students to be considered in educational planning for students with special needs. Several themes are particularly salient in the literature about the state of the practice and effects. They include: (a) the adverse effects of the practice of labeling students based on current classifications and educational placement systems; (b) the role of the learner in the instructional-learning process; and (c) the provision of a unified system of coordinated regular education and "special" education programs. Viewed collectively, these themes represent a movement toward strengthening the degree of correspondence between the learning needs of individual students and the delivery of appropriate instructional and related service supports. These themes are briefly discussed in this introductory section to provide the context for the synthesis of the research bases on individual differences and schooling effects summarized in the chapter.

Adverse Effects of Current Classification and Placement Systems

One theme that recurs in the literature is the numerous adverse effects of educational decision making and the labeling of students based upon current classification and educational placement systems that for the most part are not linked with the developmental or learning needs of students. Although these classification labels have served to marshal special education funding and other resources required to provide greater-than-usual educational and related services to students with special needs, the resulting educational placement of these students tends to have little relationship to their specific instructional programming needs. Recognizing the need for an alternative to current practices in classification and educational placement, researchers and practitioners have begun to call for the development of a data base that can be used to describe learner characteristics in terms of the cognitive and social competencies required to achieve intended learning outcomes. Such descriptions are considered essential for the design of effective educational interventions and the development of meaningful Individualized Education Programs (IEPs).

This call for a shift toward instructionally relevant descriptions of learner characteristics and needs parallels a growing dissatisfaction with traditional measures of learning ability, aptitude, and social and personality attributes. These measures are designed primarily for normative and predictive purposes. They do not provide information concerning the diversity of cognitive, affective, and social variables. Increasingly, attention is being directed to the dynamic nature of the instructional-learning process, and its role in mediating distinct types of learning and thereby improving performance. Researchers have begun to examine learner characteristics as being, in part, evolutionary products of an individual student's interactions with fluid and complex learning environments that include variables such as teacher behaviors and attitudes, program design features, and peer relationships. Increasingly, these variables are considered to be intrinsic to learning processes and academic performance and are therefore critical to the successful planning and provision of effective education.

There is a growing realization that the ability to alter learner characteristics is linked directly to our knowledge of the learning process, and that different competencies and attributes are required by individual students to succeed in different types of learning. Such developments in the conceptualization and description of individual differences contrast sharply with both the traditional view of learner characteristics as static qualities, and with the practice of classifying and labeling students in groups according to rather grossly defined categories. Furthermore, building upon the changing views of learner characteristics and the learning process will make it possible to enhance the potential for a wide range of students to succeed in a variety of learning tasks (cf. Corno & Snow, 1986; Wang & Lindvall, 1984).

The Active Learning Role of the Student

Another notable theme in the literature is the changing conception of the role of the learner in the instructional-learning process. Recent research suggests that learning essentially involves the learner in an active process of both external and internal adaptation. External adaptation occurs in the ideas and content that are to be learned, and in the modes and forms in which content is presented to the learner. Internal adaptation takes place in the learner's mind, as new content is assimilated and internal mental structures are modified to accommodate it. Thus, students are seen as active processors, interpreters, and synthesizers of information. They are expected to take responsibility for managing, monitoring, and evaluating their own learning, and for playing an instrumental role in adapting the learning environment to the demands of the instructional-learning process. Students' ability to perform this role is influenced highly by their prior knowledge and skills, as well as by their self-perceptions of cognitive and social competence. Those learner characteristics that are associated with an effectively functioning active learner role have come to be instructionally relevant, individual differences in learning (cf. Corno & Snow, 1986; Wang & Peverly, 1986).

A Coordinated Educational Program Delivery System

Another salient theme in the recent literature is the challenge to apply all forms of extant knowledge (as derived from research on teaching and school effectiveness, and from experience in the implementation of innovative educational practices) to the structuring of a coordinated, well-managed, and inclusive universal educational system that effectively meets the instructional and related service needs of individual students. These needs should be met based on the students' diagnosed needs, rather than on the eligibility criteria of special or compensatory educational programs (which generally are not relevant to the identification of specific learning needs). The goal of this system would be to provide a wide variety of educational and related services that meet the learning needs of the individual students, and to the maximum extent possible, in regular classroom environments.

Although a large number of students with special needs, if not all, are no longer physically isolated in the schools, instruction for these remains largely based on a "second system" program that is separate from the regular educational system. The current second system approach to providing special education and other categorical programs, such as Chapter 1, bilingual and migrant education, tends to implement these programs in a disjointed fashion. In addition, there is little interaction with regular education or other similar remedial and compensatory programs (cf. Gartner & Lipsky, 1987; Wang, Reynolds, & Walberg, 1988).

Intensified efforts to base instructional planning on a broadened range of student learning characteristics, particularly during the last 10 years, have led to the development of innovative programs and practices. These programs and practices enhance schools' capabilities to ensure high-quality educational opportunities for *all* students in regular classroom settings, including and particularly those with poor prognoses for school success. The significant progress that has been made in research on teaching and school effects (cf. Kyle, 1985; Wittrock, 1986) provides an extensive knowledge base on educational alternatives for improving schooling practice. By contrast, there is no distinct research base to support a continuation of the traditional segregated approach that provides instruction for students according to special education categories, particularly the categories for the various mild or moderate handicap conditions such as learning disability, mild mental retardation, and mild behavioral disorders (Allington & Johnston, 1986; Brophy, 1986; Heller, Holtzman, & Messick, 1982; Reschly, 1984; Reynolds, 1984; Ysseldyke & Thurlow, 1983).

Ethnocultural and Social-Psychological Effects

Recent findings on the relationships among ethnic and social class status, school achievement, and special education classifications have brought to attention two relevant patterns. First, there is evidence of similarities between the learning needs of students who are formally classified as disabled and other low-achieving, but nonclassified, students (Allington & Johnston, 1986; Brophy, 1986; Deshler, Schumaker, Alley, Warner, & Clark, 1982; Heller et al., 1982; Mercer, 1973; Ysseldyke, Algozzine, Shinn, & McGue, 1982). Second, there is a correlation between minority or low socioeconomic status and low achievement (e.g., Broman, Nichols, & Kennedy, 1975; Child Trends, Inc., 1985; Hodgkinson, 1985; Mare, 1981; Ramey & Campbell, 1979). The intersection of these two patterns has resulted in a disproportionate placement of black and other minority children in special education classes and programs (Anderson & Anderson, 1983; Educational Testing Service, 1980; Heller et al., 1982; Pink, 1982; Polloway & Smith, 1983; Ysseldyke, Algozzine, & Richey, 1982).

Bias in assessment strategies, placement decisions, and referral rates are frequently cited as reasons that students from selected ethnic and social class status groups traditionally have been overly represented in special education (cf. Brantlinger & Guskin, 1987; Heller et al., 1982). Biased assessment at any level of the instructional process (e.g., including screening, classification/placement, instructional planning, individual student evaluation, and program evaluation) can influence the type of education that children receive. Court actions such as that of *Larry P. v. Riles* (1979), have singled out the use of IQ tests as an example of biased assessment procedures. Cultural differences can result in biased grade assignment, classification of deviance, and teacher expectations that lead to referral for special education and related services (Duffy, Salvia, Tucker, & Ysseldyke, 1981; Reschly, 1984). Although the Education for All Handicapped Children Act of 1975 (PL 94–142) mandates that the procedures for the assessment and classification of students with special needs be selected and administered in ways that are not racially, culturally, or sexually discriminatory, implementation of PL 94–142 has fallen far short of this mandate.

Tracking procedures and discriminatory counseling are examples of practices noted to have been among the factors that result in inferior education for poor and minority children (Weinstein, 1983). In particular, "tracking," which is sometimes referred to as "homogeneous ability grouping," has been found to deprive low-achieving students of self-respect, stimulation by higher achieving peers, and helpful teacher strategies and expectations (Cave & Davies, 1977; Eder, 1981; Pink, 1982). Special education programs that are separated from the regular school curriculum are a kind of tracking, insofar as they segregate and differentiate students for instruction according to ability level (Madden & Slavin, 1983).

The social class and racial compositions of schools have also been found to affect learner characteristics and academic achievement. The majority of low-income parents interviewed by Brantlinger (1985) perceived class discrimination in school settings, and they described their schools as inferior to those in higher income districts. Students with disabilities from certain minority groups face especially difficult problems in their efforts to gain access to, and benefit from, appropriate educational interventions. These groups include: children in rural communities that have limited educational resources; American Indian children, who tend to be isolated geographically and segregated from mainstream American society; children of migrant workers, whose nomadic lifestyle adversely affects the accessibility and continuity of the educational services that are available to them; and children with limited proficiency in English, whose problems with assessment and educational programming are largely language related.

The home environment is another social factor noted by Brantlinger and Guskin (1987) as having a significant impact on the learning characteristics of students with special needs. Differences in the cognitive styles of students from particular ethnic groups have been attributed to socialization patterns that are reinforced in the home. Research has focused on identifying educationally relevant variables, such as the physical environment of the home, the emotional and verbal responsiveness of parents, parents' aspirations, and family cohesiveness and harmony (e.g., Adams, Campbell, & Ramey, 1984; Laosa, 1980; Mink, Meyers, & Nihira, 1984). In reviewing the research in this area, as noted by Henderson (1981), one must be mindful of the substantial variation in cognitive style and other socialization patterns *within* ethnic groups. Examining the process of socialization and cognition, the interrelationships of these processes, and the ethnocultural differences among individuals and subgroups is a complex undertaking; it requires much sensitivity and scientific rigor.

Learner Characteristics and Classification Practices in Special Education

One of the fundamental assumptions of research and theory related to the education of children and youth with special needs is that the educational and related service support needs required in special educational programming for children with mild disabilities are sufficiently different from those of students who are not disabled. However, findings

from Reschly's (1987) review of research and practice support the
ment that the relationships among learner characteristics, classific   ,
placement, and instruction in special education are by no means clear-
cut, consistent, reliable, or valid. These and related issues are discussed
in this section under two headings: Classification of Students with Special
Needs, and The Research Base on Differences Between Students Classified as Mildly Disabled and Other Students (which includes those considered to be low achieving and/or "academically at risk").

Classification of Students with Special Needs

Current systems for classifying students with special needs are probably best understood as the product of diverse forces, countervailing
trends, historical accident, and compromise among competing constitu-
encies (Reschly, 1987). Classification processes tend to be uniform and
consistent only insofar as they typically draw from three sets of guidlines:
the federal definitions of handicap conditions, generally framed dimensions of behavior, and the medical and social models of exceptionality.

The regulations for implementing PL 94–142, as summarized in the
Federal Register (1977), provide brief definitions of 11 handicap conditions: deaf, deaf-blind, hard-of-hearing, mental retarded, multihandicapped, orthopedically impaired, other health impaired, seriously
emotionally disturbed, specific learning disability, speech impaired, and
visually handicapped. These definitions are used in determining the
eligibility of state and local educational agencies for federal funding
to support special education services. However, the federal legislation
actually provides very little specification or direction for the classification of special education students. As a result, there is considerable
variation in classification criteria and procedures across states and local
school districts. Other chapters in this volume describe the variability,
and sometimes arbitrary nature of current classification criteria (see, for
example, the chapters by Keogh and Reynolds).

Seven general dimensions of behavior, or individual characteristics,
tend to be used in various combinations further to define each of the
handicap conditions designated by federal law. The first four dimensions—intelligence, achievement, social behavior and emotional adjustment, and communication/language—are applied principally in the
classification of students with handicaps such as educable mental retardation, learning disability, and serious emotional disturbance. The
remaining dimensions—sensory status, motor skills, and health status—
focus on physical handicap conditions, which often co-exist with one or
more of the first four dimensions. According to Reschly (1987), current
classification systems also incorporate a mixture of models for defining
and determining exceptionality (cf. Hobbs, 1975a, 1975b). Among

these, the medical and social system models are most prominent. In fact, much of the questioning in recent years in regard to the meaning of exceptionality and the basis for identifying handicaps has been precipitated by confusion of these two models.

Mercer and Ysseldyke (1977) delineated three characteristics of the *medical model*. First, the medical model attributes abnormal patterns of behavior or development to underlying biological pathology. Second, it is cross-cultural; that is, the same underlying biological abnormalities cause approximately the same deficits in behavior regardless of social status or cultural group. Finally, it is a deficit model that views biological anomalies as inherent. Certain handicap conditions defined by federal law—specifically, deaf, deaf-blind, hard-of-hearing, multihandicapped, orthopedically handicapped, other health impaired, visually handicapped, and certain levels of mental retardation—are probably best regarded as medical model handicaps.

For the most part, there tends to be little controversy over the classification of students as disabled under the medical model, and there is nearly universal agreement regarding the importance of early diagnosis and early intervention. Moreover, application of the medical model does not generally result in over representation of economically disadvantaged or minority students. Medical model disabilities can range in severity, and are of relatively low prevalence. Less than 20% of the total population of classified disabled children, and less than 2.5% of the overall school-age population, have been reported to exhibit medical model disabilities (Algozzine & Korinek, 1985).

In contrast to the medical model, the *social system model* is based on a strongly ecological perspective (Mercer, 1979). Deviant behavior or abnormal patterns of development are attributed to discrepancies between what is learned in a cultural context and the expectations for normal behavior in specific social roles and settings. The federally defined handicaps of mental retardation, serious emotional disturbance, specific learning disability, and speech impairment can be regarded as social system model disabilities. The prevalence of such conditions is quite high: more than 80% of the students who are classified as disabled tend to be identified as having social system model conditions; these students have comprised between 7% and 9.5% of the total school-age population (Algozzine & Korinek, 1985).

There is enormous variation in the prevalence of social system model conditions, especially across the classification of learning disability, educable mental retardation, and emotional disturbance. Among the major reasons for such within-model variation are the differences in state rules and regulations concerning definitions and classification criteria (e.g., Mercer, Hughes, & Mercer, 1985; Patrick & Reschly, 1982), and the variety of systemic factors that effect classification (e.g., Bickel,

1982; Keogh, 1983; MacMillan & Borthwick, 1980; MacMillan, Meyers, & Morrison, 1980). Systemic factors include teachers' tolerance for individual differences, the ways in which referrals are screened, the availability of options within general education for providing remedial services, and the availability of special programs.

The Research Base on Differences Between Students Classified as Mildly Disabled and Other Students

Recent research has examined the magnitude of differences in intelligence, achievement, and social/emotional characteristics among four groups of students: "average" students; low-achieving students; economically disadvantaged students; and students classified in the various mild disability categories (e.g., learning disability, mild behavioral disorders, educable mental retardation). Many of the studies of contrasted groups have been designed to delineate instruction-related characteristics of students with mild disabilities. Despite methodological concerns and technical difficulties in determining degrees of difference and degrees of overlap, research findings in this area have important implications for reforming current classification systems and for developing improved instructional practices and programs.

Overall, researchers have found large differences between students classified as mildly disabled and students with "average" levels of performance (Conner, 1983; Gresham & Reschly, 1986; Meyers, MacMillan, & Yoshida, 1978; Reschly, Gresham, & Graham-Clay, 1984; Richmond & Waits, 1978; Schumaker, Deshler, Alley, & Warner, 1983; Scott, 1979). In addition to differences in achievement, specific differences between the two groups have been reported for a variety of information-processing variables, including efficiency of learning, prior knowledge, information-processing strategies, and metacognitive operations for directing the learning process (e.g., Borkowski, Peck, & Damberg, 1983; Brooks & McCauley, 1984; Campione, Brown, & Ferrara, 1982; Conner, 1983; Hallahan & Sapona, 1984). Significant differences have also been noted in motivational, attentional, social skills, and attitudinal variables (e.g., Adelman & Taylor, 1983, 1984; Deshler, Schumaker & Lenz, 1984; Keogh, 1982; Madden & Slavin, 1983).

By contrast, only equivocal results have been reported regarding the differences between students with mild disabilities and low-achieving students. A particular subject of much controversy and debate is the apparent lack of any major differences in education-related characteristics or outcomes for students classified as learning disabled and students with low academic achievements or those otherwise considered to be academically at risk (Gartner & Lipsky, 1987; Jenkins, Pious, & Peterson, 1988; Ysseldyke, Algozzine, & Thurlow, 1983). Several review articles also noted similarities between students with mild disabilities and economically disadvantaged students, who often are members of ethnic/racial minorities (Allington & Johnston, 1986; Brantlinger & Guskin, 1987; Brophy, 1986; Jenkins, 1987). Kavale (1980), for example, reported considerable similarity in the behavioral characteristics of the two groups, including low achievement, inefficient learning, difficulties in correlated processes such as visual and auditory perception, and social/behavioral difficulties.

Finally, some researchers in special education, especially those who have focused their research on students classified under the catergory of learning disability, frequently have suggested that there are more similarities than differences among the categories of learning disability, educable mental retardation, and mild behavior disorder (Boucher & Deno, 1979). The relatively few empirical studies in this area have yielded mixed results. However, there is no evidence that the use and effectiveness of different remedial or compensatory education procedures must necessarily depend on a student's classification, particularly if the classification is learning disability or educable mental retardation. The same procedures appear to work with students of either classification (Brophy, 1986; Jenkins, 1987). Thus, further research is needed to characterize the nature and the extent of any differences among students who are classified under the various categories of mild disability conditions.

The Role of the Learner as an Individual Difference Variable in School Learning and Functioning

The extent to which students play an active role in their learning has significant implications for the functioning of successful and less-than-successful students and for the design of effective instruction (cf. Wang & Peverly, 1987). Partly as a result of increasing awareness of the research bases in cognitive-instructional psychology, effective instruction, and the processes of learning, both general and special educators have become interested in a variety of instructional strategies that can enhance students' ability to assume an active role in learning. In this section, major theoretical advances and empirical findings are summarized to characterize the extant knowledge base on the role of the learner as an individual difference variable in school learning and functioning. Also, intervention programs for cognitive strategy development are described as one means of improving students' learning efficiency and developing their higher-order cognitive skills as they acquire subject-matter knowledge.

The Role of the Learner

The role of the learner may be conceptualized as encompassing two related categories of competence: the ability to be responsible for learning behavior and its outcomes, and the ability to be strategic and self-regulating during the learning process (Wang & Peverly, 1987). The research bases to support this conceptualization are discussed in this section.

SELF-RESPONSIBILITY FOR LEARNING

The concepts of "self" and "perceptions of personal control" are salient throughout the literature on student self-responsibility. Major research efforts have addressed the causal relationship between perceptions of self and achievement by focusing on self-efficacy (Bandura, 1977); self-worth (Covington & Beery, 1976; Covington & Omelich, 1979); locus of control (Lefcourt, 1982; Rotter, 1966); motivation based on attributions of causality for success and failure (Weiner, 1976, 1979); self-evaluation maintenance (Tesser & Campbell, 1982); and perceptions and competence regarding self-responsibility for learning (Wang, 1983). Investigations of the social-psychological determinants of learning generally have been based on two interrelated hypotheses: first, that academic achievement fosters a positive perception of self; and second, that a positive perception of self is associated with achievement motivation, which in turn influences student behavior and learning.

Thus, both theory and research indicate a close relationship between school achievement and students' perceptions of their ability to exert personal control over their learning (Coleman et al., 1966; Crandall, Katkovsky, & Crandall, 1965; McCombs, 1982; Nicholls, 1979; Thomas, 1980; Uguroglu & Walberg, 1979). Students who believe they can influence their learning are more likely to succeed than those who believe learning is controlled by powerful others (e.g., teachers) or that achievement is unaffected by effort (Dweck & Elliot, 1983). Research suggests that the development of a sense of self-responsibility for learning is critical for students who have histories of academic failure and poor perceptions of self-competence and personal control: characteristics that are frequently associated with students classified as disabled (cf. Keogh, 1982). In fact, the demonstrated effectiveness of certain educational programs and practices in improving the academic progress of students with poor prognoses for achievement has been attributed, at least in part, to features designed specifically to foster internal locus of control and perceptions of self-esteem (Madden & Slavin, 1983; Wang & Walberg, 1983).

The relationship between learning performance and perceptions of personal control has received very little attention in special education research. The data base that does exist applies mainly to learning disabled students (Adelman & Taylor, 1983; Boersma & Chapman, 1981; Dudley-Marling, Snider, & Tarver, 1982; Pearl, 1982). Despite the limited research base, three patterns are salient. First, students with special needs are more likely to attribute academic as well as social and personal success and failure to forces outside themselves; that is, students with disabilities are more likely to perceive an external locus of control. Second, students with special needs are more likely to accept responsibility for failure than for success, although they generally do not recognize ability or effort as controllable determinants of either success or failure in their school learning. Finally, those students with special needs who assume high levels of responsibility for their learning tend to show greater academic achievement than those who are not self-responsible.

Intervention studies that are designed to foster self-responsibility for learning are typified by two major approaches. The first approach is characterized in the research on learned helplessness (Sabatino, 1982) and attribution retraining (deCharms, 1976; Dweck, 1975; Meyer, 1979; Schunk, 1982; Weiner, 1983). It involves interventions aimed at training students to accept responsibility for their learning success and failure. The second major approach to fostering self-responsibility for learning consists of strategies for training students to manage their own learning and behavior (Felixbrod & O'Leary, 1974; Ross & Zimiles, 1974; Wang, 1976).

SELF-INSTRUCTIVE SKILLS AND LEARNING

Students who assume an active role in their own learning are often characterized as being strategic and self-regulating or, in other words, self-instructive (Wang & Peverly, 1987). More specifically, the term self-instructive refers to students' ability to access and organize prior knowledge, as well as their ability to seek instuctional help for accessing and using the relevant knowledge and skills in new learning. By linking relevant findings from recent empirical research on learning and classroom instruction, Wang and Peverly (1987) developed an integrated conceptual model for analyzing and describing the self-instructive process and its mediating function in student learning. The model consists of four clusters of interrelated variables: learner characteristics, the classroom learning environment, the self-instructive process, and learner outcomes. These variables are viewed as highly interactive: the self-instructive process plays a mediating role in student learning and, in turn, is likely to be affected by multiple factors associated with the unique, instructionally relevant characteristics of individual learners and/or the situation-specific characteristics of the learning environment. The use of such a person-environment-process-product paradigm to examine classroom learning and instruction is supported in the contemporary experimental literature on learning and cognition (e.g., Brown, Bransford, Ferrara, & Campione, 1983; Brown, Campione, & Day, 1981; Jenkins, 1979, 1980) and by recent research on classroom instruction and the social-psychological process of learning (e.g., Bossert, 1979; Cooper & Good, 1982; DeStefano, Wang, & Gordon, 1984; Doyle, 1977; Gordon, 1983; Marshall & Weinstein, 1984; Rosenholtz & Wilson, 1980; Stipek, 1981; Weinstein, 1983).

Self-instructive skills involve both knowledge about the learning environment and the subject matter of criterial tasks, and the ability to use that knowledge in deliberate learning through strategy planning, self-monitoring and self-assessment, and self-interrogation and clarification. Some students acquire these skills on their own. However, other students can benefit from instruction on strategies they can use to improve their learning efficiency.

Students' knowledge. What students know has consistently been shown to be one of the best predictors of learning perfomance and outcomes (e.g., Bandura, 1981; Bloom, 1984; Brophy & Good, 1986; Glaser, 1984; Resnick & Ford, 1981; Walberg, 1984). Yet detailed analysis of students' knowledge characteristics is rarely considerd in either the design of school programs or the planning of classroom instruction. Moreover, when students' knowledge is considered, the focus typically is on using information on outcome variables to classify and select/exclude individual students for instruction.

Knowledge characteristics are generally described in the experimental and instructional design literature as either subject-matter knowledge or domain-general knowledge. Subject-matter knowledge refers to the specific content of the task to be learned. The relationship between subject-matter knowledge and performance in given domains is well documented (Bloom, 1976; Brown, Bransford, et al., 1983; Coleman et al., 1966; Flavell & Wellman, 1977; Glaser, 1984; Stallings, 1975; Walberg, 1984). As might be expected, successful learners are depicted as having more subject-matter knowledge than less-than-successful learners.

Domain-general knowledge encompasses a broad spectrum of knowledge related to efficient learning. In the conceptual model developed by Wang and Peverly (1987), domain-general knowledge refers to knowledge about characteristics of the task and the learning environment, perceptions of the knowledge characteristics of the self and others, and knowledge about relevant strategies for effective task performance. It has been hypothesized that domain-general knowledge plays a central role in the transfer of knowledge and skills, particularly the development of strategies or rules for problem solving and the learning of new tasks. In research on cognition and learning, domain-general knowledge is discussed most often as "metacognition" or "metacognitive knowledge."

Students' use of what they know in their learning. The second component of self-instructive skills is students' ability to use what they know in learning new tasks and to apply what they know in new situations. Earlier work in this area was highly influenced by Flavell's (1970) notion of "production deficiency," which refers to a student's failure to use knowledge spontaneously even when he or she is aware of the certain prerequisite strategies or behaviors for applying the knowledge to accomplish a goal. Production deficiency has been noted as a frequent problem for students identified as learning disabled (Kauffman & Hallahan, 1979; Torgensen, 1977), mentally retarded (Belmont & Butterfield, 1977; Brown, 1974; Campione & Brown, 1977), or hyperactive (Douglas & Peters, 1979). The results from such research suggest that children who have difficulty in learning may lack the skills to regulate or coordinate what they know about a task with efficient strategies for task completion.

Much recent work in this area focuses on the skills that are a requisite part of an individual's knowledge about his or her thought processes during learning (Brown, 1978). Findings suggest the importance of the role that students play in adapting their internal mental structures as they acquire new knowledge and solve problems (e.g., the self-regulatory process described by Brown, 1978), as well as the importance of students' roles in modifying the learning environment to accommodate their individual learning needs. Thus, metacognitive skills are considered to be critical for deliberate and efficient learning. Research has consistently found a positive correlation between students' ability to use what they know and achievement.

Studies on the use of knowledge in new learning have focused, for the most part, on planning and self-monitoring of performance. Planning involves identification, formulation, and restructuring of goals; strategy planning; and executive planning. Planning emerges sporadically when a learner undertakes a new and complex activity; it becomes increasingly stable and systematic as experience is gained in particular activities or areas of knowledge (Brown, Day, & Jones, 1983; Brown & Smiley, 1978; Scardamalia & Bereiter, 1986). Self-monitoring involves execution of solution steps (e.g., questioning, help-seeking, checking, revising), assessment and interpretation, and self-interrogation and clarification. Monitoring becomes active during the learning process. It refers to on-line management of the continually changing interrelationships of knowledge, plans, strategies, and goals en route to the completion of a task. Self-monitoring skills are influenced by task-specific features as well as by the level of students' cognitive development.

Cognitive Strategy Development

Both laboratory-based and school-based interventions have been developed explicitly to foster students' functioning as self-instructive learners. These interventions, which typically are aimed at training students to use a variety of cognitive strategies, include many of the current programs for teaching thinking skills (cf. Segal, Chipman, & Glaser, 1985). Cognitive strategy training tends to focus on ways of helping students to acquire and apply knowledge and academic skills in specific subject-matter areas, while also enhancing the development of higher-order cognitive skills such as reasoning and problem solving (cf. Palincsar & Brown, 1987). Palincsar and Brown (1987) delineated several features of effective cognitive strategy training. These features include: careful analysis of the tasks at hand, indentification of strategies that promote successful task completion, explicit strategy instruction that provides metacognitive information, feedback by teachers on the usefulness of specific strategies and the success with which they are being acquired by students, and instruction in strategy generalization.

STRATEGY TRAINING AND SUBJECT-MATTER INSTRUCTION

Findings from six recent laboratory studies on selected approaches to improving reading comprehension skills confirm the effectiveness of systematic, explicit, cognitive strategy training (e.g., Day, 1980; Kurtz & Borkowski, 1985; Miller, 1985; Pflaum & Pascarella, 1980; Schumaker, Deshler, Alley, Warner, & Denton, 1984; Wong & Jones, 1982). These studies included diverse subject samples (e.g., learning disabled students, average-achieving students, and students of different chronological ages and different cognitive/academic abilities), and used a variety of strategies, instructional modes, and assessment procedures. However, each study attended to students' metacognitive knowledge and taught strategies (e.g., identifying main idea information, self-questioning) that would promote comprehension monitoring, as well as enhance comprehension. All of the studies gradually transferred responsibility for applying a strategy from teacher to student; teacher modeling was widely used. In addition, each study was concerned with criterion-level acquisition: before students were encouraged to attempt independent application of trained strategies, efforts were made to ensure mastery based on specified criteria. One of the notable findings from among this group of studies is that informed, self-control training (i.e., training in which students were taught both the usefulness of specific strategies and ways of monitoring and evaluating their own strategy use) seemed highly effective for improving the reading comprehension skills of students with special needs.

The vast majority of research on cognitive strategy instruction has not been carried out in natural classroom settings. Classroom intervention studies by Brown and Palincsar (Brown & Palincsar, 1982; Palincsar & Brown, 1984), and by Paris and his colleagues (Paris, Cross, DeBritto, Jacobs, Oka, & Saarnio, 1984) are among the few examples. In their series of studies conducted principally by remedial reading teachers in natural reading groups, Palincsar and Brown investigated the effectiveness of reciprocal teaching for below-grade-level students. Reciprocal teaching trains students to use four strategies: summarizing (identifying information related to main ideas); generating questions (self-testing on information identified as important); demanding clarity (being able to note breakdowns in comprehension and to restore meaning); and predicting (hypothesizing what the author will discuss next). Palincsar and Brown found that, as a result of reciprocal teaching, students were able independently to refine and use all four strategies; they were able to maintain the strategies for at least eight weeks after the intervention; and they could generalize the strategies to use them in social studies and science classes. Similar findings from Paris and associates' (1984) reading studies of the instructional program, Informed Strategies for Learning, suggest improved reading awareness and applied use of comprehension strategies, especially for young and poor readers.

In the subject-matter area of written communication, cognitive strategy training studies of students with mild disabilities have focused on the subprocesses of handwriting (e.g., Kosiewicz, Hallahan, Lloyd, & Graves, 1982), correct use of syntax (e.g., Harris & Graham, 1985; Stone & Serwatka, 1982), and spelling (e.g., Drake & Ehri, 1984; Englert, Hiebert, & Stewart, 1985). Overall, findings suggest that these discrete subprocesses are responsive to training that is both explicit and comprehensive, but little evidence has been generated to indicate spontaneous transfer and/or maintenance of the trained strategies. Studies of global composition skills for students with special needs have received relatively less attention than have the various writing subprocesses. Yet cognitive strategy training in global composition would seem to hold promise for the maintenance and transfer of improved skills in written communication (Hillocks, 1984; Palincsar & Brown, 1987; Scardamalia, Bereiter, & Steinbach, 1984).

Although much research has been conducted on the strategies used by individuals to solve mathematics problems, the research on instruction in such strategies is less extensive. The work of DeCorte and Verschaffel (1981) is an example of research that combined both emphases.

Their study involved first determining the mathematics problem-solving activities and processes of their student subjects, and then instructing students in cognitive strategies that would lead to effective problem solving. As a result of cognitive strategy training, the experimental group in the DeCorte and Verschaffel study made fewer algorithmic (thinking) errors, maintained their performance over time, and spontaneously used their acquired conceptual knowledge in the solution of transfer problems.

The importance of adequate knowledge structures that students can integrate with cognitive strategies for comprehension and problem solving was demonstrated in studies by Greeno and his associates (e.g., Greeno, 1982; Riley, Greeno, & Heller, 1983), and by Lindvall, Tamburino, and Robinson (1982). This research suggests that differences in students' learning performance can be accounted for by differences in students' conceptual understanding for solving mathematics story problems. Likewise, findings from a study by Lloyd, Saltzman and Kauffman (1981) on learning disabled students suggest that the generalization of academic skills depends upon explicit instruction in both pre-skills and the strategies for applying the preskills.

In the literature on cognitive instruction in mathematics, the terms "heuristics" and "strategies" are often used interchangeably. As noted by Schoenfeld (1980), based on findings from his study of heuristic strategy instruction with college students, the use of heuristics in mathematics instruction must be grounded in an understanding of instruction as a *process* in which the teacher plays the role of coach. Findings from Marcucci's (1980) meta-analysis of research on various methods for teaching the solving of word problems in mathematics suggest that the heuristic approach is highly effective at the elementary school level.

STRATEGY TRAINING IN HIGHER-ORDER COGNITIVE SKILLS

There is growing interest in the explicit teaching of thinking skills independent of specific academic or subject-matter content. In their recent review of the literature in this area, Nickerson, Perkins, and Smith (1984) described five categories of approaches to teaching thinking skills: the cognitive-process approach, which assumes that thinking depends on fundamental processes such as comparing, categorizing, and predicting (e.g., the Instrumental Enrichment Program, Feuerstein, 1980); the heuristics approach, which focuses on problem-solving skills (e.g., the Productive Thinking Program, Covington, Crutchfield, Davies, & Olton, 1974); the approach that is grounded in the assumption that the ability to perform formal or abstract operations is normally acquired only after the ability to perform concrete operations has been developed (e.g., the program entitled Accent on the Development of

Abstract Processes of Thought, Campbell et al., 1980); the language and symbol manipulation approach (e.g., as described in books such as *The Little Red Writing Book*, Scardamalia, Bereiter, & Fillion, 1979, and reflected in the LOGO computer program, Papert, 1980); and the teaching of thinking as subject matter approach, which assumes that learning about thinking can improve one's own thinking (e.g., the Philosophy for Children Program, Lipman, Sharp, & Oscanyan, 1980).

Such approaches have been widely adopted, but there is little empirical evidence to support their relative effectiveness. The existing data (e.g., Feuerstein, 1979, 1980) suggest that teachers enjoy and approve of strategy training in thinking skills, and that they feel such training puts students into situations requiring concentration and attention. Furthermore, students working under approaches like those noted above have demonstrated improvement on standardized measures of intelligence. However, more extensive research is needed to determine whether or not strategy training in thinking skills such as reasoning and problem solving can actually enhance the acquisition of subject-matter knowledge, especially for students with special needs who repeatedly show weaknesses in the generalization and transfer of skills.

Educational Approaches That Are Adaptive to Individual Differences

Instructional experimentation and innovative program development over the past decade have focused a great deal of attention on identifying approaches that can effectively accommodate diverse learner characteristics and learning processes such as those described in preceding sections of this chapter. The adaptive instruction approach seems especially compatible with the conceptualization of instruction as a series of internal and external adaptations in which the individual student plays an active role and the learning environment flexibly accommodates his or her unique learning characteristics. Indeed, there is increasing evidence that adaptive instruction can improve schooling for general education students as well as for students with special needs (Walberg & Wang, 1987).

Adaptive instruction programs incorporate a variety of interventions or practices that have been proven effective in many different classroom settings. These interventions include mastery learning, cooperative teamwork, and individualized instructions (Wang & Lindvall, 1984). Their use is adapted to differences in teachers, classrooms, and students, and there is considerable diversity among adaptive instruction programs in terms of the degree of emphasis that is placed on particular interventions.

The following set of core features has been described as characteristic of the adaptive instruction approach (Wang & Lindvall, 1984):

1. Instruction is based on the assessed capabilities of each student.
2. Materials and procedures permit each student to progress in the mastery of instructional content at a pace suited to his or her abilities and interests.
3. Periodic evaluations of student progress serve to inform teachers and individual students of their mastery.
4. Each student assumes increasing responsibility for identifying his or her learning needs as well as the resources required to perform tasks, plan individual learning activities, and evaluate his or her mastery.
5. Alternative activities and materials are available to aid students in the acquisition of essential academic skills and content.
6. Students have opportunities to make some choices and decisions about their individual learning goals, their specific learning activities, and, consequently, their own learning outcomes.
7. Students assist each other in pursuing individual goals, and they cooperate in achieving group goals.

In their recent review of research and practice in educational provisions for individual differences, Walberg and Wang (1987) highlighted the findings from four large-scale studies (Walberg, 1984; Wang & Baker, 1985–86; Wang & Walberg, 1986; Waxman, Wang, Anderson, & Walberg, 1985). All of these studies were designed to identify critical features of widely implemented educational programs or practices that are aimed at accommodating diverse student needs, and to determine the impact the programs and practices have on classroom processes and a variety of student outcomes. Findings from the studies suggest that it is possible to incorporate selected program components into integrated, well-managed systems of education that provide for individual differences among students and produce positive outcomes. Findings from the four major, large-scale studies are summarized in this section.

Productivity Factors in Learning

Walberg's (1984) major synthesis of research on productivity factors in learning involved a summary and analysis of findings from 2,500 studies conducted over the past 50 years. Walberg identified nine factors as consistent, influential causes of learning. These "educational productivity" factors fall into three groups: student aptitude, instruction, and environment. The three student aptitude factors are ability or prior achievement, as measured by standardized tests; development, as indexed by chronological age or state of maturation; and motivation or self-concept, as indicated by personality tests or by a student's willingness to persevere in learning tasks. There are two instruction factors: the amount of time during which students engage in learning; and the quality of instructional experiences, including psychological aspects and curriculum. The four environmental factors that have been found consistently to affect learning are the educational and psychological climates of the home, the classroom social group, the peer group outside of school, and the use of out-of-school time (specifically, the amount of leisure time spent on television viewing).

It should be noted that Walberg's estimates of the effects of these various factors require replication and further study, and the educational productivity factors that were found for general education may or may not yield results for special education students. Nevertheless, the results from this major research integration comprise a sound empirical basis for future investigations of educational effects under a variety of circumstances. These investigations could include, for example, studies of related productivity factors for students with special needs.

A Quantitative Synthesis of Findings From Research on Adaptive Instruction

Waxman and associates (1985) synthesized findings from 38 studies of adaptive instruction programs that were reported in the literature between 1973 and 1982. The studies were conducted in general education classrooms of elementary and secondary schools and provided an overall subject sample of 7,200 students in kindergarten through Grade 12. Each study also produced contrasted-group or correlational results. Based on data from the studies, Waxman and associates calculated 309 statistical effect sizes to estimate the extent of positive cognitive, affective, and behavioral outcomes under the 38 adaptive instruction programs.

Of all the comparisons that were included in this quantitative synthesis, 77% were positive. The average weighted effect was 0.45; under the adaptive instruction programs, the average student scored at the 67th percentile of the control group distribution for all three categories of outcomes.

A Quantitative Synthesis of the Features and Efficacy of Mainstreaming Programs

Wang and Baker (1985–86) conducted a meta-analysis of the empirical data base developed from the mid-1970s to the mid-1980s on the practice of mainstreaming: the integration of students with special needs in regular classrooms. Data from 11 studies were subjected to two types of analysis: comparison of performance, attitudinal, and process outcomes of special education students in mainstreaming environments with the outcomes of those enrolled in segregated, special education programs;

and preanalysis and postanalysis of program outcomes of special education students enrolled in mainstreaming programs. Performance outcomes were defined to include measures of achievement in academic subject areas such as mathematics and reading. Attitudinal outcomes included measures of students' self-concept and/or their attitudes toward learning and schooling, the attitudes of mainstreamed special education students towards their regular education peers, the attitudes of general education students toward mainstreamed special education students, and the attitudes of teachers and parents toward mainstreaming. Process outcomes consisted of measures of classroom processes, such as the types of interactions between teachers and students and among students.

Overall, the results from the Wang and Baker meta-analysis suggest that programs designed for implementation of special education programs in regular classroom settings (i.e., integrating special education students and their required educational and related services as an integral component of regular education programs) tend to result in improved performance, attitudinal, and process outcomes of mainstreamed special education students. This finding is especially interesting in light of results from previous reviews that describe the effects of mainstreaming as being limited to only academic outcomes (e.g., Carlberg & Kavale, 1980; Leinhardt & Pallay, 1982; Madden & Slavin, 1983; Semmel, Gottlieb, & Robinson, 1979).

The small number of studies that met the criteria for the Wang and Baker meta-analysis, coupled with the general lack of descriptive data on specific program features and instructional practices of effective mainstreaming programs, clearly point to the need for further systematic research on the features and effects of such programs. Although certain program design features were frequently mentioned across the 11 studies (e.g., features such as continuous assessment, a variety of curriculum materials, individualized progress plans, student self-management, peer assistance, instructional teaming, and consulting teachers), few of the studies in the meta-analysis provided data that directly addressed the impact of such features on student outcomes.

A Large-Scale Observational Study of Features and Effects of Adaptive Instruction

A recent study by Wang and Walberg (1986) characterized exemplary implementations of eight, widely adopted, instructional models. The study analyzed the extent to which the models incorporate features of adaptive instruction for the explicit purpose of accommodating student differences. It also examined how combinations of these design features were implemented in the sample classrooms and investigated whether that high degree of implementation resulted in classroom processes and outcomes associated with effective instruction and learning. The instructional models included in the Wang and Walberg study were the following: Adaptive Learning Environments Model (Wang, Gennari, & Waxman, 1985); Bank Street Model (Gilkeson, Smithberg, Bowman, & Rhine, 1981); Behavior Analysis Model (Ramp & Rhine, 1981); Direct Instruction Model (Becker, Engelmann, Carnine, & Rhine, 1981); Individually Guided Education (Klausmeier, 1972); Mastery Learning (Bloom, 1968); Team-Assisted Individualization (Slavin, 1983); and the Utah System Approach to Individualized Learning (Jeter, 1980).

Data were collected from a total of 65 second-grade, third-grade, and fourth-grade classrooms at exemplary implementation sites that were recommended by the developers of the eight models. The data included information on the contextual characteristics of the implementation sites; the critical features of adaptive instruction as they were implemented in the sample classrooms; and the within-model and cross-model patterns of classroom processes, students' perceptions of self-responsibility, classroom climate, and student achievement.

Two sets of results are noteworthy. First, high degrees of implementation of adaptive instruction features were established and maintained in regular classrooms in a variety of school settings. Second, the classroom processes under the eight instructional models closely resembled the classroom processes described in the effective teaching research literature (e.g., Brophy & Good, 1986). Several models in the study produced classroom process outcomes that many students, parents, and educators greatly value. Among these were constructive student interactions, independent work, individual diagnosis and prescription, cooperative learning, and student exploration.

Program features such as the fostering of student choice and student initiative, which the effective-teaching literature suggests to be ineffective, were found by Wang and Walberg to facilitate student learning. Other features of the instructional models in the Wang and Walberg study included the use of a variety of materials and activities, the allocation of available class time for curriculum-related activities, and the prescription of learning tasks that are appropriate for students' learning needs and achievement levels. These features are also cited in the effective teaching literature as being generic to "good" instruction (Brophy & Good, 1986).

Conclusions and Recommendations

The findings from several major syntheses of research and practice clearly suggest the possibilities and potential positive impact of innovative programs and practices that can lead to the successful accommodation of the widest possible range of instructionally relevant learner characteristics in regular classroom settings. Further progress in research in this area must be made in both research design and type of variables that are studied. Discussions of some of the implications of the findings are organized under four headings for future research, program development needs, reforming the classification and placement system in special education, and the delivery of effective educational and related services for students with special needs.

Future Research

A major research agenda in this area for the coming decade is the development of effective strategies for implementing practices that improve the instruction and learning of all students, including and particularly those with special learning needs. A fundamental first step is the establishment of an extensive, descriptive data base on learner characteristics that are instructionally relevant for addressing a broad array of questions related to improving instruction and learning. The following are examples of research questions that address these and related research needs:

1. What are the important variables that cause learning? How do some of the salient and commonly agreed-upon variables, such as classroom climate, the principal's leadership, teacher expectations, teacher–student interactions, time-on-task, and so forth affect student learning performance, the classroom instructional-learning process, academic achievement, and handicap classifications and placement of students with special needs?

2. What specific aspects of the functioning of students with disabilities and/or students considered to be academically at-risk differ from the characteristics of "expert" learners? How do successful and less-than-successful students differ in terms of their ability to assume an active role in their learning? Are these learner characteristics alterable? What are some of the effective intervention strategies that foster increasing "expertise" in students who are considered academically "handicapped" or at risk of academic failure?

3. What are the salient characteristics (features) of programs that appear to be most conducive to developing student self-responsibility and competency for active self-instructive process in knowledge, and skill acquisition and maintenance?

4. How are certain alterable learner characteristics (e.g., knowledge, students' self-perception of cognitive and/or social competence, temperament, and motivation) related to students' responsiveness to cognitive strategy training and other interventions aimed at developing both subject-matter knowledge and higher-order cognitive skills?

5. Do differences in teacher styles and instructional approaches require differences in levels of student competence for assuming self-responsibility in their learning and ability to be self-instructive?

6. How can advances in cognitive-instructional research be incorporated to improve understanding and procedures for diagnosing and monitoring learning processes that are intrinsic to student achievement of subject-matter knowledge and the higher-order cognitive skills of reasoning and problem solving?

7. What specific steps can be taken to enhance the linkage between assessment (diagnosis of student learning needs and evaluation of learning outcomes) and improvement in instructional effectiveness? What types of assessment (measures and procedures) are most effective in integrating the assessment and instructional process to produce information in the service of student learning?

8. What do teachers need to know about instructionally relevant learner characteristics and state-of-the-art practices in order to increase their expertise in linking diagnosis and assessment to improve student learning?

Program Development

The extant research base reflects a great deal of agreement between the characteristics of effective programs and practices for general education students and students with special needs (cf., Brophy, 1986; Wang, Reynolds, & Walberg, 1987–89). Among these major characteristics are strategies for increasing learning efficiency, including the transfer and generalization of information-processing skills; development of cognitive skills and social competencies that facilitate adult adjustment and lifelong learning; prescription of tasks and activities that match students' learning needs and achievement levels; frequent, systematic evaluation of students' progress and timely provision of feedback; and use of a variety of materials and activities to suit the talents and needs of individual students (Reschly, 1987; Walberg & Wang, 1987).

There is a pressing need for intensified program development that builds upon current expectations and extant research findings. This work should link educators, researchers, and policymakers from general and special education in the conducting of school-based experimentations aimed at implementing, evaluating, and refining alternate programs and practices that better serve all students, including students with special needs or otherwise considered to be academically at risk. Programs and practices such as those based on the adaptive instruction approach must be sharply defined and vigorously tested if they are to stand as precedents for providing effective, efficient education for diverse student populations.

Systematic programs of research and evaluation should accompany the development and adoption of alternate instructional approaches, as well as the continuation of current interventions for students with special needs. This research should be longitudinal and comprehensive; it should cut across many of the present categorical and disciplinary boundaries; and it should test the effectiveness of specific interventions in meeting the learning needs of individual students or groups of students.

Classification System Reform

Advances in research and program development can provide the foundation for replacing the current emphasis on whom should be classified as special education students and by what criteria with a focus on introducing and maintaining educational alternatives that improve the chances of schooling success for students with special needs. The time and energy that is currently devoted to determining the eligibility of students for "special" services represent an excessively costly and inefficient use of resources (Davis & Smith, 1984; Shepard, 1983). Perhaps the most obvious inefficiency in present classification systems is the lack of linkage between the classification labels and specific eligibility criteria and instructional intervention (Reschly, 1987).

To the extent that some form of classification may continue to be necessary for the effective identification of specific learning difficulties, the reform of current systems should be guided by at least two important considerations: first, the need to establish and comply with rigorous criteria of reliability and validity; and second, the implications of nomenclature and labeling.

Reliability may be defined as the degree to which independent judges examining the same information about historical characteristics and/or currently assessable characteristics arrive at the same classification. Validity is the degree to which classification is related to specific treatments of interventions and to knowledge regarding their effectiveness. Effective classification systems would consider all relevant learning phenomena, and they would incorporate valid interventions, effective placement options, and practices for minimizing stigma. The risk–benefit ratio of the classification process should be evaluated in terms of the degree to which classification results in beneficial treatment and the degree to which labeling effects and stigma are avoided (Heller *et al.*, 1982; Reschly, 1979, 1984; Reynolds & Wang, 1983).

Suggestions for reforming current classification systems have included specific steps such as distinguishing the nomenclature for mild or educable levels of handicaps from that which is used for other levels of mental retardation. It has also been suggested that the mild handicap categories of learning disability, mild or educable mental retardation, and emotional disturbance should be combined (Reschly, 1987). Both of these ideas for reform stem from an interest in protecting students from excessive stigma. However, the most promising and dramatic reform would be to label interventions instead of children (Hobbs, 1975a, 1975b). The labeling of services may make it possible to move away from "either-or" decisions regarding classification and placement, and to concentrate instead upon instructional options that are consistent with the unique learning characteristics and educational needs of individual students.

Effective Delivery Systems

Experience in a variety of settings has shown that research and program development tend to have little impact on schooling practice unless serious attention is also given to delivery systems that support program implementation. The effective delivery of improved educational and related services for students with special needs requires organizational patterns that allow for the flexible deployment of personnel and material resources. For example, the widespread implementation of programs and practices for serving students with special needs in regular classrooms will be possible only if partnerships are established between special and general educators. The effective operation of such partnerships depends on the special educators' increased knowledge of regular school curriculum, and the collaboration of school psychologists, special education teachers, and general education teachers in curriculum-based student assessments and subsequent provision of instruction.

Curriculum-based assessments are a particularly critical element lacking in the current delivery of special and general education. Assessments that are curriculum based can produce instructionally relevant information that is useful to teachers as they make day-to-day analyses, such as where an individual student fits into a school's curriculum, what cognitive and academic skills the student uses to perform specific types of tasks, and how responsive the student is to instruction in self-instructive strategies or metacognitive processes and related strategies for improving learning efficiency.

A Final Word

The findings described in this chapter on instructionally relevant learner characteristics and the provision of instructional and related services that are effective in meeting the learning needs of the individual students are cause for optimism and for renewed determination to build upon the state of the art and the state of practice. Many research-based alternatives to traditional practices are available for further testing and widespread implementation. These alternatives are grounded in the assumption that improved learning can be expected for *all* students when information on an expanded range of learner characteristics interacts with the design of specific educational interventions for accommodating those characteristics.

References

Adams, J. L., Campbell, F. A., & Ramey, C. T. (1984). Infants' home environments: A study of screening efficacy. *American Journal of Mental Deficiency*, **89**, 133–139.

Adelman, H. S., & Taylor, L. (1983). *Learning disabilities in perspective*. Glenview, IL: Scott, Foresman.

Adelman, H. S., & Taylor, L. (1984). Enhancing motivation for overcoming learning and behavior problems. *Annual Review of Learning Disabilities*, **2**, 102–109.

Algozzine, B., & Korinek, L. (1985). Where is special education for students with high prevalence handicaps going? *Exceptional Children*, **51**, 388–394.

Allington, R. L., & Johnston, P. (1986). The coordination among regular classroom reading programs and targeted support programs. In B. I. Williams, P. A. Richmond, & B. J. Mason (Eds.), *Designs for compensatory education: Conference proceedings and papers* (VI, pp. 3–40). Washington, DC: Research and Evaluation Association, Inc.

Anderson, G. R., & Anderson, S. K. (1983). The exceptional Native American. In D. R. Omark & J. A. Erickson (Eds.), *The bilingual exceptional child* (pp. 163–180). San Diego, CA: College-Hill Press.

Bandura, A. (1977). *Social learning theory.* Englewood Cliffs, NJ: Prentice-Hall.

Bandura, A. (1981). Self-referent thought: A developmental analysis of self-efficacy. In J. H. Flavell & L. R. Ross (Eds.), *Social cognitive development: Frontiers and possible futures* (pp. 200–239). New York: Cambridge University Press.

Becker, W. C., Engelman, S., Carnine, D., & Rhine, W. R. (1981). Direct Instruction Model. In W. R. Rhine (Ed.), *Making models more effective: New directions from Follow Through* (pp. 95–154). New York: Academic Press.

Belmont, J. M., & Butterfield, E. C. (1977). The instructional approach to developmental cognitive research. In R. V. Kail, Jr., & J. W. Hagen (Eds.), *Perspectives on the development of memory and cognition* (pp. 437–481). Hillsdale, NJ: Erlbaum.

Bickel, W. E. (1982). Classifying mentally retarded students: A review of placement practices in special education. In K. A. Heller, W. H. Holtzman, & S. Messick (Eds.), *Placing children in special education: A strategy for equity* (pp. 182–229). Washington, DC: National Academy of Sciences Press.

Bloom, B. S. (1968). Learning for mastery. *Evaluation Comment,* 1(2), 74–86.

Bloom, B. S. (1976). *Human characteristics and school learning.* New York: McGraw-Hill.

Bloom, B. S. (1984). The 2 sigma problem: The search for methods of group instruction as effective as one-to-one tutoring. *Educational Researcher,* 13(6), 4–16.

Boersma, F. J., & Chapman, J. W. (1981). Academic self-concept, achievement expectations, and locus of control in elementary learning disabled children. *Canadian Journal of Behavioral Science,* **13**, 349–358.

Borkowski, J. G., Peck, V. A., & Damberg, P. R. (1983). Attention, memory and cognition. In J. L. Matson & J. A. Mulick (Eds.), *Handbook of mental retardation* (pp. 479–497). New York: Pergamon General Psychology Service.

Bossert, S. T. (1979). *Tasks and social relationships in classrooms.* New York: Cambridge University Press.

Boucher, C. R., & Deno, S. L. (1979). Learning disabled and emotionally disturbed: Will the labels affect teacher planning? *Psychology in the Schools,* **16**, 395–402.

Brantlinger, E. A (1985). Low-income parents' opinions about the social class composition of schools. *American Journal of Education,* **93**, 319–408.

Brantlinger, E. A., & Guskin, S. L. (1987). Ethnocultural and social psychological effects on learning characteristics of handicapped children. In M. C. Wang, M. C. Reynolds, & H. J. Walberg (Eds.), *Handbook of special education: Research and practice: Vol. 1. Learner characteristics and adaptive education* (pp. 7–34). Oxford, England: Pergamon.

Broman, S. H., Nichols, P. L., & Kennedy, W. A. (1975). *Preschool IQ: Prenatal and early developmental correlates.* Hillsdale, NJ: Erlbaum.

Brooks, P. H., & McCauley, C. (1984). Cognitive research in mental retardation. *American Journal of Mental Deficiency,* **88**, 479–486.

Brophy, J. B. (1986). Research linking teacher behavior to student achievement: Potential implications for instruction of Chapter 1 students. In B. I. Williams, P. A. Richmond, & B. J. Mason (Eds.1, *Designs for compensatory education: Conference proceedings and papers* (IV. pp. 121–179). Washington, DC: Research and Evaluation Associates. Inc.

Brophy, J., & Good, T. L. (1986). Teacher behavior and student achievement. In M. C. Wittrock (Ed.), *Third handbook of research on teaching* (3rd ed., pp. 328–375). New York: MacMillan.

Brown, A. L. (1974). The role of strategic behavior in retardate memory. In N. R. Ellis (Ed.), *International review of research in mental retardation* (Vol. 7, pp. 55–111). New York: Academic Press.

Brown, A. L. (1978). Knowing when, where, and how to remember. In R. Glaser (Ed.), *Advances in instructional psychology* (Vol. 1, pp 77–165). Hillsdale, NJ: Erlbaum.

Brown, A. L., Bransford, J. D., Ferrara, R., & Campione, J. (1983). Learning, understanding and remembering. In J. H. Flavell & E. Markman (Eds.), *Handbook of child psychology: Vol. 1. Cognitive development* (4th ed., pp. 77–166). New York: Wiley.

Brown, A. L., Campione, J. C., & Day, J. D. (1981). Learning to learn: On training students to learn from texts. *Educational Researcher*, **10**, 14–21.

Brown, A. L., Day, J. D., & Jones, R. S. (1983). The development of plans for summarizing texts. *Child Development*, **54**, 968–979.

Brown, A. L., & Palincsar, A. S. (1982). Inducing strategic learning from texts by means of informed, self-control training. *Topics in Learning and Learning Disabilities*, **2**(1), 1–17.

Brown, A. L., & Smiley, S. S. (1978). The development of strategies for studying text. *Child Development*, **49**, 1076–1088.

Campbell, T. C., Fuller, R. G., Thornton, M. C., Peter, J. L., Peterson, M. Q., Carpenter, E. T., & Narveson, R. D. (1980). A teacher's guide to the learning cycle: A Piagetian-based approach to college instruction. In R. G. Fuller (Ed.), *Piagetian programs in higher education* (pp. 27–46). Lincoln: University of Nebraska-Lincoln.

Campione, J. C., & Brown A. L. (1977). Memory and metamemory development in educable retarded children. In R. V. Kail, Jr., & J. W. Hagen (Eds.), *Perspectives on the development of memory and cognition* (pp. 367–406). Hillsdale, NJ: Erlbaum.

Campione, J. C., Brown A. L., & Ferrara, R. A. (1982). Mental retardation and intelligence. In R. J. Sternberg (Ed.), *Handbook of human intelligence* (pp. 392–490). Cambridge, England: Cambridge University Press.

Carlberg, C., & Kavale, K. (1980). The efficacy of special versus regular class placement for exceptional children: A meta-analysis. *Journal of Special Education*, **14**, 295–309.

Cave, R. G., & Davies, B. (1977). *Mixed ability teaching in the elementary school*. London: Ward Lock Educational.

Child Trends, Inc. (1985). *The school-age handicapped* (NCES 85–400). Washington, DC: U.S. Government Printing Office.

Coleman, J. S., Campbell, E. Q., Hobson, C. J., McPartland, J., Mood, A. M., Weinfeld, F. D., & York, R. L. (1966). *Equality of educational opportunity*. Washington, DC: U.S. Government Printing Office.

Conner, F. P. (1983). Improving school instruction for learning disabled children: The Teachers College Institute. *Exceptional Child Quarterly*, **4**, 23–44.

Cooper, H. M., & Good, T. L. (1982). *Pygmalion grows up: Studies in the expectation communication process*. New York: Longman.

Corno, L., & Snow, R. E. (1986). Adapting teaching to individual differences among learners. In M. C. Wittrock (Ed.), *Handbook of research on teaching* (3rd ed., pp. 605–629). New York: Macmillan.

Covington, M. V., & Beery, R. (1976). *Self-worth and school learning*. New York: Holt, Rinehart & Winston.

Covington, M. V., Crutchfield, R. S., Davies, L. B., & Olton, R. M. (1974). *The Productive Thinking Program: A course in learning to think*. Columbus, OH: Merrill.

Covington, M. V., & Omelich, C. L. (1979). Effort: The double-edged sword in school achievement. *Journal of Educational Psychology*, **71**, 169–182.

Crandall, V. C., Katkovsky, W., & Crandall, V. J. (1965). Children's belief in their own control of reinforcements in intellectual-academic situations. *Child Development*, **36**, 91–109.

Davis, A., & Smith, M. L. (1984). The history and politics of an evaluation: The Colorado learning disabilities study. *Educational Evaluation and Policy Analysis*, **6**, 27–37.

Day, J. D. (1980). *Training summarization skills: A comparison of teaching methods*. Unpublished doctoral dissertation, University of Illinois, Urbana.

deCharms, R. (1976). *Enhancing motivation: Change in the classroom*. New York: Wiley.

DeCorte, E., & Verschaffel, L. (1981). Children's solution processes in elementary arithmetic problems: Analysis and improvement. *Journal of Educational Psychology*, **73**, 765–779.

Deshler, D. D., Schumaker, J. B., Alley, G. R., Warner, M. M., & Clark, F. L. (1982). Learning disabilities in adolescent and young adult populations: Research implications. *Focus on Exceptional Children*, **15**, 221–227.

Deshler, D. D., Schumaker, J. B., & Lenz, B. K. (1984). Academic and cognitive interventions for LD adolescents. Annual Review of Learning Disabilities, **2**, 57–66.

DeStefano, L., Wang, M. C., & Gordon, E. W. (1984, April). Differences in student temperament characteristics and their effects on classroom processes and outcomes. In M. C. Wang (Organizer), *Temperament characteristics and learning.* Symposium presented at the annual meeting of the American Educational Research Association, New Orleans.

Douglas, V. I., & Peters, K. G. (1979). Towards a clearer definition of the attentional deficit of hyperactive children. In G. A. Hale & M. Lewis (Eds.), *Attention and cognitive development* (pp. 173–249). New York: Plenum.

Doyle, W. (1977). Paradigms for research on teacher effectiveness. In L. S. Shulman (Ed.), *Review of research in education* (Vol. 5, pp. 163–198). Itasca, IL: Peacock.

Drake, D. A., & Ehri, L. C. (1984). Spelling acquisition: Effects of pronouncing words on memory for their spellings. *Cognition and Instruction*, **1**, 297–320.

Dudley-Marling, C. C., Snider, V., & Tarver, S. G. (1982). Locus of control and learning disabilities: A review and discussion. *Perceptual and Motor Skills*, **54**, 503–514.

Duffy, J. B., Salvia, J., Tucker, J., & Ysseldyke, J. E. (1981). Nonbiased assessment: A need for operationalism. *Exceptional Children*, **47**, 427–434.

Dweck, C. S. (1975). The role of expectations and attributions in the alleviation of learned helplessness. *Journal of Personality and Social Psychology*, **31**, 674–685.

Dweck, C. S., & Elliot, E. S. (1983). Achievement motivation. In P. H. Mussen (Ed.), *Handbook of child psychology: Vol. 4. Socialization, personality, and social development* (pp. 643–692). New York: Wiley.

Eder, D. (1981). Ability grouping as a self-fulfilling prophecy: A microanalysis of teacher-student interaction. *Sociology of Education*. **57**, 151–162.

Educational Testing Service. (1980). New vistas in special education. *Focus*. **8**, 1–20.

Englert, C. S., Hiebert, E. H., & Stewart, S. R. (1985, April). *Spelling unfamiliar words by an analogy strategy.* Paper presented at the annual meeting of the American Educational Research Association, Chicago, IL.

Federal Register (1977, August). Regulations for implementing the Education for All Handicapped Children Act of 1975 (Public Law 94–142). **42**, 474–482, 518.

Felixbrod, J. J., & O'Leary, K. D. (1974). Self-determination of academic standards by children: Toward freedom from external control. *Journal of Educational Psychology*, **66**, 845–850.

Feuerstein, R. (1979). *The dynamic assessment of retarded performers: The learning potential assessment device, theory, instruments, and techniques.* Baltimore, MD: University Park Press.

Feuerstein, R. (1980). *Instrumental Enrichment: An intervention program for cognitive modifiability.* Baltimore, MD: University Park Press.

Flavell, J. H. (1970). Developmental studies of mediated memory. In H. W. Reese & L. P. Lipsitt (Eds.), *Advances in child development and behavior* (Vol. 5, pp. 182–211). New York: Academic Press.

Flavell, J. H., & Wellman, H. M. (1977). Metamemory. In R. V. Kail, Jr., & J. W. Hagen (Eds.), *Perspectives on the development of memory and cognition* (pp. 3–33). Hillsdale, NJ: Erlbaum.

Gartner, A., & Lipsky, D. K. (1987). Beyond special education: Toward a quality system for all students. Harvard Educational Review. **57**(4), 367–395.

Gilkeson, E. C., Smithberg, L. M., Bowman, G. W., & Rhine, W. R. (1981). Bank Street Model: A developmental-interaction approach. In W. R. Rhine (Ed.), *Making schools more effective: New directions from Follow Through* (pp. 249–288). New York: Academic Press.

Glaser, R. (1984). Education and thinking: The role of knowledge. *American Psychologist*, **39**, 93–104.

Gordon, E. W. (Ed.). (1983). *Human diversity and pedagogy.* Westport, CT: Mediax.

Greeno, J. G. (1982). *Forms of understanding in mathematical problem solving* (Tech. Rep. UPITT/LRDC/ONR/APS–10). Pittsburgh, PA: University of Pittsburgh, Learning Research and Development Center.

Gresham, F. M., & Reschly, D. J. (1986). Social skill deficits and low peer acceptance of mainstreamed learning disabled children. *Learning Disability Quarterly*, **9**, 23–32.

Hallahan, D. P., & Sapona, R. (1984). Self-monitoring of attention with learning disabled children: Past research and current issues. *Annual Review of Learning Disabilities*, **2**, 97–101.

Harris, K. R., & Graham, S. (1985). Improving learning disabled students' composition skills: A self-control strategy training approach. *Learning Disability Quarterly*, **8**, 27–36.

Heller, K. A., Holtzman, W. H., & Messick, S. (Eds.). (1982). *Placing children in special education: A strategy for equity*. Washington, DC: National Academy of Sciences Press.

Henderson, R. W. (1981). Home environment and intellectual performance. In R. W. Henderson (Ed.), *Parent-child interaction* (pp. 3–29). New York: Academic Press.

Hillocks, G. (1984). What works in teaching composition: A meta-analysis of experimental treatment studies. *American Journal of Education*, **93**, 133–170.

Hobbs, N. (1975a). *The futures of children*. San Francisco, CA: Jossey-Bass.

Hobbs, N. (Ed.). (1975b). *Issues in the classification of children* (Vols. 1–2). San Francisco, CA: Jossey-Bass.

Hodgkinson, H. L. (1985). *All one system: Demographics of education—Kindergarten through graduate school*. Washington, DC: Institute for Educational Leadership, Inc.

Jenkins, J. J. (1979). Four points to remember: A tetrahedral model of memory experiments. In L. S. Cermak & F. I. M. Craik (Eds.), *Levels of processing and human memory* (pp. 429–446). Hillsdale, NJ: Erlbaum.

Jenkins, J. J. (1980). Can we have a fruitful cognitive psychology? In H. E. Howe & J. H. Flowers (Eds.), *Nebraska symposium on motivation* (pp. 211–238). Lincoln: University of Nebraska Press.

Jenkins, J. R. (1987, February). Similarities in the achievement levels of learning disabled and remedial students. *Counterpoint*, p. 16.

Jenkins, J. R., Pious, C., & Peterson, D. (1988). Exploring the validity of a unified learning program for remedial and handicapped students. *Exceptional Children*, **55**(2), 147–158.

Jeter, J. (Ed.). (1980). *Approaches to individualized education*. Alexandria, VA: Association for Supervision and Curriculum Development.

Kauffman, J. M., & Hallahan, D. P. (1979). Learning disability and hyperactivity (with comments on minimal brain dysfunction). In B. B. Lahey & A. E. Kazdin (Eds.), *Advances in clinical child psychology* (Vol. 2, pp. 72–105). New York: Plenum.

Kavale, K. (1980). Learning disability and cultural-economic disadvantage: The case for a relationship. *Learning Disability Quarterly*, **3**, 97–112.

Keogh, B. K. (1982). Children's temperament and teachers' decisions. In R. Porter & G. M. Collins (Eds.), *Temperamental differences in infants and young children* (pp. 269–285). London: Pitman.

Keogh, B. K. (1983). Classification, compliance, and confusion. *Journal of Learning Disabilities*, **16**, 25.

Klausmeier, H. J. (1972). *Individually Guided Education: An alternative system of elementary schooling* (Harlan E. Anderson Lecture). New Haven, CT: Yale University, Center for the Study of Education.

Kosiewicz, M. M., Hallahan, D. P., Lloyd, J., & Graves, A. W. (1982). Effects of self-instruction and self-correction procedures on handwriting performance. *Learning Disability Quarterly*, **5**, 71–77.

Kurtz, B. E., & Borkowski, J. G. (1985, March). *Metacognition and the development of strategic skills in impulsive and reflective children*. Paper presented at the annual meeting of the Society for Research in Child Development.

Kyle, R. M. (Ed.). (1985). *Reaching for excellence*. Washington, DC: E. H. White and Co.

Laosa, L. M. (1980). Maternal teaching strategies and cognitive styles in Chicano families. *Journal of Educational Psychology*, **72**, 45–54.

Larry P. v. Riles, Civil Action No. C–71–2270, RFP (N.D. CA. 1971).

Lefcourt, H. M. (1982). *Locus of control: Current trends in theory and research* (2nd ed.). Hillsdale, NJ: Erlbaum.

Leinhardt, G., & Pallay, A. (1982). Restrictive educational settings: Exile or haven? *Review of Educational Research*. **52**, 557–578.

Lindvall, C. M., Tamburino, J. L., & Robinson, L. (1982, March). *An exploratory investigation of the effects of teaching primary grade children to use specific problem solving strategies in solving simple arithmetic story problems.* Paper presented at the annual meeting of the American Educational Research Association, New York.

Lipman, M., Sharp, A. M., & Oscanyan, F. S. (1980). *Philosophy in the classroom.* Philadelphia, PA: Temple University Press.

Lloyd, J., Saltzman, N. J., & Kauffman, J. M. (1981). Predictable generalization in academic learning as a result of preskills and strategy training. *Learning Disability Quarterly,* **4,** 203–216.

MacMillan, D., & Borthwick, S. (1980). The new educable mentally retarded population: Can they be mainstreamed? *Mental Retardation,* **18,** 155–158.

MacMillan, D., Meyers, C. E. & Morrison, G. (1980). System-identification of mildly mentally retarded children: Implications for interpreting and conducting research. *American Journal of Mental Deficiency,* **85,** 108–115.

Madden, N. A., & Slavin, R. E. (1983). Mainstreaming students with mild handicaps: Academic and social outcomes. *Review of Educational Research,* **53,** 519–569.

Marcucci, R. J. (1980). A meta-analysis of research on methods of teaching math problem solving. *Dissertation Abstracts International,* **41,** 2485A.

Mare, R. D. (1981). Change and stability in educational stratification. *American Sociological Review,* **46,** 72–87.

Marshall, H. H., & Weinstein, R. S. (1984). Classroom factors affecting students' self-evaluations: An interactional model. *Review of Educational Research,* **54,** 301–325.

McCombs, B. L. (1982). Learner satisfaction and motivation: Capitalizing on strategies for positive self-control. *Performance and Instruction.* **21**(4), 3–6.

Mercer, C. D., Hughes, C., & Mercer, A. R. (1985). Learning disabilities definitions used by state education departments. *Learning Disability Quarterly,* **8,** 45–55.

Mercer, J. (1973). *Labeling the mentally retarded.* Berkeley: University of California Press.

Mercer, J. (1979). *System of Multicultural Pluralistic Assessment technical manual.* New York: Psychological Corporations.

Mercer, J., & Ysseldyke, J. (1977). Designing diagnostic-intervention programs. In T. Oakland (Ed.), *Psychological and educational assessment of minority children* (pp. 70–90). New York: Brunner/Mazel.

Meyer, W. (1979). Academic expectations, attributed responsibility, and teachers' reinforcement behavior: A comment on Cooper and Baron, with some additional data. *Journal of Educational Psychology,* **71,** 269–273.

Meyers, C., MacMillan, D., & Yoshida, R. (1978). Validity of psychologists' identification of EMR students in the perspective of the California decertification experience. *Journal of School Psychology,* **16,** 3–15.

Miller, G. E. (1985). The effects of general and specific self-instruction training on children's comprehension monitoring performances during reading. *Reading Research Quarterly,* **20,** 616–628.

Mink, I. T., Meyers, C. E., & Nihira, K. (1984). Taxonomy of family life styles: 2 homes with slow-learning children. *American Journal of Mental Deficiency,* **89,** 111–123.

Nicholls, J. G. (1979). Quality and equality in intellectual development: The role of motivation in education. *American Psychology,* **34,** 1071–1084.

Nickerson, R. S., Perkins, D. N., & Smith, E. E. (1984). *Teaching thinking.* Cambridge, MA: Bolt, Beranek and Newman.

Palincsar, A. S., & Brown, A. L. (1984). Reciprocal teaching of comprehension-fostering and comprehension-monitoring activities. *Cognition and Instruction,* **1,** 117–125.

Palincsar, A. S., & Brown, A. L. (1987). Advances in improving the cognitive performance of handicapped students. In M. C. Wang, M. C. Reynolds, & H. J. Walberg (Eds.), *Handbook of special education: Research and practice: Vol. 1. Learner characteristics and adaptive education* (pp. 93–112). Oxford, England: Pergamon.

Papert, S. (1980). *Mindstorms.* New York: Basic Books.

Paris, S., Cross, D., DeBritto, A., Jacobs, J., Oka, E., & Saarnio, D. (1984, April). *Improving children's metacognition and reading comprehension with classroom instruction.* Paper presented at the annual meeting of the American Educational Research Association, New Orleans.

Patrick, J., & Reschly, D. (1982). Relationship of state educational criteria and demographic variables to school-system prevalence of mental retardation. *American Journal of Mental Deficiency*, **86**, 351–360.

Pearl, R. (1982). Learning disabled children's attributions for success and failure: A replication with labeled LD sample. *Learning Disability Quarterly*, **5**, 173–176.

Pflaum, S. W., & Pascarella, E. T. (1980). Interactive effects of prior reading achievement and training in context on the reading of learning disabled children. *Reading Research Quarterly*, **16**, 138–158.

Pink, W. T. (1982). School effects, academic performance, and school crime. *Urban Education*, **17**, 51–72.

Polloway, E. A., & Smith, J. D. (1983). Changes in mild mental retardation: Population, programs, and perspectives. *Exceptional Children*, **50**, 149–159.

Ramey, C. T., & Campbell, F. A. (1979). Compensatory education for disadvantaged children. *School Review*, **87**, 1711–1789.

Ramp, E. A., & Rhine, W. R. (1981). Behavior Analysis Model. In W. R. Rhine (Ed.), *Making schools more effective; New directions from Follow Through* (pp. 155–200). New York: Academic Press.

Reschly, D. J. (1979). Nonbiased assessment. In G. Phye & D. Reschly (Eds.), *School psychology: Perspectives and issues* (pp. 215–253). New York: Academic Press.

Reschly, D. J. (1984). Beyond IQ test bias: The National Academy panel's analysis of minority EMR overrepresentation. *Educational Researcher*, **13**(3), 15–19.

Reschly, D. J. (1987). Learning characteristics of mildly handicapped students: Implications for classification, placement and programming. In M. C. Wang, M. C. Reynolds, & H. J. Walberg (Eds.), *Handbook of special education: Research and practice: Vol. 1. Learner characteristics and adaptive education* (pp. 35–58). Oxford, England: Pergamon.

Reschly, D. J., Gresham, F. M., & Graham-Clay, S. (1984). *Multi-factored nonbiased assessment: Convergent and discriminant validity of social and cognitive measures with black and white regular and special education students. Final project report.* Ames: Iowa State University, Department of Psychology. (ERIC Document Reproduction Service No. ED 252034).

Resnick, L. B., & Ford, W. W. (1981). *The psychology of mathematics for instruction.* Hillsdale, NJ: Erlbaum.

Reynolds, M. C. (1984). Classification of students with handicaps. In E. W. Gordon (Ed.), *Review of research in education* (Vol. 11, pp. 63–92). Washington, DC: American Educational Research Association.

Reynolds, M. C., & Wang, M. C. (1983). Restructuring "special" school programs: A position paper. *Policy Studies Review*, **2**, 189–212.

Richmond, B. O., & Waits, C. (1978). Special education—Who needs it? *Exceptional Children*, **44**, 279–280.

Riley, M. S., Greeno, J. G., & Heller, J. I. (1983). Development of children's problem solving ability in arithmetic. In H. P. Ginsburg (Ed.), *The development of mathematical thinking.* New York: Academic Press.

Rosenholtz, S., & Wilson, B. (1980). The effect of classroom structure on shared perceptions of ability. *American Educational Research Journal*, **17**, 75–82.

Ross, S., & Zimiles, H. (1974). The differentiated child behavior observational system. In M. C. Wang (Ed.), *The use of direct observation to study instructional-learning behaviors in school settings* (pp. 4–21) (*LRDC Publication Series* 1974/9). Pittsburgh, PA: University of Pittsburgh, Learning Research and Development Center.

Rotter, J. B. (1966). Generalized expectancies for internal versus external control of reinforcement. *Psychological Monographs*, **80** (1, Whole No. 609).

Sabatino, D. A. (1982). Research on achievement motivation with learning disabled populations. In K. D. Gadow & I. Bialer (Eds.), *Advances in learning and behavioral disabilities* (Vol. 1, pp. 75–116). Greenwich, CT: JAI Press.

Scardamalia, M., & Bereiter, C. (1986). Fostering the development of self-regulation in children's knowledge processing. In S. F. Chipman, J. W. Segal, & R. Glaser (Eds.), *Thinking and learning skills: Vol. 2. Research and open questions* (pp. 563–577). Hillsdale, NJ: Erlbaum.

Scardamalia, M., Bereiter, C., & Fillion, B. (1979). *The little red writing book: A source book of consequential writing activities.* Ontario, Canada: Ontario Institute for the Study of Education, Pedagogy of Writing Project.

Scardamalia, M., Bereiter, C., & Steinbach, R. (1984). Teachability of reflective processes in written composition. *Cognitive Science*, **8**, 173–190.

Schoenfeld, A. H. (1980). Teaching problem-solving skills. *American Mathematical Monthly*, **87**, 794–805.

Schumaker, J. B., Deshler, D. D., Alley, G. R., & Warner, M. M. (1983). Toward the development of an intervention model for learning disabled adolescents: The University of Kansas Institute. *Exceptional Education Quarterly*, **4**, 45–74.

Schumaker, J., Deshler, D., Alley, G., Warner, M., & Denton, P. (1984). Multipass: A learning strategy for improving reading comprehension. *Learning Disability Quarterly*, **5**, 295–304.

Schunk, D. H. (1982). Effects of attributional feedback on children's perceived self-efficacy and achievement. *Journal of Educational Psychology*, **74**, 548–557.

Scott, L. S. (1979, August). *Identification of declassified students: Characteristics and needs of the population.* Paper presented at the annual meeting of the American Psychological Association, New York.

Segal, J. W., Chipman, S. F., & Glaser, R. (Eds.). (1985). *Thinking and learning skills: Vol. 1. Relating instruction to research.* Hillsdale, NJ: Erlbaum.

Semmel, M. I., Gottlieb, J., & Robinson, N. M. (1979). Mainstreaming: Perspectives on educating handicapped children in the public school. In D. C. Berliner (Ed.), *Review of research in education* (Vol. 7, pp. 223–279). Washington, DC: American Education Research Association.

Shepard, L. A. (1983). The role of measurement in educational policy: Lessons from the identification of learning disabilities. *Educational Measurement: Issues and Practice*, **2**, 4–8.

Slavin, R. E. (1983). *Team-Assisted Individualization: A cooperative learning solution for adaptive instruction in mathematics.* Baltimore, MD: The Johns Hopkins University, Center for the Social Organization of Schools.

Stallings, J. A. (1975). Implementation and child effects of teaching practices in Follow Through classrooms. *Monographs of the Society for Research in Child Development*, **40**(7–8, Serial No. 163).

Stipek, D. J. (1981, April). *The development of achievement-related emotions.* Paper presented at the annual meeting of the American Educational Research Association, Los Angeles.

Stone, A, K., & Serwatka, T. S. (1982). Reducing syntactic errors in written responses of a retarded adolescent through oral patterning. *Education and Training of the Mentally Retarded*, **17**, 71–74.

Tesser, A., & Campbell, J. A. (1982). A self-evaluation maintenance approach to school behavior. *Educational Psychologist*, **17**, 1–12.

Thomas, J. (1980). Agency and achievement: Self-management and self-regard. *Review of Educational Research*, **50**, 213–240.

Torgenson, J. K. (1977). The role of nonspecific factors in the task performance of learning disabled children: A theoretical assessment. *Journal of Learning Disabilities*, **10**, 27–34.

Uguroglu, M., & Walberg, H. (1979). Motivation and achievement: A quantitative synthesis. *American Educational Research Journal*, **16**, 375–389.

Walberg, H. J. (1984). Improving the productivity of America's schools. *Educational Leadership*, **41**(8), 19–30.

Walberg, H. J., & Wang, M. C. (1987). Effective educational practices and provisions for individual differences. In M. C. Wang, M. C. Reynolds, & H. J. Walberg (Eds.), *Handbook of special education: Research and practice: Vol. 1. Learner characteristics and adaptive education* (pp. 113–128). Oxford, England: Pergamon.

Wang, M. C. (1976). (Ed.). *The Self-Schedule System of instructional-learning management for adaptive school learning environments* (*LRDC Publication Series* 1976/9). Pittsburgh, PA: University of Pittsburgh, Learning Research and Development Center.

Wang, M. C. (1983). Development and consequences of students' sense of personal control. In J. M. Levine & M. C. Wang (Eds.), *Teacher and student perceptions: Implications for learning* (pp. 213–247). Hillsdale, NJ: Erlbaum.

Wang, M. C., & Baker, E. T. (1985–86). Mainstreaming programs: Design features and effects. *Journal of Special Education*, **19**, 503–521.

Wang, M. C., Gennari, P., & Waxman, H. C. (1985). The Adaptive Learning Environments Model: Design, implementation, and effects. In M. C. Wang & H. J. Walberg (Eds.), *Adapting instruction to individual differences* (pp. 191–235). Berkeley, CA: McCutchan.

Wang, M. C., & Lindvall, C. M. (1984). Individual differences and school learning environments: Theory, research, and design. In E. W. Gordon (Ed.), *Review of research in education* (Vol. 11, pp. 161–226). Washington, DC: American Educational Research Association.

Wang, M. C., & Peverly, S. T. (1986). The self-instructive process in classroom learning contexts. *Contemporary Educational Psychology*, **11**, 370–404.

Wang, M. C., & Peverly, S. T. (1987). The role of the learner: An individual difference variable in school learning and functioning. In M. C. Wang, M. C. Reynolds, & H. J. Walberg (Eds.), *Handbook of special education: Research and practice: Vol. 1. Learner characteristics and adaptive education* (pp. 59–92). Oxford, England: Pergamon.

Wang, M. C., Reynolds, M. C., & Walberg, H. J. (Eds.). (1987–1989). *Handbook of special education: Research and practice* (Vols. 1–3). Oxford, England: Pergamon.

Wang, M. C., Reynolds, M. C., & Walberg, H. J. (1988). Integrating children of the second system. *Phi Delta Kappa*, **70**, 248–251.

Wang, M. C., & Walberg, H. J. (1983). Evaluating educational programs: An integative, causal-modeling approach. *Educational Evaluation and Policy Analysis*, **5**, 347–366.

Wang, M. C., & Walberg, H. J. (1986). Classroom climate as mediator of educational inputs and outputs. In B. J. Fraser (Ed.), *The study of learning environments 1985* (pp. 47–58). Salem, OR: Assessment Research.

Waxman, H. C., Wang, M. C., Anderson, K. A., & Walberg, H. J. (1985). Adaptive education and student outcomes: A quantitative synthesis. *Journal of Educational Research*, **78**, 228–236.

Weiner, B. A. (1976). An attributional approach for educational psychology. In L. Shulman (Ed.), *Review of research in education* (Vol. 4, pp. 179–209). Itasca, IL: Peacock.

Weiner, B. A. (1979). Theory of motivation for some classroom experiences. *Journal of Educational Psychology*, **7**, 3–25.

Weiner, B. A. (1983). Speculations regarding the role of affect in achievement-change programs guided by attributional principles. In J. M. Levine & M. C. Wang (Eds.), *Teacher and student perceptions: Implications for learning* (pp. 57–73). Hillsdale, NJ: Erlbaum.

Weinstein, R. S. (1983). Student perceptions of schooling. *The Elementary School Journal*, **83**, 286–312.

Wittrock, M. C. (Ed.). (1986). *Handbook of research on teaching* (3rd ed.). New York: Macmillan.

Wong, B., & Jones, W. (1982). Increasing metacomprehension in L.D. and normally achieving students through self-questioning training. *Learning Disability Quarterly*, **5**, 228-238.

Ysseldyke, J. E., Algozzine, B., & Richey, L. (1982). Judgment under uncertainty: How many children are handicapped? *Exceptional Children*, **48**, 531–534.

Ysseldyke, J. E., Algozzine, B., Shinn, M. R., & McGue, M. (1982). Similarities and differences between low achievers and students classified learning disabled. *Journal of Special Education*, **16**, 73–85.

Ysseldyke, J. E., Algozzine, B., & Thurlow, M. (1983). On interpreting institute research: A response to McKinney. *Exceptional Child Quarterly*, **4**, 145–147.

Ysseldyke, J. E., & Thurlow, M. L. (1983). *Identification/classification research: An integrative summary of findings* (Research Rep. No. 142). Minneapolis: University of Minnesota, Department of Educational Psychology.

Effectiveness of Differential Programming in Serving Handicapped Students

KENNETH A. KAVALE

University of Iowa

What makes special education special? In a general sense, the answer lies in a variety of special services and practices, including curriculum, materials, methods, and techniques that are not routinely used in regular education settings. Special education is designed to respond to the unique learning characteristics of students whose needs cannot be met within the standard school context. The special education program typically is highly individualized and aims at either remediation—correction of special academic or social problems, or compensation—alternative procedures to aid students in overcoming specific academic or social problems, or both. Although viewed generally as a separate system, special education may be delivered within a context ranging from complete segregation to full integration. Regardless of the level of integration with regular education, special education is ultimately defined by the special activities with which it has come to be associated. The question becomes one of whether these different practices demonstrate a level of efficacy sufficient to demonstrate the practicality of special education.

Debate continues to rage over the efficacy of special education. Even though decisions have come to rely increasingly upon empirical evidence, the data have not been unequivocal. Decisions about intervention efficacy have thus become entwined in political and ideological rhetoric associated with different schools of thought about special education. Kauffman (1981) suggested that these schools of thought can lead to a sense of cynicism and despair because they have, at times, provided more false hopes and easy solutions than real progress. The result is found in the periodic surfacing of the basis question: Is special education special? (Milofsky, 1974). Implied here is whether or not special education can be justified on a cost-benefit analysis basis. With special education costs exceeding regular education costs by as much as one and one-half to four times (Wilkerson & Jones, 1976), it becomes important to determine whether the costs are justified in terms of outcome effectiveness.

Many of the concerns over the effectiveness of differential programming are philosophical in nature but specific issues can be addressed through an evaluation of the extant research. The major difficulty under this heading was to define appropriate programming alternatives that could be applied comprehensively across students and settings but, at the same time, were different enough to clearly be defined as special education practices. These programming alternatives span a wide continuum and offer no natural framework for investigating the primary issue related to their effectiveness. Therefore, a framework needed to be imposed upon the general topic to delimit the boundaries. Five subtopics were then agreed upon to address the major concerns in the area of differential programming. The selected subtopics were not exhaustive but did provide a comprehensive perspective about the nature of special education practices in providing services to handicapped students.

The five subtopics could be grouped into three levels of specificity. One level assesses specific concerns (e.g., cognitive-behavioral training for basic skills, and programming independent living skills); a second level deals with general theoretical and philosophical concerns embodied in special education practices (e.g., diagnostic-prescriptive teaching models); and a third level focuses on general concerns about the manner in which intervention practices are best integrated and coordinated (e.g., the relationship between instructional programming and placement options). The primary and secondary issues addressed in these subtopics provide an overview of the effectiveness of the practices which have come to define special education. Ultimately, the effectiveness of these practices will determine whether or not special education is special enough to warrant their inclusion in programming for handicapped students. Thus, the question is whether or not these practices actually do reveal special education as a useful alternative to and improvement upon regular education.

Curriculum Considerations

A basic consideration in educating children with special needs is the question of what should be taught. This question is answered through the concept of curriculum which, in its broadest sense, encompasses what the learner learns in a learning situation. Although curriculum is an important concern for regular education, the past 10–15 years have shown a neglect of this topic in special education. The heterogeneity of special education populations along with policies emphasizing individual education may account for the neglect of curriculum issues. Before instructional strategies can be chosen, however, it is necessary to know program content in terms of what should be taught.

Morrison (1987) addressed the question of curriculum in special education, especially how curricular emphases dealing with social and vocational components (now common in special education) can be meshed with the more traditional academic focus. Curriculum can be an elusive concept and Morrison drew upon philosophical trends, empirical contributions, governmental policies, and state-of-the-art practice to detail curricular choices.

Philosophical Trends

The goals of any curricular arrangement ultimately reflect the needs and values of the society at large. Within this context, it appears that the goal for handicapped students is that they be allowed to develop into productive adulthood to the greatest possible degree. Debate begins with the best means to achieve this desired goal. Traditionally, emphasis has been on academic training as a means to promote effective functioning; however, it should also include elements of social and vocational education to round out the picture.

The question of balance among academic, social, and vocational emphases in curriculum content initiates many philosophical disputes, but Morrison suggested that, in reality, these content areas are not mutually exclusive. The reason is found in a policy which mandates appropriate education, least restrictive environment, and the Individualized Education Program (IEP). When these policy mandates are considered, it means that any goals for handicapped students must insure quality education which meets the individual student's needs within a comprehensive framework.

Empirical Contributions

Much of the decision making regarding curricular content emphases is based upon the student's handicap and age. For example, severely handicapped students have curriculum developed through three approaches: developmental, behavioral, and functional. Similarly, curriculum for mildly handicapped students is usually guided through four approaches: psychoeducational, sensory-neurological, ecological, and behavioral. These theoretical guides are used as a general framework for curriculum development and are often more appropriate for particular emphases (e.g., ecological approach for social programming). Morrison suggested that, except for degree and kind of programming, much similarity exists between theoretical curricular content for mildly and severely handicapped students; however, low-incidence handicaps (e.g., visually and hearing impaired) face unique curriculum problems. For the most part, existing curricular content must be adapted to the needs of low-incidence handicapped students.

Morrison emphasized theoretical and philosophical orientations primarily because little empirical research has been conducted to verify outcomes for differential weighting of curricular content areas. One major difficulty is the lack of consensus about what should be the major criteria for program efficacy. Typically, investigations attempt to evaluate overall models, so information about specific program features is often not considered. Thus, it is difficult to evaluate the success of individual components and to make judgments about the efficacy of each curricular content area in relation to the total curriculum package.

Without empirical evidence, the organization and emphasis of curriculum content tends generally to be a judgmental process contingent upon the nature of the handicapping condition, the age of the target students, and the values of those making curriculum decisions (e.g., teachers, parents). Morrison described the sources through which an entire curriculum package is put together. A major source is found in curriculum guides, an integral part of most school districts. These guides typically include tasks which represent a scope and sequence for activities to be taught. Another source is found in the unit method, which structures tasks around areas of interests and emphasizes application in real settings. Finally, special education has seen curriculum development projects aimed at systematic construction that includes consideration of child variability, material availability, institutional setting, and teacher characteristics. The prototypical example is the Social Learning Curriculum (Goldstein, 1975) developed to enhance social competence. Recently, similar effects have been attempted for career education (e.g., Brolin's (1982) Life Centered Career Education).

Governmental Policies

Morrison next described how decisions are arrived at regarding program content emphases. If any model and its guide or products are not adopted intact, then decisions need to be made about how a total package will be developed. A first step is to prioritize goals and objectives. When a consensus on this prioritization is achieved among teachers, administrators, parents, and community, then the process becomes one of matching these goals to the individual needs of the consumers (i.e., the handicapped students themselves). This is critical in order to prevent the curriculum from becoming the primary focus at the expense of the student. The IEP process is designed to coordinate goals and individual needs with the overall objective of a comprehensive curriculum aimed at maximizing the "criterion of ultimate functioning." The process has been further refined through activities aimed at aligning curriculum like "curriculum maps" or the "Individualized Critical Skills Model."

Morrison concluded that curriculum in special education has been influenced by historical, philosophical, political, theoretical, and empirical sources. Public Law 94-142, particularly the mandate for IEPs, has provided a structure for decisions regarding curricular content for handicapped students. With a means of prioritizing goals and matching them to individual student needs, the IEP has rationally focused on balancing academic, social, and vocational emphases in providing a total curriculum package. The process, however, is by no means settled because little consensus has emerged about the question of integration and emphasis of the various content areas. The paucity of research has made it difficult to answer satisfactorily questions such as (a) Should one content area be preferred above the others? (b) What should the order of prioritization be? (c) Are the content areas best taught in concert in an integrated curriculum? Morrison warned that research alone is not the final answer because research too often focuses on simplistic or policy-related questions. Thus, research can provide only partial answers because too much is based on philosophical considerations that are bound to differ among those making curriculum decisions.

State-of-the-Art Practice

Finally, curriculum matters in special education need to be placed in the context of schools in general, and regular education in particular. Morrison suggested that the relationships are best considered within the framework of the effective school research. By examining what makes schools effective, it will be possible to define the best arrangements for merging regular and special education practices to produce the strongest curricular structure for handicapped students.

Diagnostic-Prescriptive Teaching

In its most traditional sense, diagnostic-prescriptive teaching should not be a controversial issue. The concept implies the creation of an individualized program based upon assessment data and available resources. Peter (1965) described a comprehensive diagnostic-prescriptive model wherein individual diagnostic data are considered in relation to the individual problem, situational factors, and the school environment in formulating teaching techniques.

Colarusso (1987), however, demonstrated how this concept has been more narrowly defined and how it polarized the field of special education. One view, termed the Process Model, grew out of the medical model and stressed the need to train underlying abilities that are prerequisite to academic learning. Kirk (1963) and others championed this model during the 1960s, and it became the predominant model, especially in the emerging field of learning disabilities. This section will review research on diagnostic prescriptive teaching in order to emphasize the impact of controversy in the field.

Research Integration

Beginning in the late 1960s, questions arose about the Process Model. Many of these questions were raised by behaviorists who objected to the training of underlying processes at the expense of what can be observed. The behaviorists focused on actual tasks which were analyzed with respect to how the skill could be improved directly. The emphasis was on the actual academic learning task and came to be called the Task Model.

Colarusso demonstrated how the term diagnostic-prescriptive teaching became inexorably linked to the Process Model and thus became a source of continuing controversy within the context of the behavioral zeitgeist so prominent in special education during the 1970s. The problem was further compounded through an association of the diagnostic-prescriptive model with the concept of aptitude-treatment interactions. Thus, a concept that might be interpreted in a straightforward and noncontroversial manner has evolved into a long-standing controversy not easily resolved.

In its most general sense, Ysseldyke and Salvia (1974) described the critical assumptions underlying the Process Model within the diagnostic-prescriptive framework. These include the following:

1. Children enter a teaching situation with strengths and weaknesses.
2. These strengths and weaknesses are causally related to the acquisition of academic skills.
3. These strengths and weaknesses can be reliably and validly assessed.
4. There are well-identified links between children's strengths and weaknesses and relative effectiveness of instruction.

Colarusso organized the discussion to address three primary questions.

1. Do the psychological constructs of the process model exist?

2. Can these process constructs be assessed?
3. Can deficits in the process areas be remediated or trained?

DO THE PSYCHOLOGICAL CONSTRUCTS EXIST?

Colarusso explored the first question through a discussion of visual perception and found considerable variability in how perception is defined. Definitions ranged from broad to specific and included any number of different factors. This made it difficult to compare definitions across research studies. Given these difficulties, Colarusso suggested that some analyses (e.g., Arter & Jenkins, 1979) may have oversimplified their findings. Reliability and validity should not be the sole arbiters of whether or not the constructs exist. Additionally, assessment and training cannot be used unequivocally as evidence for or against process constructs. Colarusso argued that knowledge of developmental and criterion levels must be considered in discussion of process constructs. When these issues are considered, Colarusso concluded that the research is equivocal, and it is by no means clear that process constructs do not exist.

CAN PROCESS CONSTRUCTS BE ASSESSED?

In answering the question of whether or not process constructs can be assessed, Colarusso framed the discussion in terms of reliability and validity. A significant problem is the assignment of cut-off scores for reliability. A major factor not considered is the purpose of the decision which influences the desired level of reliability. Although multiple criteria would be useful for deciding levels of reliability, they are often not included, and reliability levels typically remain static. In a review of the most popular process tests, Colarusso concluded that, while a few demonstrated acceptable reliability, most tests revealed suspect reliability, particularly with respect to subtest reliability.

Validity was addressed through the notions of both criterion and construct validity. A majority of the popular process tests were found not to be good predictors of academic achievement. Tests of auditory perception and auditory-visual integration, however, demonstrated the ability to distinguish between, for example, good and poor readers. The Frostig Developmental Test of Visual Perception and the Illinois Test of Psycholinguistic Abilities (ITPA) were most often assessed for construct validity. The constructs on the Frostig test were not supported, while factor analytic studies did support the constructs of the ITPA. Findings, however, all tend to be conflicting and are, at best, inconclusive.

CAN PROCESS ABILITIES BE REMEDIATED?

Colarusso discussed the remediation of process abilities through a discussion of perceptual-motor training, psychoeducational training, and modality matching. Although the perceptual-motor training literature used different designs and analyses, reviews generally concluded that such training has little positive effect on either perceptual-motor abilities or academic functioning. In a meta-analysis of perceptual-motor training, Kavale and Mattson (1983) summarized 180 studies and found essentially no effect for any combination of variables.

Psycholinguistic training surrounds the question of whether functions of the ITPA can be trained and has produced a more focused debate. Kavale (1981), in a meta-analysis of 34 studies, concluded that all areas of psycholinguistic training were enhanced but the most impressive gains were found in Representational Level subtests including Verbal and Manual Expression. These findings were disputed on the basis of practical significance, meaning that the observed effects translate into only two to three items per subtest. What is lost in this criticism is the fact that items represent proxies for hundreds of items and the value of increased scores represents far more than two to three items.

Little support was noted for modality matching, wherein model strengths and weaknesses are identified, and then instruction is matched to capitalize upon the pattern of observed modality preferences.

State of the Practice

Colarusso concluded that the Diagnostic-Prescriptive Teaching Model remains a source of confusion for special educators. The model itself is open to varying interpretation, including a classic interpretation (Peter, 1965), a model emphasizing process concepts, a model emphasizing behavioral concepts, and finally a model combining process and task analytic features to focus on the interaction of teacher and learner (Lerner, 1981). While this debate continues, it must be understood that diagnostic-prescriptive teaching as a concept is integral to individualized instruction and hence the Individualized Education Program (IEP).

Diagnostic-prescriptive teaching has been most often associated with the process model. Surveys and interviews reveal the ingrained nature of the assumption that processes and process training are linked to the way teachers view diagnostic-prescriptive teaching. The behavioral model has offered an alternative diagnostic-prescriptive teaching sequence based on task analysis and direct instruction. Mann (1971) was among the first to criticize the fractional practices inherent in the process model and to emphasize the need for skill training directed at analyzed components. Although hierarchies of learning skills have been identified, questions have been raised over the definitiveness of such hierarchies and whether or not alternative hierarchies are equally valid. Arguments have been presented (e.g., Smead, 1977) suggesting that neither process nor skill models are complete, and they should be combined for a comprehensive intervention program. Such combinations have not been forthcoming.

Colarusso concluded that, while process training seems to be ineffective, it is not at all clear that process concepts should be abandoned. Research problems in the process area are then discussed with hopes of improving upon the past for the betterment of special education. Colarusso called for practitioners not to take a philosophical stance, but rather to become true eclectics who will select intervention strategies based on individual needs. Additionally, these intervention packages must be evaluated with new and better methods that transcend the problems found in the past. It is only in this way that special education can move towards diagnostic-prescriptive instruction in its classical sense rather than fruitless debate about particular philosophical views. The benefits will not so much be the elimination of unproductive dispute but rather improved remedial efforts for children with special needs.

Cognitive Methods

Evaluating intervention activities in special education has long been problematic because of the enormous variability inherent in special education. Variability in populations studied and application of specific techniques have confounded the search for aptitude-treatment interactions which might serve as the basis for differential programming. Given these constraints, Gerber (1987) focused on the efficacy of theoretically derived cognitive and cognitive-behavioral training (CBT) methods. The theoretical basis of CBT has made for reasonably consistent application across areas of special education.

Cognitive Research and Applications of CBT

The methods of CBT emanated from the study of learning within an information-processing framework. When applied to learning problems, cognitive models have proved useful for differentiating the needs of individual handicapped students and designing interventions for their particular needs. The seminal work in the area (e.g., Belmont & Butterfield, 1969; Brown, 1974) demonstrated how CBT methods could be used to improve inefficient information-processing strategies and make for more "intelligent" performance. Gerber showed how CBT methods were applied to the major characteristics of impulsivity and distractibility in mildly handicapped students. Before Meichenbaum and Goodman (1971) combined techniques from social learning theory (i.e., modeling) and language development (i.e., self-statement), impulsivity and distractibility were most often treated by behavior modification (operant) methods that failed to maintain and to generalize their outcomes. With the introduction of CBT methods, treatment became more comprehensive and the positive outcomes more global. The CBT methods were then extended to training basic academic skills and are now an accepted intervention for mildly handicapped students.

Focus of CBT Intervention

Gerber then addressed a fundamental question related to CBT methods: What should be their focus? Should CBT methods be applied when needed or be part of the everyday curriculum? The question really becomes one of whether CBT methods should represent a unified approach applicable across learners and across content areas. The question remains unanswered, but some investigations have looked at the problem of applying specific training methods as a means of enhancing global learning behavior. One such demonstration investigated self-monitoring behavior (Hallahan et al., 1983). Although students trained to self-monitor revealed improvement in academic productivity, the improvement was limited to drill and practice activities making it problematic whether the self-monitoring enhances the acquisition of new skills. The difficulty is how to design CBT that can induce more internally directed learning which does not replace direct instruction of new knowledge but attempts to reduce the amount of external structure needed during teaching. What needs to be known is the number of skills necessary to produce a qualitative shift towards a more general competence. Can CBT be used to teach students how they can approach learning generally?

It appears that this question has been answered in the affirmative through the concept of strategy. A strategy is viewed as a theoretical link between covert and overt mental events. Gerber warned, however, that the popularity of the concept of strategy has resulted in this less-than-rigorous application which has obscured the concept and led to its loss of explanatory power. Are strategies rote rules or abstract algorithms? The answer is important because of its implications for the design and implementation of CBT methods.

Gerber suggested that CBT is a valuable instructional tool because it provides sufficient structure to reduce response uncertainty. The various CBT techniques aim at making correct responses more probable by either organizing or reducing information. Because CBT has focused on group research, individualized principles have not been forthcoming. The general principles for educational programming, however, can be used to formulate pragmatic schema for teachers.

Experimental Intervention Methods

At a general level, CBT can be described as incorporating three types of intervention (Brown, Campione, & Day, 1981). The first is blind rule following, wherein instruction is geared to induce particular behavior, but students are not told why or what benefits might accrue. This type of instruction is analogous to typical classroom learning. Informed rule learning is a second approach where students are induced to use a strategy and are provided information about its general relevance and possible utility. The final method is termed self-control training, and uses informed rule learning with the addition of a component to teach students how to monitor, check, and evaluate these strategies. Research has documented the efficacy of self-control training, not only for specific task performance but also for more generalized self-regulation during task performance.

Instructional Research Guidelines

Gerber next described instructional guidelines culled from the research literature. The theory and method of CBT has focused on three components: (a) how to design interventions, (b) what general instructional methods should be used, and (c) what task-specific rules, algorithms, or manipulations should be taught. The first two components present generally agreed upon principles. The third component is more difficult to specify as a set of general principles. Thus, a major component remains problematic and is confounded by questions about the appropriateness of CBT for teaching basic academic skills.

CBT and Academic Learning

Basic skills are viewed as items that must be rote memorized and hence are not amenable to CBT-type activities. In fact, much of the current focus of research is aimed at understanding how CBT can be best utilized to enhance basic skills knowledge. In this regard, Gerber summarized literature describing how CBT methods have been used to aid the acquisition of basic academic skills. The most often studied area is reading, with attention focused on both decoding and comprehension. In the area of writing, CBT methods have been applied to handwriting, spelling, and composition. Arithmetic has also been studied, especially verbal problem solving. In all areas, findings have been positive but problems continue with maintenance and generalization of the acquired skills.

Gerber ended on a very positive note. Implementing CBT has been made relatively easy because methodological standards used by researchers have made translation to practice more direct. Apart from a formidable theoretical underpinning, most studies describe explicitly how teachers should act and what instructional arrangements need to be made. Nevertheless, there are, as yet, no well-developed curriculum packages, and the application of "cognitive" methods needs to be approached cautiously. Finally, Gerber made a call for more research investigating CBT methods to enhance basic skills. Cognitive variables, such as attention and memory, have been studied but have not been generalized to learning tasks found in classrooms. Gerber, however, found reason to be hopeful. What is required is a shift in attitude away from a skills approach to a general competency idea, along with greater emphasis on students assisting the learning process more on their own behalf. The desired outcome is a curriculum that transcends the normal scope and sequence of discrete skills, and thereby results in greater clarity of differential programming effectiveness.

Independent Living Skills

Because handicapped students grow older like everyone else, attention has been focused on developing, delivering, and evaluating programs aimed at enhancing independent living skills in order to insure successful transition through adulthood. Independent living skills are seen as an integral part of an appropriate education and are necessary in a total program for both mildly and severely handicapped students.

The content for independent living skills is seen as limitless and can include any skills necessary for integrated home and community living. For the severely handicapped, independent living skills involve environmental demands and a student's access and participation in daily living activities. For the mildly handicapped, independent living skills include the requirements for functioning in various life roles and settings, and they are integral to the notion of career education. For both the mildly and severely handicapped, curriculum and program development for independent skills are evident but their empirical validation appears to be lacking. Thus, the state of the art appears to be advanced over the state of the science which, in turn, has implications for the state of practice.

State-of-the-Art Curriculum

With respect to the state of the art, Irvin, Close, and Wells (1987) identified three primary curricular approaches for severely handicapped students: developmental, behavioral, and ecological. The development approach is normative in perspective and relies upon a sequenced set of activities. The behavioral approach emphasizes the experimental analysis of behavior and the use of prompting, shaping, and feedback. Community adaptation is the goal of the ecological approach. Functional age-appropriate skills are emphasized in one effort to meet the criterion of ultimate functioning. For the mildly handicapped, the primary curricular approach to emerge has been career education. Although career education has not been defined precisely, it possesses agreed-upon components including life skills education, the role of work, and career development.

Current Research

In their review of the state of the science, Irvin et al. emphasized the lack of efficacy or comparative research on independent living curricula, especially career education. As an overall evaluation, they suggested that structured instruction can promote independent living skills, but it is unclear how severity, age, setting, training, sequence, and differential instructional methods affect outcomes. The most prominent instructional technology is behavioral (e.g., shaping, task analysis, chaining), and while effective, problems exist with respect to the most appropriate and relevant criteria for judging outcomes. For the severely handicapped, the behavioral technology is most often used, but questions remain about the impact of task difficulty, level of prerequisite skills, and impact of community experience. The major problematic component is related to generalization, but significant strides are being made (e.g., general case approach, simulation, continuity of training) that have contributed to an understanding of how skills are transferred to the community. For the mildly handicapped, no single technology has emerged as most prominent; and there has, in fact, been confounding of independent living skills with academic programming, making for poor transition from school to work. The most often used methods include simulation and general case programming. Generally, community-based instruction is superior to simulation training, but questions remain about its efficacy on a cost-benefit basis.

State of Practice

Irvin et al. next dealt with the state of practice by offering descriptions of two programs for the severely handicapped and two programs for the mildly handicapped. The Oregon High School Model and the Over-21 Project were chosen to serve as exemplary models of what can be accomplished with severely handicapped students. For the mildly handicapped, the programs chosen were Life Centered Career Education: A Competency-Based Approach (Brolin, 1978) and the Lane Community College Adult Skills Development Program, the latter designed for young handicapped adults in a community college setting.

Impact of Instruction

The impact of independent living programs is next addressed. What benefits are realized from these programs? Although data on follow-up are sparse, they lead to a rather pessimistic conclusion regarding the benefits of such programs, especially for severely handicapped students. Most handicapped young adults live at home, do not have jobs, and do not participate much in outside-the-home activities. It is suggested that this situation results partially from the lack of a shared future-oriented vision between parents and professionals.

In terms of policy and program development, it is clear that a more cohesive foundation is necessary to coordinate the components about which there is general agreement. Irvin et al. emphasized the need for more research directed at development, validation, and replication of instructional programs to prepare handicapped students for independent functioning.

Placement Options and Instructional Programming

Special education has historically attempted to classify students in order to place them differentially in service arrangements. From this practice, the question arises as to whether categories of students profit from distinctly different educational programs. Additionally, teachers receive different certifications based on special education categories. Do these categorical frameworks result in improved intervention? These concerns may be viewed within an aptitude-treatment interaction paradigm and surround the basic issue of whether placement decisions mediate instructional decisions.

Efficacy Research

Epps and Tindal (1987) cast these questions within the general context of efficacy, that is, do students profit more from instruction in regular or mainstreamed settings? Mainstreaming is a difficult concept to define with precision, but it has come to be synonymous with administrative arrangements that attempt to place students in the least restrictive environment. The basic model is usually formulated within the framework of the cascade model (Deno, 1970). The focus is on setting as an independent variable that needs to be investigated to determine its influence on student achievement. In addition, the nature of the instruction and interaction in a setting is reviewed in an effort to determine program efficacy.

Epps and Tindal pointed out the serious methodological limitations that plague almost all efficacy research. It generally has been concluded that special education placement is of questionable value, but it is unclear whether this conclusion is justified on the basis of ineffective special education or methodological problems that limit findings. Five methodological concerns were examined to evaluate the validity of efficacy research: (a) population serviced—the variability among definitions used in subject selections which results in heterogeneous samples; (b) assignment to treatment—randomized selection and assignment; (c) appropriateness of measuring devices—the match between the outcome and the measure; (d) metric of analysis for dependent measures—the problematic nature of grade-equivalent scores; and (e) independent variables—a confounding of outcomes because of the lack of program description and the integrity of its delivery.

A Review of Efficacy Literature

The literature on efficacy research can be conceived of as answering five different questions, with each representing a particular historical state. The literature is extensive and Epps and Tindal first examined regular versus self-contained settings before and after 1970. Before 1970, the conclusion which emerged was that regular class students who received no special help performed better than, or as well as, special class students. Methodological difficulties limit severely any conclusion which are further confounded by the watered down nature of the curriculum that resulted in a reduction of instructional intensity.

The study singled out as the best effort prior to 1970 was that of Goldstein, Moss, and Jordan (1965). It eliminated many design flaws and did not provide overwhelming support for the superiority of special class placement. Yet even this study possessed shortcomings which must temper any conclusions. After the Goldstein *et al.* (1965) study, the trend was toward less segregation, and efficacy research focused on how much handicapped students would benefit if they spent at least part of their day in mainstreamed settings. In an analysis of five post-1970 studies, Epps and Tindal concluded that the findings were inconsistent, with some favoring special classes, some the regular class, and some finding no differences.

With increased emphasis on mainstreaming, the resource room became a favored placement option. But, when compared with both self-contained and regular classes, the results were not definitive. In fact, a review of seven studies revealed that the findings were conflicting. Resource programs appeared to be superior to regular classes but held no advantage over self-contained classes. Epps and Tindal suggested that much of this research also suffers from methodological difficulties, and then raised the question about the type of problem the handicapped student manifests. The inconsistencies in the resource room efficacy research may be due partially to a failure to differentiate repertoire problems (can't do) and motivational problems (won't do). This distinction has not been addressed and may account for the differences found in the efficacy research.

META-ANALYSIS OF EFFICACY RESEARCH

Epps and Tindal then analyzed critically the findings from quantitative syntheses of the efficacy research. They reported the findings obtained by Carlberg and Kavale (1980) and Wang and Baker (1985–86). The former found the special class a generally inferior alternative to regular class placement, but differences emerged based on categorical classification, with low IQ students doing better in regular classes and learning disabled and behaviorally disordered students doing better in special classes. Wang and Baker investigated the efficacy of mainstreaming and found empirical support for it on all program effects: performance, attitudes, and classroom processes. There were no differential effects related to student classification. Although meta-analysis is widely used, it is not without its critics and these findings have been questioned (e.g., Guskin, 1984).

SETTING AS A MACROVARIABLE

The findings of their efficacy research led Epps and Tindal to suggest that equivocation results because setting is only a macrovariable and any placement option does not guarantee effective instruction. The setting may provide teachers with the opportunity to engage in different behaviors, and these behaviors may have a greater impact on student outcomes. Consequently, special and regular education settings may differ substantially in terms of content, that is, the amount and type of instruction. These differences are studied through a process-product paradigm wherein classroom processes are observed and student achievement measured to determine how instruction relates to student outcomes.

Observational research investigating academic engaged time revealed that while special settings provide more structure and opportunity for students to be engaged, there may not be a direct relationship to more practice. In fact, comparisons between handicapped and nonhandicapped students typically show no differences in amount of engaged time. The finding of no difference was not related to level of service or change in service as a function of placement decisions. Thus, few substantive differences were found across educational settings, which suggests that setting, per se, is not highly related to functional differences in the delivery of instruction.

ANALYSIS OF INSTRUCTIONAL VARIABLES

Epps and Tindal next reviewed instructional variables that may operate within settings to produce outcome differences. One area where consensus seems to be emerging is what has come to be known as "effective teaching research." The problem seems to be a lack of specificity which prevents its comprehensive implementation in classrooms. Although the elements of effective teaching research are far from prescriptive, many have been incorporated into well-defined instructional programs. The programs described included the Adaptive Learning Environments Model (ALEM) (Wang, 1981), Active Mathematics Teaching (Good, Grouws, & Eberneer, 1983), and Direct Instruction (Becker, Englemann, Carnine, & Rhine, 1981). These programs possess considerable specificity, and their implementation may be evaluated. All possess empirical evidence about their impact on student achievement. In each case, active teaching is a central concept, as is frequent measurement and mastery monitoring.

Although placement option has been considered a form of treatment, it appears that setting, per se, is not a major factor in student outcomes and may account for inconsistent findings found in efficacy research. More important are the features of instruction that occur in the setting, but research has revealed that student classifications and placement options do not relate to distinctions in instructional approaches used. Thus, there appears to be no differential programming in serving mildly handicapped students. To make this a reality, it is necessary to move away from setting as the variable of interest and move towards investigating instructional variables that affect student outcomes.

Conclusions

The effectiveness of differential programming for handicapped students presents a mixed picture. The elements reviewed here, which represent much of the differential programming associated with special education, were found to be both effective and not effective. Perhaps the major reason for this mixed picture is the equivocal nature of the research. It lacks clear specification of populations, settings, and interventions. There is little consensus about criteria to be used, and many outcome assessments are not sensitive enough to measure change. The lack of uniformity, as well as the all too prevalent "one-shot" study, led to research findings which could not be used with confidence to make decisions about program efficacy.

Colarusso (1987) and Gerber (1987) focused on particular approaches to intervention. Diagnostic-prescriptive teaching has become associated with process training. Although process training engenders much passion, the research evidence must be considered equivocal, and the need for better research is evident. While recent research has not been forthcoming, process training has become one of the entrenched controversies in special education about which everyone has an opinion. The value of the model is still in question, and the uncertainty leading to tacit approval of the behavioral model must be guarded against. While process training in this most traditional sense (e.g., perceptual motor, pyscholinguistic) remains controversial, it is important to note that newer interventions (e.g., cognitive strategies) contain many elements of process training.

Methods of CBT were viewed as important additions to the repertoire of special education interventions because they addressed important academic and social problems manifested by handicapped students. Although promising, CBT methods require more research documenting their efficacy across students and settings. To date, most research has been of the laboratory type, and an examination of the maintenance and generalizability of CBT methods is needed. While possessing a strong theoretical base, CBT methods also require more attention on strategies for implementation. In general, CBT methods hold much promise but still require research support to enhance understanding of their value.

The issue of research support creates a tension between researchers and practitioners. Practitioners' needs are immediate, and they often choose interventions on the basis of face validity. Researchers should acknowledge this need and attempt to distill information in a form most useful for practioners. The goal should be one of mutual cooperation, wherein science and art are meshed to produce the best possible intervention and implementation.

While academic skills are an agreed upon goal, there is much less consensus about schools' responsibilities for social and vocational skills. Morrison (1987) addressed this issue through a review of curriculum issues. With few exceptions, special education appears not to have focused upon curricular concerns. Curriculum development and evaluation have not been high priorities, with the result being that special education curriculums have usually been modified regular curriculum packages. Consequently, it is uncertain whether the most important skills for handicapped students are being taught and whether or not those skills are being delivered within a developmental framework. Irvin et al. focused on programming independent living skills and emphasized their importance to prevent "life failure" for mildly handicapped students. The primary difficulty seems to be reaching consensus about what skills constitute "cultural imperatives" and how they should be weighted along with academic skills in creating an entire curriculum package. Although judgment is involved, these decisions can and should be made on the basis of empirical evidence.

Placement and programming seem not to be related. Ideally, students' needs would be identified and would influence decisions about service. Current practice, however, seems to focus on the search for a pathology that results in a label as the sole outcome. Consequently, actual intervention is highly variable and shows little relationship to the setting. The inherent variability makes research about efficacy problematic. Equivocal conclusions are the rule, and this in turn makes policy decisions problematic. While policy should be based on research, too often in special education the research difficulties create a situation wherein research follows policy.

Issues about the efficacy of differential programming thus remain unresolved. Special education is effective, but it is also not effective. The need for research is evident, but new and different methodologies should be used to enhance understanding. Decisions about what to study also need to be made. A total and unequivocal picture will probably never be attained. Thus, it is necessary to make decisions about what is promising and how these promising areas can best be studied.

The equivocal nature of differential programming makes it mandatory that regular education be considered as a possible source of special education. Special education can focus on related practices (e.g., preferral assessment, consultation), while modified regular education practices can focus on intervention. Special education must set less emphasis on the placement process and pay more attention to intervention, not in the form of particular methods, but rather as a total process incorporating student, teacher, and school. Setting alone does not make an intervention, and it appears that special education must make a concerted effort to study the entire system so the efficacy question is cast in its most general context. Special education cannot be viewed as a system apart from regular education but rather as a part of a larger system which includes regular and special education students. If special education's "special" interventions are found effective, they should be used. If not, they should be abandoned in favor of curriculum and methods that have proved effective for all students. Special education may lose some of its specialness but it will be clear which differential programming techniques are valuable and should be maintained and which lead to useless equivocation. Differential programming options may be reduced, but the benefit will be in better service delivery to handicapped students.

References

Arter, J. A., & Jenkins, J. R. (1979). Differential diagnosis-prescriptive teaching: A critical appraisal. *Review of Educational Research*, **49**, 517–556.

Becker, W. C., Engelmann, S., Carnine, D. W., & Rhine, W. R. (1981). Direct Instruction Model. In W. R. Rhine (Ed.), *Making schools more effective: New directions from Follow Through* (pp. 95–154). New York: Academic Press.

Belmont, J. M., & Butterfield, E. C. (1969). The relations of short-term memory to development and intelligence. In L. Lipitt & H. Reese (Eds.), *Advances in child development and behavior* (Vol. 4). New York: Academic Press.

Brolin, D. E. (1978). *Life centered career education: A competency based approach.* Reston, VA: Council for Exceptional Children.

Brolin, D. E. (1982). Life-centered career education for exceptional children. *Focus on Exceptional Children*, **14**, 1–15.

Brown, A. L. (1974). The role of strategic behavior in retardate memory. In N. R. Ellis (ed.), *International review of research in mental retardation* (Vol. 7, pp. 55–111). New York: Academic Press.

Brown, A. L., Campione, J. C., & Day, J. D. (1981). Learning to learn: On training students to learn from texts. *Educational Researcher*, **10**(2), 14–21.

Carlberg, C., & Kavale, K. (1980). The efficacy of special versus regular class placement for exceptional children: A meta-analysis. *Journal of Special Education*, **14**, 295–309.

Colarusso, R. P. (1987). Diagnostic-prescriptive teaching. In M. C. Wang, M. C. Reynolds, & H. J. Walberg (Eds.), *Handbook of special education: Research and practice: Vol. 1. Learner characteristics and adaptive education* (pp. 155–166). Oxford, England: Pergamon Press.

Deno, E. (1970). Special education as developmental capital. *Exceptional Children*, **37**, 229–237.

Epps, S. & Tindal, G. (1987). The effectiveness of differential programming in serving students with mild handicaps: Placement options and instructional programming. In M. C. Wang, M. C. Reynolds, & H. J. Walberg (Eds.), *Handbook of special education: Research and practice: Vol. 1. Learner characteristics and adaptive education* (pp. 213–248). Oxford, England: Pergamon Press.

Gerber, M. M. (1987). Application of cognitive-behavioral training methods to teaching basic skills to mildly handicapped elementary school students. In M. C. Wang, M. C. Reynolds, & H. J. Walberg (Eds.) *Handbook of special education: Research and practice: Vol. 1. Learner characteristics and adaptive education* (pp. 167–186). Oxford, England: Pergamon Press.

Goldstein, H. (1975). *The social learning curriculum.* Columbus, OH: Charles E. Merrill.

Goldstein, H., Moss, J. W., & Jordan, L. J. (1965). *The efficacy of special class training on the development of mentally retarded children* (Cooperative Research Project Report N. 619). Urbana: University of Illinois, Institute for Research on Exceptional Children. (ERIC Document Reproduction Service No. ED 002-907).

Good, T. L., Grouws, D. A., & Ebmeier, H. (1983). *Active mathematics teaching.* New York: Longman.

Guskin, S. L., (1984). Problems and promises of meta-analysis in special education. *Journal of Special Education*, **18**, 73–80.

Hallahan, D. P., Hall, R. J., Ianna, S. O., Kneedler, R. D., Lloyd, J. W., Loper, A. B., & Reeve, R. E. (1983). Summary of research findings at the University of Virginia Learning Disabilities Research Institute. *Exceptional Education Quarterly*, **4**(1), 95–114.

Irvin, L. K., Close, D. W., & Wells, R. L. (1987). Programming independent living skills for handicapped learners. In M. C. Wang, M. C. Reynolds, & H. J. Walberg (Eds.), *Handbook of special education: Research and practice: Vol. 1. Learner characteristics and adaptive education* (pp. 187–211). Oxford, England: Pergamon Press.

Kauffman, J. M. (1981). Historical trends and contemporary issues in special education in the United States. In J. M. Kauffman & D. P. Hallahan (Eds.), *Handbook of special education* (pp. 3–23). Englewood Cliffs, NJ: Prentice-Hall.

Kavale, K. A. (1981). Functions of the Illinois Test of Psycholinguistic Abilities (ITPA): Are they trainable? *Exceptional Children*, **47**, 496–510.

Kavale, K. A., & Mattson, P. D. (1983). "One jumped off the balance beam": Meta-analysis of perceptual-motor training. *Journal of Learning Disabilities*, **16**, 165–173.

Kirk, S. A. (1963). Behavioral diagnosis and remediation of learning disabilities. In *Proceedings of the Conference on Exploration Into the Problems of the Perceptually Handicapped Child* (Vol. 1, pp. 3–32). Chicago, IL: University of Illinois Press.

Lerner, J. W. (1981). *Learning disabilities: Theories, diagnosis, and teaching strategies* (3rd ed.). Boston: Houghton Mifflin.

Mann, L. (1971). Psychometric Phrenology and the new faculty psychology: The case against ability assessment and training. *Journal of Special Education*, **5**, 3–65.

Meichenbaum, D., & Goodman, J. (1971). Training impulsive children to talk to themselves: A means of developing self-control, *Journal of Abnormal Psychology*, **77**, 115–126.

Milofsky, C. D. (1974). Why special education isn't special. *Harvard Educational Review*, **44**, 437–458.

Morrison, G. M. (1987). Relationship among academic, social, and career education in programming for handicapped students. In M. C. Wang, M. C. Reynolds, & H. J. Walberg (Eds.), *Handbook of special education: Research and practice: Vol. 1. Learner characteristics and adaptive education* (pp. 133–154). Oxford, England: Pergamon Press.

Peter, J. J. (1965). *Prescriptive teaching.* New York: McGraw Hill.

Smead, V. S. (1977). Ability training and task analysis in diagnostic/prescriptive teaching. *Journal of Special Education*, **11**, 113–125.

Wang, M. C. (1981). Mainstreaming programs: Design features and effects. *Journal of Special Education*, **19**, 504–521.

Wang, M. C., & Baker, E. T. (1985–1986). Mainstreaming programs: Design features and effects. *Journal of Special Education*, **19**, 503–525.

Wilkerson, W., & Jones, P. (1976). *Review of special education cost studies: CEC Institute on Finance.* Reston, VA: Council for Exceptional Children.

Ysseldyke, J. E., & Salvia, J. (1974). Diagnostic-prescriptive teaching: Two models. *Exceptional Children*, **41**, 17–31.

Noncategorical Special Education

MAYNARD C. REYNOLDS

University of Minnesota
Minneapolis, Minnesota

This chapter examines noncategorical special education as an alternative to present categorical practices in the delivery of special education. The focus is on children who are "mildly handicapped," which includes most children who are educable mentally retarded, learning disabled, and emotionally disturbed; and children with mild degrees of speech, language, physical, or sensory problems. Demographic indicators point to an increasing school-age population in the future and greater numbers and proportions of children who are handicapped or "at risk" and therefore in need of specialized services.

There are eight topics in this chapter, organized in two major sections: current problems in special education programming and noncategorical solutions as alternatives to present practice.

Problems in Present Practice of Special Education Programming

Much progress has been made in extending special education and related services to children in recent years, but a number of serious problems have been growing as well. Several such problems are considered below.

Classification: Some Assumptions

As noted by Hobbs (1975) some years ago, the way children are classified is very important. It influences how they are labeled and counted in school; it determines which students are entitled to receive special education and related assistance; it may influence the kinds of assistance they will receive and where they receive it; and it relates to program organization, funding, and teacher preparation.

Several beliefs and assumptions which permeate much of this chapter need to be explained. First, classification of a child in any way "implies that the category chosen is good for something" (Robbins, 1966, p. 5). In the context of education, a classification system is assumed to be useful to the extent that it facilitates effective instruction for the individuals involved. Secondly, to criticize or oppose present systems of classification in special education is not to oppose all forms of classification. Inevitably, education involves classifying and placing students in school programs by some systematic means; and all of science involves noting similarities and developing related networks of knowledge. What is questioned here is only the present practice of categorizing children for special education, not the whole idea of classification. Thirdly, to criticize the ways we classify "exceptional" children is not to deny that the children have problems. People delivered to hospital emergency rooms usually have serious problems; the classification of their problems after arrival may or may not be valid. Similarly, the children referred to special education are not just randomly chosen. They are exceptional in various ways. It is only the ways we classify or partition these children and the school programs for them that are cast in doubt in the present discussion.

A fourth assumption in this chapter is that the classification systems useful for communication among researchers may be different from those that are useful in professional practices. Agreements on "marker variables" (Keogh, Major–Kingsley, Omori–Gordon, & Reid, 1982) and careful descriptions of both children and school situations are important for purposes of communication among researchers, especially in relation to functions of replication and generalization of results. However, all of this says little, if anything, about the usefulness of the same "markers," dimensions of analysis, or categories for practical purposes of school placement and instruction. Failure to note this important point has caused many difficulties.

A fifth and somewhat broader point is that different professions classify individuals quite differently, according to the purposes to be served and the interventions they manage. For example, a scientist may be interested in classification of disabled children according to etiology in order to learn how to prevent the disability in succeeding generations; a physician may be interested in classification according to certain metabolic processes in order to predict variations in disposition in responding to a particular drug or other form of medical treatment. Such classifications, however, are likely to be irrelevant to the teacher in deciding how to instruct the same children. Consistency across professions in classification of children should not be expected; nor should one profession "give away" to another its classification practices except under quite extraordinary conditions of mutual understanding

A sixth point for initial consideration is to acknowledge that it is legitimate for policymakers to denote certain categories of at risk children for special attention on the basis of group base rate data. For example, legislators have designated children of migrant workers and children of the poor for extra attention in school because children in such classes show a high rate of school learning difficulties. It is another matter, of course, if educators permit these policy designations to result in isolation of the children as a category for instructional purposes. Forming a separate program for the migrant child, the poor child, or children in other categories should not be necessary unless strong evidence is available to support the value of such separations. It is a theme of this chapter, based on research reviews, that excessive amounts of separation and disjointedness have developed in school programs, based on these kinds of faulty transformations of policies into educational practices.

Mildly Handicapped Children: The Focus of the Problem

The focus in this chapter is on mildly handicapped children. This is meant to include most students now classified in the schools as educable mentally retarded, learning disabled, and emotionally disturbed, plus many children who have speech and language problems and others who have physical and sensory problems without major secondary complications. The term mildly handicapped excludes from consideration children and youth who show severe/profound cognitive deficits, extreme behavior disorders, and complex multiple disabilities. At least 75% (possibly even as many as 90%, according to Algozzine & Korinek, 1985) of children now enrolled in special education programs are mildly handicapped as the term is used here. In parts of the chapter, the focus is broadened to include other categories besides those of special education.

Earlier reviews of classification problems in the schools (Heller, Holtzman, & Messick, 1982; Hobbs, 1975, 1980) and other chapters in this volume offer evidence that the present methods of classifying mildly handicapped children for special education are inadequate. This makes it difficult to synthesize research findings and creates illogical statistical variances among the States in the reported prevalence of disabilities. It also, far too often, leads to "special" treatments that are in no way specifically related to diagnostic classification. This categorical nonsystem does not appear to be evolving toward more specific and scientifically valid categories for children. On the contrary, there seems to be an increase in political and economic moves to limit and revise classification procedures by "capping" certain categories, most notably that of learning disability. Professional considerations about classification appear to be diminishing in impact, probably because of the fumbling in approaches to the problem by professionals and advocates. Increasing numbers of schools are offering mixed category, noncategorical or cross-categorical programs. In a one-year period, from the 1981–82 to 1982–83 school years, the number of noncategorical teachers employed in special education programs of the United States rose from 16,177 to 25,305 (U.S. Department of Education, 1985). In percentage terms, that is a far higher gain in a short period than for any other category considered in federal reports on implementation of Public Law 94–142.

Inconsistencies in Practices and Rates of Classification

Ysseldyke (1987) observed that probably the most critical act of classification relating to special education occurs when a teacher refers a child for study. Usually such referral is based on the teacher's judgment that the child has a learning and/or behavioral problem. From there a diagnostic team often goes on what has been described as a "search for pathology" (Sarason & Doris, 1979), resulting in categorization of the child as handicapped in special education terms. In one study of practices following referral, about 92% of referred children were tested, and of that group, 73% were categorized as handicapped in some way and given special education placements (Algozzine, Christenson, & Ysseldyke, 1982).

The designators for categories vary somewhat from one state to another, but practices in most school systems and states show a high degree of conformity with the federal reporting system, which includes the following 11 categories (*Federal Register*, 1977): deaf, deaf-blind, hard-of-hearing, mentally retarded, multihandicapped, orthopedically impaired, other health impaired, seriously emotionally disturbed (ED), specific learning disability (SLD), speech impaired, and visually handicapped. The mentally retarded category is often subdivided by state and local school authorities into three levels: a relatively large group of children at a mild or educable level (EMR), a smaller group at a moderate level, and a low-incidence group at a severe/profound level.

The team which classifies the child and determines needs for special education and related services often includes regular teachers, a psychologist, and a special educator. It must include parents, unless they choose not to participate. But usually the parties who might be expected to know the child best (regular teachers and parents) appear to have only minimal functions in team meetings (Ysseldyke, Algozzine, & Allen, 1981). Studies by Ysseldyke and his colleagues at the University of Minnesota showed that team meetings in the schools usually "consisted

largely of round-robin presentations of test data" and that "participants
. . . were for the most part individuals who had given tests to students"
(Ysseldyke, 1987, p. 259).

The classification of children into various categories has been
influenced by many factors besides those reflecting school learning and
behavior. These include sex, socioeconomic status, physical
appearance, availability of different kinds of services, and "power" of
parents (Christenson, Ysseldyke, & Algozzine, 1982; Hocutt, Cox, &
Pelosi, 1984). Understandably, this produces inconsistency in practices
and rates of classification across various school and political entities. In
one report the percentage of students classified as educable mentally
retarded was 0.49% in Alaska and at the same time 4.14% in Alabama;
learning disabled was 0.83% in New York versus 5.2% in Maryland,
and emotionally disturbed was 0.04% in Mississippi versus 3.09% in
Utah. These data show that children are as much as 75 times more likely
to be classified in a given category in some states as in others (Morsink,
Smith-Davis, & Thomas, 1987).

The lack of consistency in classification of mildly handicapped children is shown also in significant shifts across categories in hydraulic-like
fashion, that is, down in rate for one category while up in another.
Tucker (1980) reported on a situation in which there was a significant
increase in the number of children classified as learning disabled and a
concomitant decrease in students classified as educable mentally
retarded. In further analysis, he demonstrated that the shift resulted
from the reclassification of large numbers of black children from the
educable mentally retarded category to learning disabilities. Reschly
(1987) notes that the number of children classified as mentally retarded
in the United States declined by 300,000 from 1976 to 1983, while in the
same period the number classified as learning disabled increased by one
million. It appears that when the rate of classification in a given category
goes down, it is related to negative evaluation of the resulting school
placements (Cleary, 1980); presumably parents would be clamoring to
get their children into certain categories if the resulting programmatic
assignments were valued highly.

Even when criteria for placement of children in special education
programs have been specified quite clearly, practices still tend to be
unreliable. Garrison and Hammill (1970) found in one study that two-
thirds of the students classified as mentally retarded in Philadelphia
schools did not meet the criteria for that category. Shepard and Smith
(1981) reported that less than half of the students classified as learning
disabled (perceptual-communication disorder in Colorado) met the state
criteria in Colorado.

Inconsistencies in the Reporting of Research

The classification of children for research purposes suffers similar problems of inconsistency. Taylor (1980), for example, found that for a six year period, following publication of the 1973 *Manual on Terminology and Classification* by the American Association on Mental Deficiency, only 28% of the articles appearing in the two journals published by the association (*Mental Retardation* and the *American Journal on Mental Deficiency*) followed the recommended practices. Wood and Lakin (1982) found procedures for classification of children as emotionally disturbed to be so unclear in research reports as to make it very difficult to replicate studies or to make informed generalizations. Researchers have tended to accept whatever procedures have been used by school personnel in labeling children without further specification, a practice which leaves the findings virtually unintelligible.

It would be greatly helpful for communicative purposes if consensus could be achieved among researchers and leading practitioners in special education on a "marker variable" system as proposed by Smith et al. (1984) or by Keogh et al. (1982). Hopefully, the markers for the system would cover a broad range of student characteristics going beyond Keogh's proposals for the field of learning disabilities to also include, for example, variables descriptive of learning situations, process variables, and outcomes. Through the consistent use of a broad marker variable system, enforced rigorously by journal reviewers and editors, perhaps progress can be made in communication efficiency in the field.

Classification and Instructional Relevance

Conceptualizing the process of classification as relevant to instruction is another important consideration. There appears to be a fair degree of agreement on one matter: that for educational purposes, the classification system ought to support improved instruction. A special panel of the National Academy of Sciences put it this way:

> It is the responsibility of the placement team that labels and places a child in a special program to demonstrate that any differential label used is related to a distinctive prescription for educational practices . . . that lead to improved outcomes (Heller, Holtzman, & Messick, 1982, p. 94).

That is a high standard, but one to which special educators, school psychologists, and others who practice diagnosis in the schools should be held accountable.

Cromwell, Blashfield, and Strauss (1975) presented a model for diagnostic processes based on the "ABCD"s: A is comprised of historical/etiological data, and B of currently assessable characteristics. The As and Bs might encompass data of any and all sorts, but finally only those that help to choose interventions (the Cs) that lead to known outcomes (the Ds) are relevant. One can imagine that certain factors of early history (the As, such as missed school a lot in first grade, had a cruel mother) along with currently assessable characteristics (the Bs, such as low achievement in basic skills, tends to be assaultive against classmates) may be helpful in choosing a treatment program (the Cs, e.g., highly structured, one-on-one instruction in reading) which is anticipated to lead to improved outcomes (the Ds, such as better reading ability, improved attention on learning tasks, better relationships with adults). It is the Cs which are pivotal. Classifications are useful in the schools to the extent that they help in the design of, or allocation to, instructional practices that are genuinely helpful to the child.

Quite clearly, current diagnostic practices in special education represent a hodgepodge of procedures which fall far short of desired standards. A thorough history of the field would undoubtedly show that present practices regarding mildly handicapped students grew out of well-meaning intentions, probably as extensions of procedures that had validity for more extreme cases. Many of the "mild" handicaps have a history of being simple extensions from severe levels—as in starting with the blind and adding the partially sighted, starting with the deaf and adding the hard of hearing, starting with the psychotic and adding the emotionally disturbed, and starting with the idiot and imbecile, then adding the moron. The learning disability category was a late-comer (made a category by law only in the 1960s) meant to cover virtually all cases of extremely slow progress in school learning not covered by the other categories. Indeed, the feature of exclusivity of other categories is considered to be one diagnostic indicator of learning disabilities. In summary, the classification system for mildly handicapped children in school situations is flawed; indeed, at least one observer describes the situation as "scandalous" (Scriven, 1983).

Demographics

The challenge and controversy surrounding classification processes and changes in delivery systems in schools are likely to become more intense over the next several years for various reasons. During the decade 1975–1985, the first years under Public Law 94–142, special education programs grew rapidly. There was considerable focus on children with handicaps and their special needs and on implementing a major new law and related regulations. But it was also a time of decline in the general school-age (5–17 years) population of the nation and in the demand for new teachers. From 1975 to 1985, the school-age population declined from about 51 million to 44 million. It was a period of relatively easy competition for additional teachers and other resources needed to meet the requirements of PL 94–142.

As we look to the future, it is clear that the general school-age population has stopped declining and is moving upward. The Bureau of Census (1982, 1983) estimates there will be 48 million children of school age by 1995 and about 50 million by the year 2000. But even more significant, the 50 million school-age children will be different from those of the past.

Some of the ways in which the school-age population of the new future will be different are: (a) a higher percentage from economically poor families; (b) a higher percentage from minority families; (c) increasing proportions living with one or neither natural parent; and (d) increasing proportions surviving low birth weight or congenital anomalies. All of these conditions are associated with higher than average rates of disability and need for special education and related services (Child Trends, 1985; Reynolds & Lakin, 1987; Zill, 1985).

It is clear that the numbers of children in the United States who are handicapped and/or at risk in a significant problematic way and in need of specialized help in the schools will increase over the next decade, both in absolute numbers and in percentage of the total child population. Equally, it is clear that advocates for these children during this period will be working in a more difficult economic and political context than in the past. Improving the effectiveness and efficiency of programs, including changes in classification practices, will have growing importance.

Special Education Funding

Making changes in present classification practices is particularly difficult because systems of special education funding are frequently linked to categorical approaches. In many states, local school districts receive extra funding whenever a child is categorized as handicapped in some approved way and then placed in a special program. The district may experience financial disincentives if children are instructed without traditional labeling in noncategorical programs, even if what they receive is indeed quite "special." Advocates for special education, often organized in narrow categorical groups, tend to be apprehensive about changes that may threaten financial supports for programs they've fought for, and more so when there is the possibility that dropping the categorical labels may cause the children to lose legal rights (such as Individualized Educational Programs, due process, etc.).

A further obstacle to change in special education practices arises from widespread feelings of distrust. In the early 1980s attempts were made to repeal PL 94–142 and to fold the Federal special education funds into a larger set or "block" of grants. Advocates for handicapped children opposed and defeated this move, but there is still widespread concern that the hard-fought victories for handicapped children could be lost if policies expressed in PL 94–142 are allowed to erode in any way. The dominant attitude in the advocacy community appears to be one of holding fast to present policies and regulations at all costs.

Alternatives to Present Practice

In the following section of this chapter, attention is given to some of the possible solutions of the problems outlined above, giving special attention to improved practices in referral and classification of children.

Reducing Referral Rates

An obvious way to solve some of the problems of classifying and labeling children in the schools is to reduce the rate at which the first initial step in the whole process occurs: the referral of children by regular teachers. Referrals result in shifting "ownership" of problems through special placements of children. Reducing referral rates is a difficult and complex issue; it touches upon attitudes as well as technical procedures. To be more than a mere mechanical, rule-enforced reduction, fundamental changes are required in mainstream school environments, including added supports to mainstream teachers and more preventively-oriented early education programs. Policies are leaning strongly toward fewer special education referrals, and some schools are mandating a virtual shutdown on such referrals until consultation and various prereferral interventions are tried in mainstream classes. All of these matters are topics for this section of the chapter and for longer treatment by Nevin and Thousand (1987).

Fortunately, there is a relatively new and impressive body of research on effective schools and effective instruction which can be used in seeking improved mainstream instruction and less need for referrals. This body of knowledge is taking a central place in the renegotiation of responsibilities between regular and special educators (Brookover, Bendy, Flord, Schweitzer, & Wisenbaker, 1979; Good, 1983; Walberg, 1984). Characteristics of effective schools include strong administrative leadership to establish high expectations for achievement, clear specification of goals, precise sequencing of the curriculum, and an orderly and safe learning environment. Effective instructional practices include high teacher directedness, expanded time on academic tasks completed with success, frequent monitoring and corrective feedback on student work, homework (checked by teachers), mastery-type assessments, and individualized pacing of the curriculum. It seems very likely that mainstream school programs in which improvements in these domains are being attempted will result in fewer referrals of children for special education.

A number of specific approaches to improvement of the mainstream environment have been proposed and evaluated with positive results. For example, methods of creating positive interdependencies among children in heterogeneous groups have been invented and carefully evaluated. Meta-analyses reported by Johnson, Maruyama, Johnson, Nelson, and Skon (1981) have shown that "cooperative goal structuring" produces a positive effect size of about three-fourths of a standard deviation on academic variables and impressive gains on social variables. The method involves mutual helpfulness among students when working in carefully structured groups. Nevin, Johnson, and Johnson (1982) and Johnson and Johnson (1981) have shown specific positive effects on the handicapped students using these methods. Peer and cross-age tutoring also shows positive results for handicapped children, probably because it provides a means of implementing principles of effective instruction (Jenkins & Jenkins, 1981).

Chalfant has advanced an idea for teaming by regular teachers to offer mutual help and support in dealing with instructional problems and with pupils who are problematic (Chalfant, Pysh, & Moultrie, 1979). Teacher Assistance Teams (TATs), created on appointment by school principals or by teacher choices, are used to provide "day-to-day peer problem solving groups for teachers" (Chalfant et al., 1979, p. 83). In an evaluation of 23 different TAT operations involving 200 problem children, it was found that in 133 cases the problems were resolved sufficiently to prevent referral to special education.

The TAT model is one example of the broad efforts now being made to try prereferral strategies with students who are experiencing learning or behavior problems in the regular classrooms. School psychologists and special educators are rapidly developing consultation skills in order to try to improve opportunities for children at a prereferral level. This kind of intervention was recommended by the National Academy of Sciences Panel (Heller et al. 1982) as one means of reforming practices related to special education placement. Graden, Casey, and Bonstrom (1985) have shown that work by school psychologists to establish prereferral interventions can reduce referral rates to special education, but evaluation studies are only beginning to appear in this domain; much remains to be tried and evaluated.

Descriptions of the consultation model in practice and evidence of its utility is mounting quite impressively (Idol-Maestas, Nevin, & Paolucci-Whitcomb, 1985; Knight, Meyers, Hasazi, Paolucci-Whitcomb, & Nevin, 1981). Miller and Sabatino (1978) showed that student gains were as positive for "consulting" as for other special education practices and, in addition, regular teacher behaviors appeared to be slightly improved. The schools of Vermont have operated a consulting teacher model on virtually a statewide basis for a number of years; Knight et al. (1981) found impressive results for the Vermont model both in student gains and increased teacher skill.

An important aspect of efforts to strengthen the mainstream as a resource for exceptional students is preparing regular teachers for expanded functions and for collaborative work with other school personnel. Summaries of efforts in teacher preparation have been provided in a number of sources, including Grosenick and Reynolds (1978) and Sharp (1982). Most of the literature on teacher preparation for mainstreaming is merely descriptive, but some works are carefully analytic (Reynolds, 1980) and quite persuasive concerning the domains in which teacher education will need to be changed or enhanced in order to implement a successful mainstreaming program.

Intervention at the early education level presents another opportunity to serve children effectively in ways that reduce referrals to special education. It is not yet clear that the specific achievement gains shown by children enrolled in early education programs will persist after the children reach ordinary school-entrance ages and enter regular schools. There are not yet enough studies of good design to be clear about long-range benefits (White & Casto, 1984). However, the Lazar and Darlington (1982) summary of follow-up studies of subjects in 12 major early education projects started in the 1960s indicates that early education may result in as much as a 50% reduction in later referrals of children to special education. Weikert, Bond, & McNeir (1978) showed comparable positive long-range outcomes specifically for students enrolled in their Perry Preschool Project.

Clearly, a massive renegotiation is occurring in the relationships between regular and special education, with the aim of making regular education more powerful in accommodating individual differences and reducing the rates at which students are placed in "special" stations for their schooling. This renegotiation is a response to the "least restrictive environment" principle enunciated in Public Law 94–142 and in other public policies. Many approaches are being tried, including the full implementation of the "effectiveness" principles concerning instruction and schools, the broader development of early childhood programs, and new models for collaboration by regular and special teachers (and psychologists, social workers, nurses, etc.). Impressive gains are evident in many of the programs. There may be little respite for regular teachers, however, for as they accommodate mildly handicapped pupils in the mainstream, pressures mount to include the moderately and severely handicapped as well—but that is a story for another time and place.

Noncategorical Special Education Programs

One reason for reworking the present structure of special education for mildly handicapped students is that so little evidence is available to support present practices. Morsink (1984) did an extensive review of textbooks for teachers of students classified as learning disabled, educable mentally retarded, and emotionally disturbed. Her conclusion was that the texts failed to indicate that specific teaching strategies and materials were effective for one category as opposed to others. On the other hand, research on effective methods for instruction of students in the several categories suggests that the same methods tend to be successful across at least three large categories—learning disability, educable mental retardation, and emotional disturbance (Algozzine, 1984; Morsink, Branscum, & Boone, 1984: Valcante, 1984). It is important to note that observations about methods of teaching are not about curriculum and some feel that the curricular requirements are distinctly different among the categories. Further study is needed on these issues.

Ideas emerging in the effectiveness literature have bearing here when they have been applied systematically in programs. Larivee (1982) constructed instruments for describing effective teachers and used them in observations in a variety of classroom situations, leading to the conclusion that behaviors that were effective for teachers in general were effective with mildly handicapped students as well. Algozzine, Algozzine, Morsink, and Dykes (1984) found a number of the effectiveness factors to be present in special education classes and that teacher behaviors did not differ by category of exceptionality. Morsink et al. (1987) propose four common clusters of effective methodologies for mildly handicapped students: (a) teacher directedness; (b) high density of academic responding, with feedback; (c) contingent reinforcement for appropriate behavior; and (d) instruction adapted to individual needs.

Many school districts now operate special education programs organized on a noncategorical, mixed categorical, or multicategorical basis. In the case of noncategorical programs, the children are not classified in traditional ways; in mixed or multicategorical programs the children are classified in traditional ways, but more than one category of students are permitted to be served in the same setting and usually by one teacher. Friend and McNutt (1984) report that 49 states have resource rooms classified as noncategorical or multicategorical. Large numbers of early and secondary education programs are noncategorical in nature. Unfortunately, very few evaluative data have been provided concerning such programs.

In one of the studies, Dulle and Childs (1985) compared categorical and crosscategorical approaches in resource rooms and special classes.

A total of 229 students, classified as learning disabled, educable mentally retarded, and emotionally disturbed were included, but data were complete through posttesting on only half of them. The researchers concluded that categorical and crosscategorical approaches were equally effective, but acknowledged several methodological problems in their research. They noted that some parents and professionals had objected to the crosscategorical programs.

The largest and most comprehensive study of mixed-category programs was conducted in Pennsylvania (Sage & Fensom, 1985). Working on a contract with the Pennsylvania State Department of Public Instruction, Sage and Fensom used stratified sampling procedures to establish a representative set of mixed-category special education programs. Researchers visited each site and interviewed people who were the most involved, including parents, teachers, and administrators (regular and special education). They concluded that the mixed-category programs tended to be successful except in situations where there was clear neglect of principles that would be important in any school program. For example, some unsuccessful programs had excessively large numbers of exceptional students placed in the mixed-category program. There is a danger that when program requirements are loosened in one way, they may go out of control in broader ways, perhaps in response to economic pressures.

Morsink et al. (1987) have noted the possibility that the development of multicategorical programs may reflect shrinking fiscal and personnel resources rather than professional considerations. Such approaches can be just an administrative convenience and cost-saving device. Also, there is a danger that multicategorical programs designed for mildly handicapped students might slip into enrolling severely handicapped students in inappropriate ways, making the teaching situation very difficult. Several survey studies have suggested a number of practical concerns about multicategorical grouping, fearing abuses of valuable principles of instruction and of pupil placement (Noel, Smith-Davis, & Burke, 1985; Smith-Davis, Burke, & Noel, 1984).

Teacher Preparation for Noncategorical Programs

It would be possible to categorize children, yet serve them in multicategorical programs conducted by noncategorical special education teachers. But that is not generally the way programs have been organized. Historically, special education teachers have been prepared, certified or licensed, and employed in the categorical streams corresponding to the categories used for children. That is, learning disability teachers teach learning disabled children and educable mental retardation teachers teach educable mentally retarded pupils and so on; but that situation is changing.

In 1973, a national Delphi survey was reported which predicted a trend toward noncategorical approaches in teacher preparation and certification (Reynolds, 1973). The survey asked respondents, mostly teachers, teacher-educators, and administrators, to make predictions for five-year (to 1978) and ten-year periods (to 1983) into the future. Reynolds interpreted his results to indicate that there would be a movement towards a lesser number of categories of special education teacher certification, probably coming down from eight or nine (the average number of different types of special education teaching certificate licenses available in the several states) to just five special education areas: (a) hearing, (b) vision, (c) speech-hearing-language, (d) severe-profound handicaps, and (e) mildly handicapped. The last would represent the noncategorical approach in services for mildly handicapped pupils. Blackhurst, Bott, and Cross (1987) find that the trend, in fact, is consistent with Reynolds' predictions, but at a slower pace than was anticipated. They note that considerable controversy exists about this trend.

A number of studies on components of categorical teacher education programs have shown more similarities than differences across categories. Blackhurst, McLaughlin, and Price (1977) analyzed four categorical teacher preparation programs and found significant similarities in program components. Newhouse (1981) examined program objectives of several categorical programs and found much repetition. In a questionnaire study of active teachers in three categories (learning disabilities, emotional disturbance, and mental retardation), Carri (1985) found that there were more similarities than differences in skills and competencies judged important by the teachers employed across the several categories.

In 1977, 11 states offered some form of generic or noncategorical certification (Gilmore & Argyros, 1977). Two years later the number of states offering such certification had increased to 14, according to Barresi and Bunte (1979). In another study conducted in 1979, Belch found that 11 states had noncategorical certification clearly in place but that 12 others were making plans for such certification. Smith-Davis et al. (1984) reported that by 1984 half the states had some form of multi-categorical certification, but that most also offered the more traditional categorical certificates. The number and percentage of colleges offering noncategorical preparation tends to correspond quite closely with trends in certification requirements. Geiger (1983), in a survey of college programs, found that about 46% of colleges involved in special education teacher preparation offered a noncategorical program: about equal to the percentage of states ofering some form of generic special education certificate.

The literature contains several useful models for the design of noncategorical teacher preparation programs and for the treatment of the issues involved (Blackhurst, 1977, 1983; Blackhurst et al., 1977; Stephens & Joseph, 1982; Vallecorsa, 1983). Little evaluation of the emerging teacher preparation programs has been conducted. Blackhurst, Cross, Nelson, & Tawney (1973) and Nelson, Berdine, & Boyer (1976) report formative evaluation data. A study by Idol-Maestas, Lloyd, and Lilly (1981), which presented data on the academic performance of children representing a variety of diagnostic classifications while served by noncategorical resource/consulting teachers, points the way for needed studies.

The "Waiver for Performance" Approach

To address some of the problems of changing the structure of special education, Reynolds and Lakin (1987) proposed what they term a "waiver for performance" approach. (For some people the idea of "waivers" may seem negative in tone. Perhaps it would be preferable to speak of "experimental permits" with the "waiver" aspect being only incidental to the more positively-framed experimental approaches.) It is intended to be a moderately proactive strategy, one which leaves major laws and policies intact, but permits carefully selected school districts and states to undertake experimental programs and to exercise more-than-usual flexibility through waivers of some regulatory requirements. In return for receiving waivers or permits for experimentation, the school officials would be responsible for submitting performance data, showing how well the program worked in producing desired outcomes, and in particular, how the rights of handicapped children were assured.

Several communities, for example, might submit plans for use of noncategorical, curriculum-based classification systems in which a student's current rate of progress (or lack thereof) in the school's curriculum would determine whether he or she received special assistance at any given time. A school district might agree to run parallel categorical identification systems (traditional as well as curriculum-based) for an experimental period (e.g., 3-5 years), or compare performance in the experimental system with that in a traditional program in a neighboring school district to test the accountability features of the new system. Through study of the parallel systems, researchers could check to see whether the experimental system would identify all or most of the children now identified as learning disabled, emotionally disturbed, or educable mentally retarded; whether school officials could be held equally accountable for services to the children under the experimental arrangement; whether services could be provided on a cost-effective basis; whether the experimental program would lead to equal or improved academic, social, and psychological benefits to students traditionally identified as handicapped; and/or whether it could provide benefits to nonhandicapped students as well. Under the waiver for performance strategy, it would be necessary for governmental agencies to assure that funding now provided under the various categories would not be reduced for participating districts during the experimental period. In return, districts would assure governmental agencies that all legal requirements (e.g., due process rights, preparation of IEPs, etc.) would be satisfied.

The waiver for performance strategy would require careful consideration of proposals by state boards of education and federal officials before they granted waivers of various policies, rules, and regulations. Plans would have to be made to ensure deliberations on policy matters, to give policy leaders the opportunity to decide on the kinds of outcome data required, and to schedule reviews of data on outcomes.

Reynolds and Lakin (1987) propose that the waiver policy and related experiments be extended to areas beyond contemporary special education. It was noted in the National Academy of Sciences study (Heller et al. 1982), for example, that the distinctions between special education programs and programs for disadvantaged students (such as those served in Chapter 1 programs) have little or no credibility. Most Chapter 1 programs provide tutoring for students whose progress in reading and/or arithmetic is slow. Many learning disability programs do the same, which means that the distinction between Chapter 1 students and learning disabled students is marginal. Under a broad waiver for performance strategy, programs combining the student assessment, teaching, and program evaluation resources of special education and Chapter 1 probably would be popular. Hopefully, experimental efforts would encompass other categorical programs as well, such as migrant education, bilingual education, English as a Second Language instruction, and Indian education.

If a number of school districts and states entered into waivers for performance experiments, they could occasionally be brought together with external participants in the evaluation (e.g., university faculty, advocates, parents) to share their experiences and data. A special research community would thus be created to help summarize and disseminate results of the studies and to stimulate discussion of related policy issues.

The waiver for performance approach would put research into a central position in trying to identify promising alternative diagnostic and instructional practices, administrative arrangements, and means of resource allocation that respond to critical problems in categorical education programs. This strategy would offer possibilities for data-based policy and regulatory changes. While such a strategy would encourage alternatives to current practice, it need not threaten in any way the rights of handicapped children to a free and appropriate education.

Program Alternatives

The Reynolds–Lakin proposal assumes that a variety of responsible but different approaches to revisions in the structuring of special education programs for mildly handicapped children are feasible. Some features of revised programs which they considered especially promising were the following:

USE OF CURRICULUM–BASED MEASUREMENT (CBM)

This feature is used in identifying children needing special education and in monitoring student progress. It assumes that the basic starting point in special education should be with curriculum, and that children should be identified for special help when their progress in the curriculum is troublesome or slow. The CBM approach is proposed as an alternative to present practices, which depend heavily on measures of children's presumed predispositions for learning. For example, school psychological studies sometimes put more emphasis on intelligence and other dispositional traits than on school learning itself. The distinctions in these studies between so-called learning disabled and educable mentally retarded children depend more on dispositional analysis than on curriculum-based measurement. A variety of carefully developed CBM systems are now available and ready for full testing. Advocates of CBM believe that their procedures result in cost reductions and in data that are more useful to teachers when compared with present measurement and classification practices.

USE OF BROAD SYSTEMS OF INDIVIDUALIZED INSTRUCTION

Some school districts will wish to try comprehensive instructional systems that involve individualizing programs for all children. In such a system, mildly handicapped students may be expected to learn efficiently while they remain in regular classes, especially if special education teachers and paraprofessionals are redeployed into the mainstream classes to help operate the total system of individualization.

One such total system is known as the Adaptive Learning Environments Model (ALEM), developed at the University of Pittsburgh (Wang, 1981). At its core is a managment system for individualizing instruction and teaching students to take considerable self-responsibility for managing their own progress through the curriculum. It has a detailed monitoring system to reflect the degree of implementation of the model, a teacher-training system, and a parent involvement program. Under the ALEM, regular and special education teachers coordinate their work in developing comprehensive curricula to teach students with widely ranging levels of ability and academic status. The ALEM focuses on teaching basic skills, but it is not a teaching method; it is a total system for providing adaptive education. The National Association of School Psychologists has published a volume which includes a variety of additional "alternative educational delivery systems" (Graden, Zins, & Curtis, 1988).

DIMENSIONAL RATHER THAN CATEGORICAL DIAGNOSIS

A basic choice to be made in any diagnostic enterprise is between categorical and dimensional approaches. If one believes there are basic "types" or taxons involved (categories "carved by nature," which would exist whether or not special education existed), the choice would be categorical. Otherwise, the choice should probably be dimensional, in which case one combines various measures and observations of individuals, in ways that are relevant to decisions to be made, but without any assumptions about types or categories. For example, in dimensional approaches measures of reading ability or of psychological attributes are expressed directly by scores, assuming a continuum, rather than in categories such as "mentally retarded." In their review of the 1980 edition of the *Diagnostic and Statistical Manual* of the American Psychiatric Association, Eysenck, Wakefield, and Friedman (1980) wrote, in a brief section looking to the future, that "categorical diagnosis must be replaced with dimensional assessment. . . ." (p. 185). They went on to point out that categorical diagnosis may be appropriate when there is a "specific causal species of pathogen," "major gene defects," or "specific dietary deficiencies," but most problems encountered in school are not of these kinds and "the alternative to categorical diagnosis is dimensional assessment." Why use categories, they asked, when "the single score on the intelligence dimension provides much clearer information" (p. 186)?

Reynolds and Balow (1972) made similar suggestions some years earlier, suggesting weather phenomena as an analogy. If temperature, humidity, and atmospheric pressure can be measured quite reliably and validly, why not use the measures directly and fully to characterize the weather on a particular day rather than simply describing it as "hot and muggy?" In studying children, some important dimensions such as intelligence and achievement can be described with good validity on the basis of careful testing or observations. Why not leave it at that, with as much precision as possible? Such an approach assumes, of course, that some means of identification, such as "progress in curriculum," will be used instead of the traditional categories to identify children for special education. The variables chosen for attention in that framework would be those that predict dispositions to respond to particular forms of instruction.

A COMPOSITE APPROACH

The preceding approaches can be combined, and in fact, doing so appears to be advantageous in the integration of instructional and child study processes. Consider a hypothetical scenario presented by Reynolds and Lakin (1987).

First, children are identified on the basis of progress-in-curriculum variables. It might be declared policy, for example, that all children whose rates of progress through the basic skills curricula fall below the 20th percentile (based on local norms) will be identified for special study and for cooperative, detailed planning with parents. This procedure does not suggest any particular typology; it suggests instead that there is a wide range in children's responsiveness to the instruction offered in school and that there ought to be a definite (reliable, universally applied) system for dealing with students and situations when progress is lacking or very slow.

Second, a careful study of the instructional and broader life situation of the child in question is made. The National Academy of Sciences panel (Heller et al., 1982) suggested that an analysis should be made first of the classroom and the child's broader life situation, and that treatment should also begin there. In structuring the study, attention would go mainly to variables shown in the effectiveness literature to be related to improved instruction and learning.

Assuming that the school is doing everything possible as part of its regular operations to conduct programs effectively and systematically, and that specialists are deployed to consult with regular classroom teachers to develop the necessary modifications in the program for students showing problems, it is likely that some students still will not show adequate progress. Inevitably, 20% of the students will fall below the 20th percentile on local norms for progress in reading, arithmetic, and other subjects. (I make no special point about the 20th percentile, except that there is some evidence that this boundary point tends to pick up all or nearly all of the so-called mildly handicapped students. Other break points may serve well in particular situations.) These children are the ones proposed for special study in this hypothetical scenario.

The third step is to proceed to intensive study of the children who show the least progress. Psychologists and other professionals assist in the studies, not by classifying the children in traditional ways but by helping teachers and parents in the search for improved approaches to instruction. Data are assembled as indicators of how the child's environment might be better arranged and how instruction might be improved, both at school and at home. Measurements are treated mainly as variables exept when there is evidence supporting a typology. The purpose of the diagnostic process is to create a more promising environmental arrangement and instructional process for each child. We have not thrown away IQs, data on cognitive processes, findings of neurological studies, or anything else that might have validity and be helpful, but the entire process of diagnosis has been disciplined and focused on the one topic of increasing the child's mastery of important skills and knowledge.

Many other approaches to practical improvement of education for mildly handicapped children undoubtedly can and will be proposed. By insisting on careful evaluation of alternative approaches it is reasonable to hope that improved approaches will be created and tested carefully.

Conclusions

Special education programs for mildly handicapped children are greatly in need of improvement, especially in diagnosis and classification, which are unreliable and inefficient. At the present time, it is virtually impossible to evaluate programs in a generally meaningful way, or to create a useful knowledge base, because there has been so little clarity about the characteristics of students in the various programs. Present practices of classification in special education are of little practical use but highly expensive. Facts of demography make it clear that the schools of the nation face a growing challenge of teaching the increasing numbers of children who are handicapped or at risk. Economic and political forces are operating with increasing effect to change the basic profile of special education programs. The resulting structure of school programs for mildly handicapped children is increasingly a source of frustration—intellectually, morally, and professionally—for many educators, school psychologists, and administrators. Designing and implementing change in such a context is very difficult, especially because funding systems tend to reward and perpetuate present practices. A strategy for change is proposed in which selected school districts and states would be given special permits and assurances to support experimental efforts for new program designs without financial disincentives. A basic element in such experimental efforts should be the testing of broader, noncategorical approaches to special education. Through careful evaluation of new experimental programs, an improved basis for policies affecting school programs for mildly handicapped and other marginal students hopefully will emerge.

References

Algozzine, B., Christenson, S., & Ysseldyke, J. (1982). Probabilities associated with the referral to placement process. *Teacher Education and Special Education*, 5, 19–23.

Algozzine, B., & Korinek, L. (1985). Where is special education for students with high prevalence handicaps going? *Exceptional Children*, 51, 388–397.

Algozzine, K. (1984). Specialized competencies for EMH teachers: A review of the literature. Gainesville, FL: University of Florida, Department of Special Education.

Algozzine, R., Algozzine, K., Morsink, C., & Dykes, M. K. (1984). *Summary of the 1983–84 ESE classroom observations, using COKER*. Gainesville, FL: University of Florida, Department of Special Education.

Barresi, J., & Bunte, J. (1979). *Special education certification practices: A summary of a national survey*. Paper prepared for the Policy Options Project. Reston, VA: The Council for Exceptional Children.

Belch, P. J. (1979). Toward noncategorical teacher certification in special education—myth or reality? *Exceptional Children*, 46, 129–131.

Blackhurst, A. E. (1977). Competency-based special education personnel preparation. In R. D. Kneedler & S. G. Tarver (Eds.). *Changing perspectives in special education* (pp. 156–182). Columbus: Charles E. Merrill.

Blackhurst, A. E. (1983). A department evaluates curriculum change. In D. M. Brinkerhoff, T. Brethower, T. Hluchyj, & J. Nowakowski (Eds.), *Program evaluation: A practitioner's guide for trainers and evaluators—Sourcebook/casebook* (pp. 303–324). Boston: Kluwer-Nihoff Publishing.

Blackhurst, A. E., Bott, D. A., & Cross, D. P. (1987). Noncategorical special education personnel preparation. In M. C. Wang, M. C. Reynolds & H. J. Walberg (Eds.), *Handbook of special education: Research and practice: Vol. 1. Learner characteristics and adaptive education* (pp. 313–329). Oxford, England: Pergamon Press.

Blackhurst, A. E. Cross, D. P., Nelson, C. M., & Tawney, J. W. (1973). Approximating noncategorical teacher education. *Exceptional Children*, 39, 284–288.

Blackhurst, A. E., McLoughlin, J. A., Price, L. M. (1977). Issues in the development of programs to prepare teachers of children with learning and behavior disorders. *Behavioral Disorders*, 2, 157–188.

Brookover, W. B., Bendy, C. H., Flord, P. K., Schweitzer, J., & Wisenbaker, J. (1979). *School systems and school achievement: Schools can make a difference*. New York: Praeger.

Carri, L. (1985). Inservice teachers' assessed needs in behavioral disorder, mental retardation, and learning disabilities: Are they similar? *Exceptional Children*, 51, 411–416.

Chalfant, J., Pysh, M., & Moultrie, R. (1979). Teacher assistance teams: A model for within building problem solving. *Learning Disabilities Quarterly*, 2, 83–86.

Child Trends, Inc. (1985). *The school-age handicapped*. (NCES 85–400). Washington, DC: U.S. Government Printing Office.

Christenson, S., Ysseldyke, J. E., Algozzine, B. (1982). Institutional and external pressures influencing referral decisions. *Psychology in the Schools*, 19, 341–345.

Cleary, A. (1980). (Quoted in) *APA Monitor*, November 1980, 11, 7.

Cromwell, R. I., Blashfield, R. K., & Strauss, J. S. (1975). Criteria for classification systems. In N. Hobbs (Ed.), *Issues in the classification of children* (Vol. 1, pp. 4–25). San Francisco: Jossey-Bass.

Dulle, P., & Childs, P. (1985). *Categorical vs cross-categorical programming*. Paper presented at International Conference of the Council for Exceptional Children, April 30, 1985, Anaheim, California.

Eysenck, H. J., Wakefield, J. A., & Friedman, A. F. (1980). Diagnosis and clinical assessment: The DSM III. *Annual Review of Psychology*, 34, 167–193.

Federal Register. (1977, August 23). Washington, DC: U.S. Office of Education.

Friend, M., & McNutt, G. (1984). Response room programs: Where are they now? *Exceptional Children*, 51, 150–155.

Garrison, M., & Hammill, D. (1970). Who are the retarded? *Exceptional Children*, **38**, 13–20.

Geiger, W. L. (1983). *1983 national directory of special education teacher preparation programs*. National Information Center for Handicapped Children and Youth, P.O. Box 1492, Washington, DC, 20013.

Gilmore, J. T., & Argyros, N. S. (1977). *Special education certification: A state of the art survey*. Albany, NY: The State Education Department Office for the Education of Children with Handicapping Conditions.

Good, T. L. (1983). Classroom research: A decade of progress. *Educational Psychologist*, **18**, 127–144.

Graden, J. L., Casey, A., & Bonstrom, O. (1985). Implementing a pre-referral intervention system: Part II, The data. *Exceptional Children*, **51**, 487–496.

Graden, J. L., Zins, J. E., & Curtis, M. J. (Eds.) (1988). *Alternative educational delivery systems: Enhancing instructional options for all students*. Washington, DC: National Association of School Psychologists.

Grosenick, J., & Reynolds, M. C. (Eds.) (1978). *Teacher education: Renegotiating roles for mainstreaming*. Reston, VA: Council for Exceptional Children.

Heller, K. A., Holtzman, W., & Messick S. (1982). *Placing children in special education: A strategy for equity*. Washington, DC: National Academy Press.

Hobbs, N. (1975). *Issues in the classification of children*. San Francisco: Jossey-Bass.

Hobbs, N. (1980). An ecologically oriented service-based system for the classification of handicapped children. In E. Salzinger, J. Antrobus, & J. Glick (Eds.), *The ecosystem of the "risk" child* (pp. 271–290). New York: Academic Press.

Hocutt, A. M., Cox, J. L., & Pelosi, J. (1984). An exploration of issues regarding the identification and placement of LD, MR, and ED students. In *A policy-oriented study of special educations service delivery system, phase 1: Preliminary study* (RTI Report No. RTE/2706–06/OIES). Durham, NC: Research Triangle Institute, Center for Educational Studies.

Idol-Maestas, L., Lloyd, S., & Lilly, M. S. (1981). Implementation of a noncategorical approach to direct service and teacher education. *Exceptional Children*, **48**(3), 213–219.

Idol-Maestas, L., Nevin, A., & Paolucci-Whitcomb, P. (1985). *Facilitators' manual for collaborative consultation: Principles and techniques*. Reston, VA: Project RETOOL, Council for Exceptional Children.

Jenkins, J. R., & Jenkins, L. M. (1981). *Cross age and peer tutoring: Help for children with learning problems*. Reston, VA: Council for Exceptional Children.

Johnson, D. W., Maruyama, G., Johnson, R., Nelson, D., & Skon, L. (1981). The effects of cooperative, competitive and individualistic goal structures on achievement. *Psychological Bulletin*, **89**, 47–62.

Johnson, R., & Johnson, D. (1981). Building friendship between handicapped and nonhandicapped students: Effects of cooperative and individualistic instruction. *American Educational Research Journal*, **18**(4), 415–423.

Keogh, B. K., Major-Kingsley, S., Omori-Gordon, H. P., & Reid, H. (1982). *A system of marker variables for the field of learning disabilities*. New York: Syracuse University.

Knight, M., Meyers, H., Hasazi, S., Paolucci-Whitcomb, P. & Nevin, A. (1981). A four year evaluation of consulting teacher services. *Behavior Disorders*, **6**, 92-100.

Larivee, B. (1982). Identifying effective teaching behaviors for mainstreaming. *Teacher Education and Special Education*, **5**, 2–6.

Lazar, I. & Darlington, R. (1982). Lasting effects of early education: A report from the consortium for longitudinal studies. *Monographs of the Society for Research in Child Development*, **47**, (Serial no. 195).

Miller, T., & Sabatino, D. (1978). An evaluation of the teacher consultant model as an approach to mainstreaming. *Exceptional Children*, **45**, 86–91.

Morsink, C. (1984). *Teaching special needs students in regular classrooms*. Boston: Little, Brown.

Morsink, C., Branscum, G., & Boone, R. (1984). *Specialized competencies for SLD teachers: A review of related literature*. Gainesville, FL: University of Florida, Department of Special Education.

Morsink, C., Smith-Davis, J., & Thomas, L. (1987). Noncategorical special education programs: Process and outcomes. In M. C. Wang, M. C. Reynolds, & H. J. Walberg (Eds.),

Handbook of special education: Research and practice: Vol. 1. Learner characteristics and adaptive education (pp. 287–311). Oxford, England: Pergamon Press.

Nelson, C. M., Berdine, W. H., & Boyer, J. R. (1978). The evolution of a non-categorical competency-based special education methods course. *Journal of Special Education Technology*, **2**(2), 37–46.

Nevin, A., Johnson, R., & Johnson, D. (1982). Effects of group and individual contingencies on academic performance and social relations of special needs students. *Journal of Social Psychology*, **116**, 41–59.

Nevin, A., & Thousand, J. (1987). Avoiding/limiting special education referrals. In M. C. Wang, M. C. Reynolds, & H. J. Walberg (Eds.), *Handbook of special education: Research and practice: Vol. 1. Learner characteristics and adaptive education* (pp. 273–286). Oxford, England: Pergamon Press.

Newhouse, J. (1981). A cross-disciplinary special education preparation program: An undergraduate experimental model. *Journal of Teacher Education*. **32**(4), 38–41.

Noel, M., Smith-Davis, J., & Burke, P. J. (1985). *Personnel to educate the handicapped: 1984 status report*. College Park, MD: Institute for the Study of Exceptional Children and Youth.

Reschly, D. J. (1987). Learning characteristics of mildly handicapped students: Implications for classification, placement and programming. In M. C. Wang, M. C. Reynolds, & H. J. Walberg (Eds.), *Handbook of special education: Research and practice: Vol. 1. Learner characteristics and adaptive education* (pp. 35–58). Oxford, England: Pergamon Press

Reynolds, M. C. (1973). *Delphi survey: A report of rounds I and II*. Reston, VA: The Council for Exceptional Children.

Reynolds, M. C. (Ed.) (1980). *A common body of practice for teachers: The challenge of Public Law 94–142 to teacher education*. Washington, DC: The American Association of Colleges for Teacher Education.

Reynolds, M. C., & Balow, B. (1972). Categories and variables in special education. *Exceptional Children*, **38**, 357–366.

Reynolds, M. C., & Lakin, K. C. (1987). Noncategorical special education for mildly handicapped students. In M. C. Wang, M. C. Reynolds, & H. J. Walberg (Eds.), *Handbook of special education: Research and practice: Vol. 1. Learner characteristics and adaptive education* (pp. 331–356). Oxford, England: Pergamon Press.

Robbins, L. L. (1966). An historical review of classification of behavior disorders and one current perspective. In L. D. Eron (Ed.), *The classification of behavior disorders* (pp. 1–37). Chicago: Aldine Publishing Co.

Sage, D. D., & Fensom, H. C. (1985). *A study of mixed category special education programs in the Commonwealth of Pennsylvania*. Final report to the Pennsylvania Department of Education, Bureau of Special Education, Syracuse, New York.

Sarason, S. & Doris, J. (1979). *Educational handicap, public policy, and social history*. New York: Free Press.

Scriven, M. (1983 January). Comments on Gene Glass. *Policy Studies Review*, **2** (Special No. 1), 79–84.

Sharp, B. L. (Ed.) (1982). *Dean's Grant Projects: Challenge and change in teacher education*. Washington, DC: American Association of Colleges for Teacher Education.

Shepard, L. A. & Smith, M. L. (1981). Evaluation of the identification of perceptual-communicative disorders in Colorado: Final report. Boulder, CO: University of Colorado, College of Education. (ERIC Document Reproduction Service No. 1 ED 216037).

Smith, D., Deshler, D., Hallahan, D., Lovitt, T., Robinson, S., Voress, J., & Ysseldyke, J. (1984). Minimum standards for the description of subjects in learning disabilities research reports. *Learning Disabilities Quarterly*, **7**, 112–225.

Smith-Davis, J., Burke, P. J., & Noel, M. (1984). *Personnel to educate the handicapped in America: Supply and demand from a programmatic viewpoint*. College Park, MD: University of Maryland: Institute for the Study of Exceptional Children and Youth.

Stephens, T. M., & Joseph, E. A. (1982). Decategorizing teacher preparation in special education. *Education and Treatment of Children*, **5**(4), 395–404.

Taylor, R. L. (1980). Use of the AAMD classification system: A review of recent research. *American Journal of Mental Deficiency*, **85**, 116–119.

Tucker, J. A. (1980). Ethnic proportions in classes for the learning disabled: Issues in nonbiased assessment. *Journal of Special Education*, **14**, 93–105.

U.S. Department of Education. (1985). *Seventh annual report to Congress on the implementation of Public Law 94–142: The Education for All Handicapped Children Act*. Washington, DC: U.S. Department of Education.

Valcante, G. (1984). *Specialized competencies for teachers of mildly emotionally handicapped students: A review of literature*. Unpublished manuscript. Gainesville, FL: University of Florida, Dept. of Special Education.

Vallecorsa, A. L. (1983). Cross-categorical resource programs: An emerging trend in special education. *Education*, **104**(2), 131–136.

Walberg, H. J. (1984 May). Improving the productivity of America's schools. *Educational Leadership*, **41**, 19–27.

Wang, M. C. (1981). Mainstreaming exceptional children: Some instructional design considerations. *Elementary School Journal*, **81**(4), 195–221.

Weikart, D. P., Bond, J. T., & McNeir, J. T. (1978). *The Ypsilanti Perry Preschool Project: Preschool years and longitudinal results* (Monographs of the High/Scope Educational Research Foundation No.3). Ypsilanti, MI: High/Scope Press.

White, K. R. & Casto, G. (1984). *An integrative review of early intervention efficacy studies with at-risk children: Implications for the handicapped*. Logan, UT: Early Intervention Research Institute, Utah State University.

Wood, F. H., & Lakin, K. C. (1982). Defining emotionally disturbed/behaviorally disordered populations for research purposes. In F. H. Wood, & K. C. Lakin (Eds.), *Disturbing, disordered or disturbed: Perspectives on the definition of problem behavior in educational settings* (pp. 29–48). Reston, VA: Council for Exceptional Children.

Ysseldyke, J. E. (1987). Classification of handicapped students. In M. C. Wang, M. C. Reynolds, & H. J. Walberg (Eds.), *Handbook of special education: Research and practice: Vol. 1. Learner characteristics and adaptive education* (pp. 253–271). Oxford, England: Pergamon Press.

Ysseldyke, J. E., Algozzine, B., & Allen, D. (1981). Regular education teacher participation in special education team decision making. *Elementary School Journal*, **82**, 160–165.

Zill, N. (1985, June 25). "How is the number of children with severe handicaps likely to change over time?" Testimony prepared for the Subcommittee on Select Education of the Committee on Education and Labor, U.S. House of Representatives.

Mild Mental Retardation: Persistent Themes, Changing Dynamics, and Future Prospects

DANIEL J. RESCHLY

Iowa State University

Mild mental retardation has a venerable past as part of the exceptional child classification system. The first special education programs in most cities and states were established for students classified as mildly mentally retarded. As recently as 1975, mild mental retardation had the highest incidence of the 11 handicapped student classifications specified in federal legislation. Over the past 10 years, mild mental retardation has declined significantly on several dimensions, including numbers of mildly mentally retarded students served in special education programs, amount of research published in leading journals, and numbers of teachers and other professionals trained with primary interest in mild mental retardation.

In this chapter, the current status of the mild mental retardation diagnostic construct will be analyzed from the perspective of seven persistent themes relating to fundamental problems. The discussion will lead to an analysis of factors influencing changes in mild mental retardation and other mild handicaps, followed by suggestions for likely future prospects. Special attention will be devoted to the state of current practices and the potential knowledge that could be applied in mild mental retardation programs.

Mild Mental Retardation Diagnostic Construct

Mental retardation is defined as ". . . significantly subaverage general intellectual functioning existing concurrently with deficits in adaptive behavior . . ." (Grossman, 1983, p. 1). The classification system developed by the American Association on Mental Deficiency (AAMD), generally regarded as the most authoritative source of information on mental retardation, has been adopted, often with slight modifications, in the special education rules of most state departments of education. These rules generally govern the classification and placement of school-age children into various special education programs for handicapped students, including those who are mildly mentally retarded. Common variations of the AAMD system used by states include different terminology (e.g., mental handicap or mental disability), different classification criteria (e.g., defining the IQ cut-off as general intellectual functioning below 80, 75, or 70), and varying approaches to assessment and decision making with adaptive behavior. Despite these variations, mild mental retardation is fundamentally a handicapping condition based on very low intellectual functioning and deficits in adaptive behavior.

Mild mental retardation is one of the four levels of mental retardartion specified in the AAMD *Classification in Mental Retardation* (Grossman, 1983). These levels are designated by the adjectives of mild, moderate, severe, and profound. The implicit assumption is the AAMD system is that the principal differences between levels are matters of degree, or quantitative, rather than in the basic nature of the underlying handicap. Unfortunately, this is an erroneous assumption.

The highest level in the AAMD system, mild mental retardation, usually involves general intellectual functioning in the range of about IQ 55 to IQ 70 or 75, or the bottom 5% (when IQ equals 75) to the bottom 2.3% (when IQ equals 70). Persons classified as mildly mentally retarded typically are not recognized as handicapped prior to school entry, and most are not officially classified as retarded during their adult years. However, they do have difficulties in adjustment during their adult years. They do not magically melt into the normal population (Edgerton, 1984), unrecognized as being different, as was thought earlier (e.g., Mercer, 1973). Persons classified as mildly mentally retarded typically do not display physical signs of mental retardation and there is no identifiable underlying physical cause for their intellectual and adaptive behavior deficiencies.

The more severely retarded, encompassing the bottom three levels designated by the AAMD, involves an IQ range from below 25 to about 55. In contrast to the mildly mentally retarded population, the more severely retarded are nearly always diagnosed as handicapped prior to school entry, often within a few days or weeks of birth. Furthermore, the more severely retarded virtually always display physical anomalies; nearly all are regarded as handicapped in various social roles and contexts; and the handicap is permanent (lifelong).

The fundamental differences between mild mental retardation and the more severe levels of mental retardation involve the degree to which the condition is a permanent lifelong handicap, the degree to which there is an underlying biological anomaly, and whether the deficits are comprehensive in affecting different roles and contexts. A persistent problem in mild mental retardation is the misunderstanding of the basic diagnostic construct that arises in large part because AAMD places all levels of mental retardation on the same continuum. This causes additional stigma for the mildly mentally retarded population because the characteristics of the more severely retarded are often mistakenly ascribed to them. This particular problem could be addressed through changing the classification system, or through special education reforms.

Students classified as mildly mentally retarded typically have experienced prolonged and severe achievement problems. Studies of mildly mentally retarded students indicate that most have repeated grades at least once, sometimes twice, and most had been placed in regular education remedial options such as Chapter 1 (Mercer, 1973; Reschly & Kicklighter, 1985). Referral for consideration of classification as handicapped and possible placement in a special education program nearly always occurs after persistent educational failure and after other options such as Chapter 1 have proven to be inadequate. Once referred, these students usually receive a comprehensive evaluation, including: (1) screening for sensory problems, such as visual or hearing deficits; (2) administration of individual tests in achievement and general intellectual functioning; and (3) assessment of adaptive behavior through interviews with significant others such as teachers and/or parents. Students who meet the state-mandated criteria for classification as mildly mentally retarded are then placed, pending parental permission, in a special education program—typically a resource teaching program (RTP) or a self-contained special class. The use of the RTP option varies considerably across states and districts. RTP involves part-time special education with most of the school day spent in a regular classroom. In contrast, self-contained special classes usually involve most, if not all, of the school day.

The cause or etiology of mild mental retardation is unknown and controversial. The incidence of mild mental retardation is clearly associated with poverty circumstances. Further, minority groups with high incidence of poverty circumstances are often overrepresented in mild mental retardation programs. Overrepresentation of minority students in mild mental retardation programs has led to placement litigation in the federal courts.

The relationship between poverty circumstances and mild mental retardation is very complex. The paradox of this relationship is represented well by the following generalizations, both of which have firm support from empirical studies. First, the overwhelming majority of mildly mentally retarded students come from poverty circumstances.

Second, the overwhelming majority of students from poverty circumstances are never classified as mildly mentally retarded and do not meet the intellectual or adaptive behavior criteria for the mild mental retardation diagnosis. This seeming paradox is understandable when the rather low base rate for mild mental retardation is considered. The prevalence of mild mental retardation in schools varies from under 1% to about 4% depending on the state involved.

The official classification of mild mental retardation is most likely to occur with persons during the school-age years, roughly age 5 to 17. Students classified as mildly mentally retarded are more likely to be male than female, more likely to be from poverty circumstances, and more likely to have minority status (for minority groups overrepresented in poverty). Such students generally do not have physical symptoms suggestive of mental retardation or any other handicap, and have no identifiable biological anomaly that would account for the mental retardation.

Persistent Themes and Unresolved Issues

A number of fundamental issues in research and delivery of services reflect long-term debates and enduring concerns. On many of these issues there are sharp disagreements. These issues deal with fundamental questions such as: Who is properly classified as mildly mentally retarded? Why do persons develop the mild mental retardation handicap? Can mild mental retardation be prevented or remedied through early interventions? And what services are needed by persons classified as mildly mentally retarded?

Meaning of the Diagnostic Construct and Mild Mental Retardation Classification Criteria

The mild mental retardation diagnostic construct has undergone a number of significant changes over the last three decades. Prior to about 1960, mental retardation, including mild mental retardation, was believed to be based on biological anomalies and was regarded as permanent, that is lifelong (Doll, 1941). Revisions in the AAMD classification system beginning about 30 years ago (Heber, 1959) through the most recent revision (Grossman, 1983), have regarded mental retardation as neither permanent nor restricted to a biological origin. The basic question and a longstanding persistent theme is whether or not mental retardation should be restricted to those persons who have relatively permanent handicapping conditions with a biological origin. Permanence and biological origin are, of course, attributes of the more severely retarded, but not the mildly mentally retarded.

Classification criteria are closely related to the meaning of the diagnostic construct. More stringent or more lenient classification criteria to define the upper boundary of mild mental retardation have the potential effect of changing fundamental characteristics of the diagnostic construct. For example, if the upper boundary was IQ of 55, then the diagnostic construct of mild mental retardation would acquire the permanence and biological anomaly characteristics. On the other hand, if the upper boundary on general intellectual functioning was shifted to some point considerably higher than an IQ of approximately 70, say to IQ of 85, as was the case with an earlier edition of the AAMD classification system (Heber, 1959), the diagnostic construct of mild mental retardation acquires far more potentially eligible persons who also have considerably milder degrees of handicap.

Subtle changes in IQ cut-off have considerable effects on the population of persons who might be classified as mildly mentally retarded. For example, the percentages of persons who obtain IQ scores below 70 and 75 in the general population are 2.3 and 4.7%, respectively. A seemingly small change, shifting the IQ cut-off from 70 to 75, has the practical effect of *doubling* the percentage of persons who might be classified as mildly mentally retarded.

Adaptive behavior is another significant influence on the mild mental retardation diagnostic construct and classification criteria. Depending on adaptive behavior conception, assessment procedures, and decision-making guidelines, use of adaptive behavior could virtually eliminate the population of students now classified as mildly mentally retarded (Mercer, 1979; Polloway, 1985; Reschly, 1981; 1986, 1988). If adaptive behavior is restricted to out-of-school social role performance, assessed through interviewing the parent, and a very stringent guideline for determining the existence of a deficit (such as greater than two standard deviations below the population mean), 70% or more of the population of students currently classified as mildly mentally retarded would no longer be so classified. Classification criteria exert a significant influence on the mild mental retardation diagnostic construct.

Prevention and Remediation

A prominent theme throughout twentieth century American psychology has been the degree to which human development can be accelerated through cognitive interventions. But, the complexities of these preventive or remedial efforts need to be recognized (Kramer, Piersel, & Glover, 1988; Taylor, 1988). The strong association of mild mental retardation with poverty circumstances suggests the possibility of environmental etiology. The role of an environmental etiology is further supported by the AAMD classification scheme which suggests (but does not require) an etiology of psychosocial disadvantage for most persons classified as mildly mentally retarded (Grossman, 1983; MacMillan, 1982; Reschly, 1986; 1988; Robinson & Robinson, 1976).

The efforts to prevent or remediate the cognitive and social competence limitations fundamental to mild mental retardation are extremely complex and controversial (Taylor, 1988). The most famous of these efforts, the Milwaukee Project, appeared to produce dramatic gains in a population of students known to be at high risk for the development of mild mental retardation during the school-age years (Garber & Heber, 1981). The Milwaukee Project involved a highly structured cognitive enrichment program beginning during infancy and continuing through the first five years. However, serious questions have been raised over the years concerning the credibility of those findings (Page, 1972; Sommer & Sommer, 1983). Recent, credible research by Ramey & Campbell (1984) provides reason for optimism about remedying the underlying cognitive and social competence deficits associated with mild mental retardation, but their results were not as dramatic as reports from the Milwaukee Project.

A variety of other preventive and remedial efforts have been established and evaluated, usually with mixed results and with continuing debates over methodological considerations. In addition to early cognitive stimulation, preventive/remediation efforts have attempted to control risk factors such as teenage pregnancy, poor nutrition, and inadequate medical care (*Prevention Strategies that Work* 1979).These efforts should continue and may, over the long term, substantially reduce the mild mental retardation risk for persons in poverty circumstances.

Fundamental Cognitive Processes

A theme closely related to prevention and remediation is research on the fundamental cognitive processes associated with mild mental retardation. Kramer et al. (1988) provided a review of the literature on basic learning and information processing characteristics of students classified as mildly mentally retarded. They, along with Campione, Brown, and Ferrara (1982), have identified basic differences between mildly mentally retarded and normal students. These differences have to do with efficiency of information processing, the fund of knowledge brought to a problem-solving situation, the use of problem-solving strategies, and the ability to exercise deliberate control over learning, memory, and problem-solving processes (called metacognition). The critical and still-unsolved problems in cognitive training of mildly mentally retarded students involve the more complex rather than the simple cognitive processes. Although considerable advances have been achieved demonstrating that mildly mentally retarded students can be taught to use strategies in solving problems, the intractable problems to date are transfer of strategy use to new situations, and spontaneous unaided consideration and selection of appropriate strategies (Campione et al., 1982; Kramer, et al., 1988).

The problems with strategy transfer and selection are probably part of more pervasive cognitive limitations, termed "ability to profit from incomplete instruction" by Campione et al. (1982). Incomplete instruction refers to several instructional variables, such as the need for more time, greater structure, more concrete examples, and more supervised practice to achieve mastery. The cognitive deficits in mild mental retardation become cumulative at older ages and higher grades. Mildly mentally retarded students have increasing problems, not just because of inefficient information processing and a need for more complete instruction, but also because of a smaller fund of knowledge from prior learning. The information from basic cognitive research has important implications for educational programs.

Education Programming

Vast changes have occurred in the provision of educational programs for mildly mentally retarded students. Over the 10-year period from 1975–1985, the number of students in mild mental retardation programs declined by over one-third (Polloway & Smith, 1983, 1988; Reschly, 1988). Part of this decline can be explained as superficial shifting of students' classification from mild mental retardation to specific learning disability (Tucker, 1980). This change in designation may also have involved changing the placement from a special class to a resource program, since learning disabled students are more likely to be in resource programs and mildly mentally retarded students are somewhat more likely to be in self-contained special classes.

The reasons for the changes in numbers of mildly mentally retarded students are complex and multifaceted (Polloway & Smith, 1983, 1988; Reschly, 1988). The early placement litigation consent decrees and injunctions generally upheld plaintiffs and claims of discrimination based on minority overrepresentation in mild mental retardation special classes. Thus, legal pressure prompted greater care in mild mental retardation classification and more stringent mild mental retardation eligibility criteria. The stricter criteria involved tougher IQ guidelines and more emphasis on adaptive behavior (Reschly, 1988). These changes in classification criteria are probably sufficient to explain the 33% decline in mild mental retardation.

The current group of students classified as mildly mentally retarded and placed in special education programs is probably more seriously handicapped than its predecessor 20 years ago (MacMillan and

Borthwick, 1980). Older studies of the mildly mentally retarded population (e.g., Mercer, 1973) indicated persistent and severe educational difficulties, for example, repeating grades prior to being referred and placed in special education. Due to more stringent classification criteria, the current mildly mentally retarded population probably has more serious problems than these earlier populations described by Mercer and others.

The fundamental question for students classified as mildly mentally retarded is not whether they need some sort of remedial or compensatory services. Their educational problems are persistent and serious. The question today is what kinds of services are needed, in what sort of settings, and with what degree of involvement with regular education. At the elementary level, the balance of opinion seems to lean toward emphasizing the use of regular education programs and options to the greatest extent possible, with use of resource programs when necessary and placement in self-contained special classes as a last resort. At the high school level, the choices may become more limited because of the large discrepancy between the performance of mildly mentally retarded students and the averages attained by other students.

Increasingly, as the mildly mentally retarded student progresses through the grades, dilemmas are faced concerning degree and kind of curricular emphasis. Should the curriculum for mildly mentally retarded students in high school emphasize further efforts to teach basic literacy skills such as reading and basic computations? Emphasize content areas such as science and social studies? Emphasize the acquisition of social competencies which are known to be related to early adult adjustment? Or emphasize vocational technical skills, including supervised work experiences? All of these are important and needed by mildly mentally retarded persons. Similar dilemmas are faced with specific learning disability students (Deshler, Shumaker, Lenz, & Ellis, 1984), but the degree of discrepancy from average levels of performance is not as large with learning disabled students, and they generally master basic literacy skills to a greater degree.

There is little solid empirical evidence to guide crucial decisions in the areas of educational programming. The empirical evidence firmly establishes the large discrepancy between the education achievement of mildly mentally retarded students and age and grade averages. These discrepancies eventually become large enough to require some kind of alternative curriculum. The degree to which the alternative curriculum requires a different setting, such as an RTP or a self-contained special class, is at issue, particularly during the elementary grades. The absence of strong empirical evidence leads to decisions about setting based on opinion or philosophical principles. The principle of "least restrictive environment" suggests that mildly mentally retarded students should be placed in regular education to the greatest extent possible. Trends over the past 10 years have generally followed that principle, particularly at the elementary level. Further evidence of progam effects and possible differential benefits of different settings need to be assessed, preferably with criterion-referenced, curriculum-based measures rather than norm-referenced survey instruments. These latter instruments may provide a more valid basis for assessing program effects (Deno, 1985; Shapiro & Lentz, 1985; Shinn, Tindal, Spira, & Marston, 1987).

Adult Adjustment

The adjustment of adults classified as mildly mentally retarded during their school-age years has fundamental and far-reaching implications for the development of educational programs. Mildly mentally retarded adult adjustment is enormously difficult to study for a variety of reasons. The most useful studies apply a longitudinal design in which the same persons are followed throughout their adult years. The few studies that provide data of this nature are discussed by Zetlin (1988).

One of the basic questions is whether persons earlier classified as mildly mentally retarded are identifiable as handicapped during their adult years. If not, perhaps classification during the school-age years is a disservice to these persons due to the stigma of being classified as mildly mentally retarded. Or conversely, perhaps classification during the school-age years assists individuals in acquiring social competencies and vocational skills which improve their chances for successful adult adjustment. In either case, adult adjustment results have profound implications for mild mental retardation programs.

Longitudinal studies indicate that persons classified as mildly mentally retarded during their school-age years are typically not *officially* classified during their adult years. This generalization appears to be true for about 60–80% of them (Baller, Charles, & Miller, 1967). Good adult adjustment seems to be related to acquisition of social competencies, such as interpersonal skills, acquisition of positive attitudes toward work, and avoidance of maladaptive behaviors. Specific vocational or occupational skills are also important. The positive influence of a "bene-factor" has been identified in several longitudinal studies, e.g., Baller et al. (1967) and Edgerton (1967, 1984). The benefactor assists with more complex interactions (e.g., with employers, with institutions such as state and federal government, and in management of money).

Recent evidence (Koegel & Edgerton, 1984) suggests that students classified as mildly mentally retarded do not magically melt into the general population as adults. In fact, it appears that the same kind of skill deficiences that lead to the original referral and placement in special education continue to cause difficulties in the adult years. Problems with understanding abstract relationships, dealing with concepts of time and number, use of basic literacy skills in coping with the environment, and understanding complex relationships with institutions (e.g., Social Security benefits, income taxes, etc.), continue to cause serious difficulty. These difficulties lead to other people recognizing the mildly mentally retarded individual's intellectual and adaptive behavior limitations. Although most mildly mentally retarded persons are not officially classified as handicapped during their adult years, they do continue to exhibit skill deficiencies which identify them as less competent and handicapped to others in their environment.

The evidence on adult adjustment has implications for development and delivery of school programs. Many of the findings have already been incorporated in school progams (e.g., the stress on social competencies and acquisition of vocational skills). Further application of these findings might include attempts to teach skills in seeking appropriate assistance in complex interactions with societal institutions. These help-seeking skills may become increasingly important as traditional sources of assistance (neighbors or family members) become increasingly unavailable due to social and geographic mobility.

Social Competence

The realm of social competence has vast implications for the mild mental retardation diagnostic construct and school programs. Social competence, which includes the domains of social skills and adaptive behavior (Reschly & Gresham, in press), is crucial to the development of good adjustment in the adult years. Furthermore, social competence difficulties often seriously complicate the adjustment of mildly mentally retarded and other mildly handicapped students in school and other settings (Gresham, 1982; Gresham & Reschly, in press). Social competence is therefore critical to appropriate classification of persons as mildly mentally retarded and to effective remedial and compensatory programming.

If social competence must be deficient for a person to be properly classified, then objectives concerning development of social competencies should be a part of the individualized special education program. Currently, social competencies are taught in mild mental retardation special class, but frequently ignored in resource programs.

Poverty and Mild Mental Retardation

A final theme prominent in the literature throughout the twentieth century is the link between poverty and mild mental retardation. This link is complex. As noted earlier, the overwhelming majority of mildly mentally retarded persons *do* come from poverty circumstances; however, the overwhelming majority of persons in poverty circumstances do not become mildly mentally retarded.

The link between poverty and mild mental retardation has become even more controversial due to the overrepresentation of minority students in mild mental retardation special education programs. This overrepresentation was studied thoroughly by a panel appointed by the National Academy of Sciences (Heller, Holtzman, & Messick, 1982). The panel considered a variety of issues, including complex interactions of poverty, minority status, and human development. The panel succeeded in identifying the most relevant question, specifically, "Why is overrepresentation viewed as a problem?" rather than, "Why does it occur?" The panel reasoned that overrepresentation is a problem if students are invalidly referred, inappropriately assessed, or placed in ineffective programs. The panel then went on to identify crucial principles related to effective educational programming in regular and special education. These crucial principles placed primary emphasis on the development and utilization of a variety of remedial and compensatory efforts within regular education prior to (and in place of, where possible) classification as handicapped and placement in special education. These principles are quite consistent with the special education reform movement discussed in a subsequent section of this chapter.

The link between poverty, minority status, and mild mental retardation has resulted in extremely controversial and divisive placement litigation over the past 20 years (Reschly, 1988). Court opinions in the placement litigation cases have been very different, despite similar evidence and virtually identical facts (Reschly, Kicklighter, & McKee, in press, a,b,c). This litigation has been one of the most important influences on changing the mild mental retardation diagnostic construct toward development of more stringent classification criteria. Further developments through litigation are possible, particularly since two major, contradictory opinions have been upheld by the United States Circuit Courts of Appeal (*Larry P. v. Riles*, 1979, 1984; *Marshall v. Georgia*, 1984, 1985).

The persistent themes in the mild mental retardation literature provide the context for the influence of the special education reform movement on mild mental retardation programs. These fundamental issues, though far from resolved, represent key challenges which any program for mildly mentally retarded students, whether in regular or special education, must address through crucial decisions about program setting, eligibility of students, programming objects, and intervention strategies or methods. Suggestions for addressing many of these issues will be discussed in the context of the developing special education reform movement.

Special Education Reform and Mild Mental Retardation

A number of dynamic factors are likely to produce significant changes in the mild mental retardation diagnostic construct and in the services provided to students who are now classified as mildly mentally retarded. These factors present significant problems in the current system and in advances in basic knowledge and technology.

Changing Dynamics

There are four major influences which establish the basis for the current special education reform movement. These four influences are consistent in one extremely important way—all strongly suggest a far closer relationship between regular and special education. This closer relationship might influence all facets of the current system for providing educational services to handicapped students, including basic diagnostic constructs, classification criteria, intervention or instructional objectives, placement options, instructional methods, and evaluation of outcomes.

LITIGATION

One of the most important influences on special education reform is placement litigation. Although the court decisions are now contradictory concerning whether or not minority overrepresentation in mild mental retardation special education programs is legal, the threat of litigation and the outcomes of the early cases have already influenced mild mental retardation, and that influence will continue. The litigation influence was apparent in the development of more stringent classification criteria, the significant reduction in students classified as mildly mentally retarded, and the increased care devoted to evaluation of students who might be classified as mildly mentally retarded. Part of this increased care involves greater emphasis on assessment of adaptive behavior, and insuring that regular educational alternatives for students with learning problems are exhausted prior to consideration of mild mental retardation classification and placement.

NATIONAL ACADEMY OF SCIENCES REPORT

A report from the National Academy of Sciences (Heller, et al., 1982) provided strong support for changes in special education and increased utilization of regular education. The nature of some of those changes was discussed in a previous section of this chapter. The NAS report strongly supported the use of a variety of alternatives for students with learning and behavioral problems. The report also proposed careful identification of intervention objectives rather than internal, non-observable traits, such as general intellectual functioning, as the basis for determining eligibility for special programs.

ADVOCACY GROUPS AND PROFESSIONAL ASSOCIATIONS

A number of policy statements were developed by key advocacy groups and influential professional associations in the early to mid-1980s. Two of these policy statements are particularly important. The position statement developed by the National Association of School Psychologists and the National Coalition of Advocates for Students (NASP–NCAS, 1985) stongly emphasized the development of a variety of remedial education alternatives without labeling students as handicapped. A companion paper, *Rights Without Labels* (1986), was endorsed by both of these associations. Another influential policy statement was developed by the Mental Retardation Subdivision of the Council for Exceptional Children (Polloway, 1985).

RESEARCH INTEGRATION PROJECT AND FEDERAL POLICY

A federally funded research integration project conducted thorough reviews of theory, research, and practice concerning the education of mildly handicapped students, including students classified as mildly mentally retarded. These reviews reached similar conclusions across a number of areas of exceptionality. In general, the conclusions were: (1) too much emphasis is placed on attempts to classify children according to underlying internal traits; (2) greater emphasis needs to be devoted to developing a wide range of alternatives for students with learning or behavioral problems; and (3) these alternatives need to be provided within regular education to the greatest extent possible (Wang, Reynolds, & Walberg, 1987–1989). The results of the research integration project were part of the basis for the development of the "regular education initiative" in the Federal Office of Special Education and Rehabilitation Services (Will, 1986a, b).

The dynamics of current changes in special education are diverse and broad. They include federal court opinions, a major report by the most prestigious scientific organization in the United States, policy statements by professional associations and advocacy groups, and a major synthesis of theory, research, and practice recommending changes in federal policy.

Increased Placement and Programming Options

Perhaps the most important change for students now classified as mildly mentally retarded is the development of a wider variety of placement and programming options. When Dunn (1968) severely criticized programs for students classified as mildly mentally retarded, virtually all mildly mentally retarded students were in largely self-contained, segregated (in the sense of being physically separate from regular education) special classes. Over the past 20 years there has been increased emphasis on other special education placement options, such as part-time resource teaching programs. Special education reform promises to increase programming and placement options still further, using a variety of technological innovations and grouping procedures (Graden, Casey, & Bonstrom, 1985; Grimes & Reschly, 1986; Wang & Birch, 1984). This broader continuum of options will allow a much closer match between characteristics of students and instructional/psychological interventions designed to meet their unique needs.

Social Competence: Assessment and Interventions

The relevant knowledge and the useful technology concerning assessment and development of effective social competence interventions have improved at a rapid pace over the past decade (Cartledge & Milburn, 1985; Gresham, 1982, 1983, 1988; Gresham, Elliott, & Black, 1987; Gresham & Reschly, in press; Goldstein, Sprafkin, Gershaw, & Klein, 1980; McGinnis & Goldstein, 1984; Stephens, 1987; Walker et al: 1983). These advances will be useful with nearly all students classified now as mildly handicapped, especially mildly mentally retarded students. Regardless of what may or may not happen with the classification system, and the mild mental retardation diagnostic construct, the need for social competence interventions and the relationship of social competence to successful adult adjustment will not change.

Changes in the Mild Mental Retardation Diagnostic Construct

A change in the mild mental retardation diagnostic construct is anticipated due to difficulties created by placing mild mental retardation in the same continuum as the more severe levels of mental retardation. These problems were discussed in an earlier section of this chapter. There are three possible changes in the mild mental retardation diagnostic construct. First, mild mental retardation might be separated from other levels of mental retardation through a fairly simple and straightforward change in name (e.g., Polloway & Smith, 1983; Reschly, 1982). This change of name might involve using some term that is less likely to confuse mild mental retardation with the more severe levels , as well as being behaviorally specific and descriptive of the basic problems in mild mental retardation (i.e., acquiring intellectual and social competencies). More appropriate names for mild mental retardation would be educationally handicapped or learning handicapped. A change in the name is the least drastic of the possible changes that might occur.

A second plausible change in the mild mental retardation diagnostic construct would be combining mild mental retardation with the other mildly handicapped conditions, specific learning disability and emotional disturbance/behavioral disorders. The development of a cross-categorical classification has been debated in the past and was advocated as one of the possible changes in the research integration project (Reynolds & Lakin, 1987). Using the generic category of mild handicapped would have a positive effect on students now classified as mildly mentally retarded because there is less stigma associated with specific learning disability and emotional disturbance/behavioral disorders. Students would still be classified as handicapped, although less emphasis, time, and expense would be devoted to determining whether or not the individual was "really" learning disabled, emotionally disturbed/ behaviorally disordered, or mildly mentally retarded. A recent reform plan proposed in New Jersey would combine the current three categories into a generic mild handicap classification (*A Plan to Revise Special Education in New Jersey*, 1986).

The most drastic change that could occur in the mild mental retardation diagnostic construct would be to completely eliminate the classification of students as handicapped but, at the same time, continue to provide remedial or compensatory educational services in regular education. The elimination of classification is contemplated by the policy paper, *Rights Without Labels* (1986). This paper, as well as the NCAS–NASP (1985) position statement, suggests delivering services to students based on kind and degree of discrepancies from typical levels of performance in the regular curriculum. The only classification (really not a classification at all) would be to specify as precisely as possible the student's current progess in relation to the basic curriculum adopted by the school. This particular approach might involve simply specifying the skills and competencies the student has mastered and those that have not been mastered. It should be feasible within basic literacy areas, such as reading and mathematics, at the early and middle grade levels, but may be less successful at the secondary level. The elimination of classification approach represents the most drastic change in mild mental retardation and other diagnostic constructs.

Summary

There have been dramatic changes in the mild mental retardation diagnostic construct over the past 20 years. These changes have generally involved development of more stringent classification criteria and reductions in the numbers of students classified as mildly mentally retarded and placed in special education programs. These changes have occurred in response to a variety of influences, particularly litigation in the Federal District Courts and concerns about overrepresentation of minority students in mild mental retardation programs. The persistent themes in the mild mental retardation literature throughout the 20th century address the identification and treatment of significant deficits in general intellectual functioning and social competence, and the need for interventions to help overcome these difficulties in approximately 2–3% of students. These themes are likely to remain, regardless of whether there is a mild mental retardation classification or whether classification as such is eliminated. Recent developments provide an optimistic outlook concerning assessment and intervention, particularly in the area of social competence. The social competence assessment procedures and intervention programs hold great promise for improving the adult adjustment of students not classified as mildly mentally retarded. These assessment procedures and interventions will be useful in whatever administrative arrangements and placement patterns emerge from the present special education reform movement. Improved assessment, more effective programming, and better opportunities for successful adult adjustment will remain critical goals for all students now classified as mildly mentally retarded.

References

Baller, W., Charles, D., & Miller, E. (1967). Mid-life attainment of the mentally retarded. *Genetic Psychology Monographs*, **75**, 235–329.

Campione, J. C., Brown, A. L., & Ferrara, R. A. (1982). Mental retardation and intelligence. In R. J. Sternberg (Ed.). *Handbook of human intelligence* (pp. 392–490). Cambridge: Cambridge University Press.

Cartledge, G., & Milburn, J. F. (1985). Social skill assessment and teaching in the schools. In T. R. Kratochwill (Ed.). *Advances in school psychology* (Vol. III, pp. 175–235). Hillsdale, NJ: Erlbaum.

Deno, S. L. (1985). Curriculum-based measurement: The emerging alternative. *Exceptional Children*, **52**, 219–232.

Deshler, D. D., Schumaker, J. B., Lenz, B. K., & Ellis, E. (1984). Academic and cognitive interventions for LD adolescents: Part II. *Annual Review of Learning Disabilities*, **12**, 67–76.

Doll, E. A. (1941). The essentials of an inclusive concept of mental deficiency. *American Journal of Mental Deficiency*, **46**, 214–219.

Dunn, L. (1968). Special education for the mildly retarded: Is much of it justifiable? *Exceptional Children*, **35**, 5–22.

Edgerton, R. B. (1967). *The cloak of competence: Stigma in the lives of the mentally retarded.* Berkeley, CA: University of California Press.

Edgerton, R. B. (Ed.) (1984). *Lives in process: Mentally retarded adults in a large city.* Washington DC: American Association on Mental Deficiency.

Garber, H. L., & Heber, R. (1981). The efficacy of early intervention with family rehabilitation. In M. J. Begab, H. C. Haywood, & H. L. Garber (Eds.), *Psychosocial influences in retarded performance: Volume II. Strategies for improving competence* (pp. 71–87). Baltimore: University Park Press.

Goldstein, A. P., Sprafkin, R. R., Gershaw, N. J., & Klein, P. (1980). *Skillstreaming the adolescent: A structured learning approach to teaching prosocial skill.* Champaign, IL: Research Press.

Graden, J. L., Casey, A., Bonstrom, O. (1985). Implementing a prereferral intervention system: Part II. The data. *Exceptional Children*, **51**, 487–496.

Gresham, F. M. (1982). Misguided mainstreaming: The case for social skills training with handicapped children. *Exceptional Children*, **48**, 422–433.

Gresham, F. M. (1983). Social skills assessment as a component of mainstreaming placement decisions. *Exceptional Children*, **48**, 422–433.

Gresham, F. M. (1987). Social skills assessment as a component of mainstreaming placement decisions. *Exceptional Children*, **49**, 331–336.

Gresham, F. M. (1988). Social competence and motivational characteristics of learning disabled children. In M. C. Wang, M. C. Reynolds, & H. J. Walberg (Eds.), *Handbook of special education: Research and practice: Vol. 2: Mildly handicapped conditions* (pp. 283–302). Oxford, England: Pergamon Press.

Gresham, F. M., Elliott, S. N., & Black, F. L. (1987). Teacher-rated social skills of mainstreamed mildly handicapped and nonhandicapped children. *School Psychology Review*, **16**, 78–88.

Gresham, F. M., & Reschly, D. J. (1986). Issues in the conceptualization, classification, and assessment of social skills in the mildly handicapped. In T. R. Kratochwill (Ed.), *Advances in school psychology* (Vol. VI). Hillsdale, NJ: Erlbaum.

Grimes, J. P., & Reschly, D. J. (1986). *Relevant Educational Assessment and Intervention Model (RE–AIM).* (Project proposal funded by the United States Department of Education) Des Moines, IA: Iowa Department of Education, Bureau of Special Education.

Grossman, H. J. (Ed.) (1983). *Classification in mental retardation.* Washington, DC: American Association on Mental Deficiency.

Heber, R. (1959). A manual on terminology and classification in mental retardation. *American Journal of Mental Deficiency Monograph Supplement*, **64**(2).

Heller, K., Holtzman, W., & Messick, S. (Eds.) (1982). *Placing children in special education: A strategy for equity.* Washington, DC: National Academy Press.

Koegel, P., & Edgerton, R. B., (1984). Black "six hour retarded children" as young adults. In R. B. Edgerton (Ed.), *Lives in process: Mildly retarded adults in a large city.* (pp. 145–171). Washington, DC: American Association on Mental Deficiency.

Kramer, J. L., Piersel, W. C., & Glover, J. A. (1988). Cognitive and social development of mildly retarded children. In M. C. Wang, M. C. Reynolds, & H. J. Walberg (Eds.), *Handbook of special education: Research and practice: Vol. 2. Mildly handicapped conditions.* (pp. 43–58). Oxford, England: Pergamon Press.

Larry, P. v. Riles 495 F. Supp. 926 (N. D. Cal 1979) (decision on merits). United States Court of Appeals, Ninth Circuit, N. 70–427. Jan 23, 1984, Trial Court Decision Affirmed.

MacMillan, D. (1982). *Mental retardation in school and society* (2nd ed.). Boston: Little, Brown, & Co.

MacMillan, D. L., & Borthwick, S. (1980). The new mentally retarded population: Can they be mainstreamed. *Mental Retardation*, **18**, 155–158.

Marshall et al. v. Georgia. U. S. District Court for the Southern District of Georgia, CV482–233, June 29, 1984; Affirmed (11th Cir. No. 84–8771, Oct. 29, 1985).

McGinnis, E., & Goldstein, A. (1984). *Skillstreaming the elementary school student.* Champaign, IL: Research Press.

Mercer, J. (1973). *Labeling the mentally retarded.* Berkeley, CA: University of California Press.

Mercer, J. (1979). *System of Multicultural Pluralistic Assessment Technical Manual.* New York: Psychological Corporation.

NASP–NCAS Position Statement: *Advocacy for appropriate educational services for children.* (1985). Washington, DC: National Association of School Psychologists and National Coalition of Advocates for Students.

Page, E. B. (1972). Miracle in Milwaukee: Raising the IQ. *Educational Researcher,* **1**, 8–16.

Polloway, E. A. (1985). Identification and placement in mild mental retardation programs: Recommendations for professional practice. *Education and Training of the Mentally Retarded,* **20**, 218–221.

Polloway, E. A., & Smith, J. D. (1983). Changes in mild mental retardation: Population, programs, and perspective. *Exceptional Children,* **50**, 149–159.

Polloway, E. A., & Smith, J. D. (1988). Current status of the mild mental retardation construct: Indentification, placement, and programs. In M. C. Wang, M. C. Reynolds, & H. J. Walberg (Eds.), *Handbook of special education: Research and practice: Vol. 2. Mildly handicapped conditions* (pp. 7–22). Oxford, England: Pergamon Press.

A plan to revise special education in New Jersey (1986). Trenton, NJ: State Department of Education, 225 W. State St., CN500, Trenton NJ 08625.

Prevention strategies that work (1979). Report to the President, President's Committee on Mental Retardation. Washington DC: Offices of Human Development Services, United States Department of Health and Human Services.

Ramey, C. T., & Campbell, F. A. (1984). Preventive education for high risk children: Cognitive consequences of the Carolina Abecedarian Project. *American Journal of Mental Deficiency,* **88**, 515–523.

Reschly, D. J. (1981). Evaluation of the effects of SOMPA measures on classification of students as mildly mentally retarded. *American Journal of Mental Deficiency,* **86**, 16–20.

Reschly, D. J. (1982). Assessing mild mental retardation: The influence of adaptive behavior, sociocultural status and prospects for nonbiased assessment. In C. Reynolds & T. Gutkin (Eds.), *The handbook of school psychology* (pp. 209–242). New York: Wiley Interscience.

Reschly, D. J. (1986). Economic and cultural factors in childhood exceptionality. In R. T. Brown & C. R. Reynolds (Eds.), *Psychological perspectives on childhood exceptionality: A handbook* (pp. 423–466). New York: Wiley Interscience.

Reschly, D. J. (1988). Minority MMR overrepresentation: Legal issues, research findings, and reforms, and reform trends. In M. C. Wang, M. C. Reynolds, & H. J. Walberg (Eds.), *Handbook of special education: Research and practice: Vol. 2. Mildly handicapped conditions* (pp. 23–41). Oxford, England: Pergamon Press.

Reschly, D. J., & Gresham, F. M. (1986). Adaptive behavior and the mildly handicapped. In T. R. Kratochwill (Ed.), Advances in school psychology (Vol. VI). Hillsdale, NJ: Erlbaum.

Reschly, D. J., & Kicklighter, R. H. (1985). *Comparison of black and white EMR students from Marshall v. Georgia.* Paper presented at the Annual Convention of the American Psychological Association, Los Angeles. (ERIC ED 271 911).

Reschly, D. J., Kicklighter, R. H., & McKee, P. (in press a) *Recent placement litigation Part I: Regular education grouping: Comparison of Marshall (1984, 1985) and Hobson (1967, 1969).* Manuscript submitted for publication. Ames, IA: Department of Psychology, Iowa State University.

Reschly, D. J., Kicklighter, R. H., & McKee, P. (in press b). *Recent placement litigation Part II: Minority EMR overrepresentation: Comparision of Larry P. (1979, 1984, 1986) with Marshall (1984, 1985) and S–1 (1986).* Manuscript submitted for publication. Ames, IA: Department of Psychology, Iowa State University.

Reschly, D. J., Kicklighter, R. H., & McKee, P. (in press c). *Recent placement litigation Part III: Analysis of differences in Larry P., Marshall, and S–1 and implications for future practices.* Manuscript submitted for publication. Ames, IA: Department of Psychology, Iowa State University.

Reynolds, M. C., & Lakin, K. C. (1987). Noncategorical special education for mildly handicapped students. A system for the future. In M. C. Wang, M. C. Reynolds, & H. J. Walberg (Eds.), *Handbook of special education: Research and practice: Vol. I, Learner characteristics and adaptive instruction* (pp. 331–356). Oxford, England: Pergamon Press.

Rights Without Labels (1986). New Orleans: Advocacy Center for the Elderly and Disabled.

Robinson, N., & Robinson, H. (1976). *The mentally retarded child* (2nd ed.). New York: McGraw-Hill.

Shapiro, E. S., & Lentz, F. E. (1985). Assessing academic behavior: A behavioral approach. *School Psychology Review*, **14**, 325–338.

Shinn, M. R., Tindal, G. A., Spira, D., & Marston, D. (1987). Practice of learning disabilities as social policy. *Learning Disability Quarterly*, **10**, 17–28.

Sommer, R., & Sommer, B. A. (1983). Mystery in Milwaukee: Early intervention, IQ, and psychology textbooks. *American Psychologists*, **38**, 982–985.

Stephens, T. M. (1987). *Social skills in the classroom*. Columbus, OH: Cedars Press.

Taylor, R. L. (1988). Psychological intervention with mildly retarded children: Prevention and remediation of cognitive skills. In M. C. Wang, M. C. Reynolds, & H. J. Walberg (Eds.), *Handbook of special education: Research and practice: Vol. 2. Mildly handicapped conditions* (pp. 59–75). Oxford, England: Pergamon Press.

Tucker, J. (1980). Ethnic proportions in classes for the learning disabled: Issues in nonbiased assessment. *Journal of Special Education*, **14**, 93–105.

Walker, H. M., McConnell, S., Holmes, D., Todis, B., Walker, J., & Golden, J. (1983). *The Walker Social Skills Curriculum: The ACCEPTS programs*. Austin, TX: Pro-Ed.

Wang, M. C., & Birch, J. W. (1984). Comparison of a full-time mainstreaming program and a resource room approach. *Exceptional Children*, **51**, 33–40.

Wang, M. C., Reynolds, M. C., & Walberg, H. J. (Eds.). (1987–1989). *Handbook of special education: Research and practice* (Vols. 1–3). Oxford, England: Pergamon Press.

Will, M. C. (1986a). Educating children with learning problems: A shared responsibility. *Exceptional Children*, **52**, 411–415.

Will, M. C. (1986b). *Educating students with learning problems—A shared responsibility*. Washington, DC: United States Department of Education, Office of Special Education and Rehabilitation Services.

Zetlin, A. G. (1988). Adult development of the mildly retarded. In M. C. Wang, M. C. Reynolds, and H. J. Walberg (Eds.), *Handbook of special education: Research and practice: Vol. 2. Mildly handicapped conditions* (pp. 77–90). Oxford, England: Pergamon Press.

Issues in the Education of Behaviorally Disordered Students*

FRANK H. WOOD

University of Minnesota

This chapter summarizes the literature available on important issues of policy and practice in the education of behaviorally disordered students. The term behaviorally disordered is used to define students labeled "seriously emotionally disturbed" in federal legislation and called by a variety of labels in state and local school districts. The topics addressed include the assessment of students who are potentially eligible for special education, procedures followed in making decisions about eligibility and placement, interventions and their efficacy and suitability for generalizing, personnel preparation, and interagency cooperation. Various conclusions and recommendations are reviewed in the broad context of the special challenges behaviorally disordered students present to educators, as well as the characteristics of behaviorally disordered students in general.

Unmet educational needs are the sole justification for the special educational interventions mandated by Public Law 94–142, the Education for All Handicapped Children Act. To be eligible for special services as behaviorally disordered, a student must be consistently failing to progress in school and behaving in a manner causing concern to others. The law calls for adaptations in regular educational programs to meet the unique needs of eligible students, with services provided in a setting as much like the regular classroom as possible. However, students may be removed from the regular setting when it is in their best interests as learners and when their behavior is so disturbing to teachers or other

* Besides drawing on the behavioral disorders literature prepared by other participants in this project, the author was assisted in the preparation of this summary by suggestions from the project directors and their staff, and from members of the Project Advisory Committee, particularly Dr. Steven Lilly. The author assumes responsibility for the final summary and recommendations.

students that it creates an unacceptable learning situation for all. While this caveat is not addressed specifically to students identified as behaviorally disordered, it is probably applied to them with greater frequency than to students with other handicapping conditions.

Terminology and Definition: A Fundamental Problem

The group of students labeled "seriously emotionally disturbed" or "behaviorally disordered" is quite heterogeneous. Several clusters of problem behavior emerge consistently in the literature and in the discussions of professionals. Most behaviorally disordered students display behavior from more than one cluster. To be eligible for special education under the provisions of Public Law 94–142 as interpreted by the U.S. Supreme Court in Board of Education of the Hendrick Hudson Central School District v. Amy Rowley, *et al.* (1982), they must demonstrate some signs of the first problem—failure to make satisfactory academic progress—and at least one other.

1. *Unsatisfactory academic achievement without evidence of sensory or cognitive disability*: As discussed in Smith, Wood, and Grimes (1988), presence of an achievement problem is a fundamental requirement for eligibility for special education services. Diagnosis in this cluster is done by educators with assistance from psychologists or other professionals in order to rule out alternative explanations. Typical interventions are individualized instruction and the use of alternative curricula.

2. *Emotional Disturbance*: Diagnosis of emotional disturbance usually requires confirmation of an educator's preliminary evaluation by psychologists or psychiatrists. Interventions include changes in the educational program to accommodate the emotional needs of the student and the use of cognitive-emotional interventions such as those discussed by Carpenter and Apter (1988).

3. *Behavior excesses and deficits*: Diagnosis may be done by either educators or psychologists. Interventions focus on training of adaptive behavior through the manipulation of contingent environmental events and use of some cognitive-emotional interventions such as modeling. This literature has been reviewed by Nelson and Rutherford (1988).

4. *Disruptive behavior*: Diagnosis is done by educators with confirmation from other professionals. Interventions stress control and suppression with occasional use of seclusion or other punishing consequences. Law-violating disruptive behavior leads to the application of the label "delinquent."

In some states and local school districts, students do not need to show much difficulty with academic learning to qualify as behaviorally disordered if some of the other problems listed are shown to a sufficient degree.

By custom or law, the prerogative of certifying the applicability of a specific cluster label to a student with a problem rests with different professional groups, acting alone or as members of interdisciplinary teams. These labels tend to refer to one specific aspect of the student's problem, being narrow rather than broad in suggesting possible causative factors. Since each professional group also "owns" a particular cluster of interventions considered most effective for students with a particular label, there may be rivalry among the groups about which problem cluster is primary in the case of an individual student.

There is no conclusive evidence about how this narrow specification affects the education of behaviorally disordered students. But for those who wish to review and summarize the literature relating to this handicap (psychiatric, psychological, sociological, and educational), it is devastating. Authors use a bewildering variety of terms, usually catering to the editorial practice of the journal in which they are publishing. They seldom provide a specific description of subject behavior(s). Recommendations for dealing with this fundamental problem will be summarized later, but since its effects are so pervasive, it seems appropriate to give it special attention at this point.

Different professional perspectives and the difficulty of assessing student status in each of the cluster areas mentioned will continue to make it difficult to solve this problem. For example, Tallmadge, Gamel, Munson & Hanley (1985) noted the wide differences among the states in terminology and practice and the related confusion about who should be receiving services. They concluded that only major changes would make any real differences.

> In the absence of more comprehensive changes than have been considered to date, it would probably be unwise to introduce any changes of terminology or definition at this date. Present laws and regulations have been in place long enough for State and local education agencies to adapt to them. Any change would require a substantial amount of readaptation. Even a change that could be expected to have minimal long-range effects would cause a good deal of nonproductive short-term scurrying about by parties forced to make adjustments. (p. 116)

Tallmadge et al. conclude by recommending no change. Their recommendation was supported by Department of Education Secretary William J. Bennett in a letter to Senator Lowell P. Wiecker (June 28, 1985) accompanying their report to the Congress. The view that the problem cannot be solved or that the cost of solution outweighs any possible benefits is either wise or lamentable depending on one's personal perspective and interests. The following section will discuss suggestions for constructive responses.

Identification and Placement

The problems created by nonstandardized terminology and definitions are addressed directly in Smith, Wood, and Grimes (1988). In addition to presenting a detailed discussion of the history and present dimensions of these problems, they looked for a basis for solutions in the literature.

Descriptions of the characteristics of behaviorally disordered students typically generate cluster patterns similar to those previously described. A two-cluster picture of problem behavior will contrast "acting-out" or aggressive behavior with withdrawn or "anxious" behavior. The most common source of descriptive data is ratings by parents, teachers, or others who work closely with the students described. These ratings have been shown to be subject to bias that consistently focuses raters on aggressive, disruptive behavior; and this bias can be manipulated by investigators. For example, the label "emotionally disturbed" carries its own negative bias for a rater observing a student who has been thus labeled. Persons using such ratings when making decisions about eligibility and placement need to remain sensitive to the possibility of bias, and future research may wish to study ways to minimize selective bias now that its frequent presence has been demonstrated.

There is serious cause for concern regarding evidence of the negatively biasing effects of minority radical identification and lower socioeconomic status. The experimental evidence is limited, but the patterns revealed are consistent enough with the evidence for other kinds of bias in ratings to suggest moving quickly to give priority to controlling or eliminating these biasing effects.

The practical influence of biased ratings on the labeling and placement of students is not clear. Because of the negative connotations of the behaviorally disordered-type labels, there may be some tendency among persons making such decisions (including parent participants in Individualized Education Program teams) to use other, more positive disability labels, if they permit appropriate placement. It has been observed that the number of students labeled "learning disabled" has increased over the last decade in the same proportion that the group carrying the less positive label "mentally retarded" has decreased. During the same period, the number of students labeled "behaviorally disordered" has increased very slowly or remained constant. Changes in public policy have led to reclassification of some students formerly considered "mildly mentally retarded." Will there be changes in the future that may lead to a similar reclassification of students as behaviorally disordered? We do not know, but the wide range of actual incidence of students served under this label or one of its variants suggests it is possible.

Concern also exists over one of the so-called "exclusionary clauses" in the present federal definition, that which excludes students classified as 'socially maladjusted" unless they are also "emotionally disturbed." Bower, (1982) the author of much of the language of the federal definition, has ridiculed this clause as meaningless while others have criticized it for its punitive intent.

Specific Conclusions and Recommendations

S. Lilly (personal communication, July 9, 1985) suggested that there may be no solution to the problems of terminology and definition. He urged that we consider the option of simply recognizing this as inevitable, and then move on to deal pragmatically with any service problems that may be created. It may not be necessary to solve this problem before moving on to other practical issues. Applying this idea, we would give up our efforts to define more precisely the characteristics of large groups of behaviorally disordered students, since we know that individuals typically show wide variations in the presence of underlying cluster behaviors. We would seek instead to improve the quality and usefulness of our descriptions of individuals. Models based on the collection and use of different kinds of assessment data have been proposed (e.g., Wood, Smith, & Grimes, 1985).

"Usefulness" of assessment data implies concern not only for the task of making decisions about eligibility and placement, but also about short-and long-term instructional outcomes. Which classification systems are most subject to misuse? What is the rationale for retaining terminology that lacks educational relevance? Do "better" descriptions lead to "better" services? We should also give attention to the effects of different kinds of information and procedures on the decision-making process, again seeking to develop criteria related to "usefulness." For example, "entrance" and "exit" criteria may be of more value than "eligibility" criteria. Multiple measures have been suggested as important for understanding the relative role of student and environmental factors in the development and solution of problems. Research addressing these issues may eventually enable us to establish the educational relevance, or irrelevance, of categorical labels—a factor that must be weighed against their traditional importance in controlling funding and limiting eligibility. By taking this somewhat different approach to the issue of terminology and definition, we may eventually find that it was at least in part a "phony" issue or that our initial sidestepping has brought us to a more fruitful angle of attack.

Interventions

Two pairs of authors have reviewed the literature describing interventions used with behaviorally disordered students. Nelson and Rutherford (1988) reviewed behavioral interventions covering the variety of behavior enhancement and reduction procedures. Carpenter and Apter (1988) reviewed cognitive-emotional interventions. The term intervention covers a broad array of approaches which have emerged from developmental and social perspectives, including social skills training, ecological interventions, and affective education.

Research on behavioral interventions is characterized by commitment to a common methodology and reporting style. Subjects, specific "target behaviors," interventions, and outcomes are carefully described in terms of observable behavior. Time series designs, which call for numerous observations of the target behavior(s), are typically employed. Changes in behavior are related to observed environmental events. Usually these events are systematically manipulated to demonstrate their relationship to the observed behavior changes.

Research on cognitive-emotional interventions is much more variable in methodology and reporting style. Characteristics of subjects and interventions are hypothesized to be complex. Subject characteristics include those which are internal, the presence of which must be inferred since they cannot be observed directly. Interventions are assumed to have internal as well as external effects. Criteria for outcomes typically interrelate internal and external directly observable factors. Design flaws and weaknesses in measures of key variables are common in the published research on cognitive-emotional interventions (Carpenter & Apter, 1988).

Nelson and Rutherford demonstrated the power of interventions based on behavioral principles. They noted that there is evidence for some prejudice against the use of these interventions, based mostly on misinformation but sometimes a result of faulty practice. They argued persuasively that these interventions should be taught to teachers and administrators working with behavioral disorders in students, noting that most of the problems reported in using them can be traced to limited or poor training or to failure by school systems to support the hard work required for their effective implementation. The authors took a critical look at the research literature in this area, noting that it tends to be overbalanced in favor of reporting successes. Taking a position that reflects the confidence and maturity that has developed among proponents of behavioral interventions, they suggested that there may be benefit in moving beyond the repeated demonstration of "what works" to look at reasons why it does not work in some cases.

Carpenter and Apter had a much more mixed bag of literature to summarize and discuss. Some interventions (e.g., the teaching of self-management skills) are basically extensions of behavioral interventions with a cognitive dimension added in verbal coaching and self-reporting. Indeed, as Carpenter and Apter pointed out, many of these interventions are "hybrids." They are the result of largely informal and undocumented experiments with combined intervention strategies devised by professionals working in a particular setting or with a more or less homogeneous group of students. Most descriptions of interventions are primarily pragmatic, although some are more theory-based than others. The empirical base for the efficacy of most of these interventions is seldom more than one or two published studies, and field evaluation is often informal and cursory. Carpenter and Apter noted that many professionals who attempt to implement these interventions have limited, inadequate training in their application and theoretical rationales, so that sharing of common terminology may be misleading. Major differences may exist between programs given the same label.

Both groups of reviewers suggested that it is time to look at the interactions between specific characteristics of subjects (behavioral disorders) and interventions for which effectiveness has been demonstrated. Attention must be given to the influence of age, cognitive development, sex, and cultural or familial influences, as well as problem type. They also expressed concern about the relationship between possible cultural and socioeconomic bias in the identification and placement of students in programs for the behaviorally disordered, and the types of interventions prescribed. Are some classes of students at risk for the application of more aversive interventions? This is a policy issue of obvious importance.

The relative orderliness and clarity of the behavioral literature is impressive. Nelson and Rutherford suggested that behavioral methodology can serve as a model for studying other client-centered interventions. This suggestion deserves serious consideration, and indeed, some of the most persuasive research on cognitive-emotional interventions has involved some application of observation and time series designs. Examples of this are studies in self-instruction and self-management, social skills training, and even life space interviewing. However, as the focus of attention expands to include the other factors mentioned, the task of retaining orderliness and clarity will become exceedingly difficult and expensive. As the numbers of subjects and dimensions of subject behavior increase, clear descriptions of subject behavior become more difficult. As the complexity of interventions increases, the challenge of sorting out potentially important factors is multiplied.

Complex criteria for success (e.g., measuring client satisfaction with change as well as observed change itself) must be first measured, then evaluated in cost-benefit analyses. The problem will be most acute when efforts are made to study the effectiveness of ecological intervention programs which are conceptually convincing but difficult to research. Where do we begin? Perhaps the answer is to use behavioral methodology as a foundation in all research on interventions, letting it carry us as far along the way as possible. At the same time we must accept the need to supplement this approach with measures of group status at specified points in times, the use of "untreated" comparison groups whenever possible, and an analysis of qualitative information as has been done in the study of projects like Re-Ed (Montgomery & Von Fleet, 1978).

Specific Conclusions and Recommendations

Both groups of authors concluded with calls for continuing research focused in the ways suggested above. They noted that the present reward structure (research support, job security and salary, publication policies) does not encourage educators to move in these directions. Fundamental policy changes favoring longer range commitment to educational research are needed if we are to make substantial progress in this direction. We will also need to give thoughtful attention to methods of disseminating the results of research. Complex research products do not lend themselves to traditional methods of dissemination, such as 50-minute presentations and eight-page journal articles.

The implications of these findings for assessment of behavioral disorders are obvious. Both pairs of authors mentioned the related assessment methodology problems, and underlined the need for improved coordination between assessment focused on identification and placement and assessment focused on differential treatment and evaluation of change.

The authors asserted that many effective interventions fail in application because the personnel using them lack sufficient training in their use. They suggested the need for longer preservice training of teachers and administrators, continuing inservice training, and blocks of time for pursuing advanced training. Nelson and Rutherford predicted that demands for higher levels of professional performance will not yield results unless accompanied by changes in the reward structure for practitioners. The same principles that apply to maintenance and generalization of desirable behavior by behaviorally disordered students apply to maintenance and generalization of desirable behavior by their teachers.

In discussing evidence for the effectiveness of structured cooperative learning (Johnson & Johnson, 1975, 1983), Carpenter and Apter mentioned that methods which have been demonstrated to be effective with special needs students were developed through research with regular class populations. Attention has been called to the research on effective teaching, which has also been developed primarily through studying teaching and learning in regular classrooms. Special educators need to be alert to developments taking place in regular education that may increase the ability of regular programs to accommodate learners with special needs (including behavioral disorders), as well as add to the effectiveness of special education interventions. Knowledge and use of effective interventions need to spread both ways.

Personnel Preparation

The preparation of educators to work with behaviorally disordered students would seem to be a topic that would attract much attention from researchers. Zabel (1988), however, found little empirical research as he reviewed the literature on teacher preparation. Of the research that exists, only a small part deals specifically with the training of teachers for this particular group of special needs students. Much of his information is, therefore, opinion, plan, or policy recommendation with little empirical evidence for support. Zabel was careful to highlight this feature of his sources. This summary will generally present opinions representative of the thinking in the field, calling attention to supporting data whenever it exists.

Sensitive educators agree that it is desirable to provide special services to students with special needs without removing them from the regular classroom whenever this is possible. The principle of providing students with an education in the least restrictive or most "normal" environment is clearly stated in Public Law 94–142. Yet, on the whole, discussions about the skills needed by regular classroom teachers focus on the management of academic instruction rather than management of large groups or the teaching of social skills. Expertise in the latter seems critical if larger numbers of behaviorally disordered students are to be maintained in regular classrooms.

Zabel reviewed the most widely publicized discussions of schools and educators, and they tend to be highly critical. These reports point to declining support for higher education in general, and teacher preparation programs in particular, and a decline in the number and quality of prospective teachers attracted to training programs because of the relatively low status of the profession and limited financial incentives. The expansion of employment opportunities for women, for whom teaching was formerly one of the few open professions, has also contributed to this lack of new recruits. The solutions proposed have tended to focus on the issue of personnel and training program quality, calling for higher standards for admission to colleges of education, the adoption of "five-year" programs in which an expanded amount of general liberal arts or science coursework would be followed by one year of professional training in pedagogy, and national or state written examinations for licensing candidates (cf. Special Section on Teacher Education, 1985).

Discussion of the need for increased resources to fund improved training and related research is often neglected or even absent, as is attention to the inadequate financial incentives for teachers. But without support or incentives, there is little reason to expect teachers to undertake the special preparation needed to serve behaviorally disordered students effectively in regular or special settings.

Before going further with the need for better support and incentives, we should address the question, "Do we know what we need to know if we are to do a better job?" Zabel's review suggested that the answer is "no." The basic developmental work, including research, has not been done in either regular or special education. We have already discussed the confusion in our identification and placement procedures and the weaknesses in our knowledge of the effectiveness of interventions commonly used to manage behaviorally disordered students.

Zabel found a similar weakness in the literature regarding the skills needed by regular teachers. While there has been some promising work on effective teaching (e.g., Evertson, Hawley, & Zlotnick, 1984), few of the published lists of teacher competencies or program descriptions have been subjected to field validation. "Validation," if found, is typically based on ratings done by assumed "experts," usually teachers or teacher trainers. Shores, Roberts, and Nelson (1976) described one of the few reported investigations of teacher competence in which pedagogical skills were validated by comparisons with student achievement. They noted that "undoubtedly, the time and expense involved in researching teacher competencies through this model is prohibitive for most training institutions" (p. 131). Their research was supported by federal funds. At present, it is not clear whether those teacher skills seen as desirable are actually being taught to prospective teachers, and/or whether they are then being applied in classroom settings, and/or whether the result is improved student achievement and behavior. In this regard, Zabel believes that the trend of the 1970s toward "competency-based teacher education programs" has peaked and is receding, leaving little empirical data to show whether or not it was an improvement over traditional practice.

According to Zabel, the literature has suggested that the skill needs of teachers working with behaviorally disordered students differ in important respects from those needed by teachers working with learning disabled or mentally retarded students; these are the two labeled groups who appear to overlap most frequently with the behaviorally disordered group. Competency lists proposed for "behavioral disorders" are expanded in the areas of behavior management and social skill teaching, and in some instances, give less attention to skills related to academic instruction. If this difference is significant, and the discussion is not enlightened by much empirical evidence, then teachers in these special areas and teachers prepared in "noncategorical" and regular teacher preparation programs lack the skills needed to teach behaviorally disordered students effectively. The obverse may also be true: behavioral disorders teachers may not be prepared to meet the academic needs of their students adequately. Extrapolating from this discussion, Zabel hypothesizes that many teacher educators may be inadequately prepared to train prospective teachers in methods for effectively managing the behavior of disturbed and/or disturbing students.

What do we know about the personal characteristics of teachers of behaviorally disordered students? Here there are two related questions: What are the characteristics of persons attracted to this teaching specialty? What characteristics are desirable in such teachers? There is little evidence on either of these questions. Behavioral disorders teachers have relatively higher attrition rates and a higher frequency of reported job stress and other factors related to job burnout. This can mean either that persons with the wrong characteristics are being attracted, and the mismatch does not become obvious until they are actually teaching, or that the job itself is inherently more stressful than most. The latter interpretation is the one usually favored by teachers and teacher trainers, but most efforts to date have focused on describing the problem rather than investigating its causes.

Working on the assumption that the problem rests primarily with the job rather than the people, Zabel and others have advocated that training programs give more attention to developing stress resistance and stress dissipation skills in their teacher trainees, and that school districts provide inservice training and support. While the largest single cost may occur to the person who leaves the profession to which they have devoted several years of preparation, a significant loss also occurs to administrators who have invested in training newly recruited teachers.

Specific Conclusions and Recommendations

Education in general, and teacher training in particular, appear to suffer from chronically overinflated expectations and chronically inadequate resources. Rather than choosing good candidates for teaching, scientifically training them, and carefully supervising their initial teaching experiences until we are certain they can manage on their own, we appear to admit almost everyone who shows interest, to expose them to plausible but untested training experiences, and to assume that the profession is well served through the crude sorting process that takes place after they are in the field. There are some hopeful areas in the picture Zabel provided, but on the whole the preparation of professional personnel appears to be governed almost entirely by the opinions of teacher trainers, and these opinions change rapidly in response to the whiplash of critics possessing equally limited factual information. We need systematic developmental research, and we owe much to the small number of pioneers Zabel has discovered. They are laying the foundations for the larger work which must be done.

Cooperative Interface

The public schools are assigned the responsibility of providing appropriate educational programs for special needs students, including those with severe behavioral disorders. The schools have the additional responsibility of providing supplemental services to help students make educational progress. For behaviorally disordered students, such supplemental services may include psychotherapy (Grosenick et al., 1982). Many behaviorally disordered students will need services typically provided by other agencies—for example, welfare, mental health, and correctional. The schools have the responsibility of coordinating such services in the educational interests of students.

The complex process of coordination has been given various names: interagency cooperation, interagency collaboration, and cooperative interface. Huntze, (1988) used all of these terms interchangeably. To define the process, she used a definition from page one of the Midwest Regional Resource Center Task Force report (1979).

> Interagency cooperation is "a process which: encourages and facilitates an open and honest exchange of ideas, plans, approaches, and resources across disciplines, programs, and agencies; enables all participants jointly to define their separate interests and mutually indentified needed changes in order to best achieve common purposes; and utilizes formal procedures to help clarify issues, define problems and make decisions." (p. 199)

Interagency cooperation has its origin in the perception by agency personnel that clients need a wide range of services, but services should not be duplicated. The need to coordinate services becomes greater as resources shrink. Other factors contributing to the present sense of need are a recent change in federal policy which has led to a withdrawal of federally funded services to children and youth, and a decrease in the federal funds provided to state agencies serving them. Public discussion focuses attention on the efficient use of tax monies in a time of national budget deficits. Interagency cooperation is generally believed to make possible the provision of better services at lower costs.

Legal "mandates" in the form of legislation and court decisions have also played a role in creating a strong sense of need for more cooperation, although as Huntze pointed out, most of these "allow," rather than obligate, agencies to cooperate. Public Law 94–142 is particularly significant because of the requirement that the state education agency acts as the single state agency responsible for seeing that special needs students receive the services they need to benefit from education. The use of teams in decision making, another feature of this law, has also encouraged educators to work cooperatively with representatives of noneducational specialties. However, Huntze pointed out that much of this cooperative activity has been interdisciplinary rather than inter-agency collaboration, since all participants are employed by the same agency (i.e., the school). The guidelines published as the Education Division General Administrative Regulations (EDGAR) also encourage cooperation with other agencies. Huntze believes that cooperative agreements among state agencies are now very common, but she fears that many of these may be "paper" agreements with little actual impact on practice.

Huntze's survey of the extant literature on interagency cooperation led her to conclude that there is relatively little research on the topic. A variety of models were suggested, however, which build on points in existing research. The models reviewed include discussions of fundamental considerations, specific steps to be followed, and how barriers may be overcome. Several practices emerged as common suggestions from the models reviewed: financial sharing, acceptance of a joint working philosophy, development of a common working vocabulary, joint administration of program, and state support via facilitating agreements. Some writers have also suggested procedures for evaluation.

The state of practice trails behind the ideals suggested by the models. This lag results from the complexity of the problems faced plus institutional inertia. Among the illustrations noted are a failure of formal agreements at the state level to lead to working relationships at state or local levels. However, Huntze feels that more is going on than is apparent. A great deal of promising activity never gets into the literature.

Specific Conclusions and Recommendations

What can be done to encourage interagency collaboration? At the federal and state level. Huntze urged that development of formal inter-agency agreements should be pursued because they provide the framework needed. She believes that the value of the effort to create interagency interface may lie not only in the product, but in the experience of working together itself (Hershberger, 1981). A broad knowledge base, going beyond parochial agency concerns and including as much solid financial and demographic data as possible, needs to be developed. Useful methods to support these activities include supportive or mandating legislation, the creation of interagency commissions or task forces, and the development of procedures for resource allocation and monitoring. Incentives should be stressed; discentives that arouse resistance include the threat of penalty or finding that cooperation leads to the loss of agency resources.

Huntze suggested that most creative, functional interagency agreements are developed by personnel working at the local level, whether or not their efforts are strongly supported by state level agencies. She believes that most collaborative efforts result from the work of committed individuals and suggested the usefulness of the designated "case manager" role, analogous to the sole responsible agency concept, in supporting their efforts. Training of personnel may also facilitate interagency cooperation. Such training should take place on both the preservice and inservice levels.

Systematic research on this important topic is needed. Huntze feels that evaluation of specific cases of interagency cooperation should be data based to the greatest extent possible, but that data-based research on all the aspects of broader agreements may not be possible. Interagency collaboration may be more effectively studied using naturalistic research methods. Application of simulation approaches, such as those used in other policy research, may also be useful.

General Conclusions and Recommendations

What general recommendations can be made based on the knowledge about the state of the art and the state of practice gathered by the authors mentioned in this chapter?

IDENTIFICATION AND PLACEMENT

Efforts by educators to clarify the terminology used to describe the problems of behaviorally disordered students have been unsuccessful. There is no unanimity among educators about appropriate common terminology; the variations in different states and professional journals make this clear. Other professional groups retain considerable control over the labeling/eligibility process and prefer their customary labels. The Department of Education has chosen to permit this variability rather than to impose a common usage by rule.

While it would reduce some dissonance if a common terminology and definition were in use, the authors involved in this summary have suggested that it may make sense to step over this problem for the present. There is general agreement that those students we have been calling behaviorally disordered are an extremely heterogeneous group with only a few shared characteristics. Their behavior is disturbing to others because of its disruptive impact on others or its apparently destructive effects on themselves, and because of this behavior, they are having difficulty progressing in school. Having agreed on these general characteristics, educational researchers might find it most useful to turn their attention to describing carefully the specific characteristics of each behaviorally disordered student. The use of multiple measures has been discussed in some detail by Wood et al., (1985) and others.

The next steps will be to study how these more specific characteristics of individual students interact with the placements assigned to them, their response to interventions, and the long- and short-term outcomes from services provided. Careful attention needs to be given to the interaction between the use of specific descriptive terms which have been shown to be related to decision maker bias and decision making. Indeed, decision making in this area deserves careful study. Note that what is being suggested here is more of an individual case study approach than a large group methodology to study aptitude/treatment interactions.

INTERVENTIONS

An approach to identification that focuses on describing educationally significant characteristics of individuals fits well with the call by both Nelson and Rutherford (1988) and Carpenter and Apter (1988) for greater attention to the interaction between problem type and response to intervention. In the case of behavioral and some cognitive-emotional interventions, the interventions are well enough specified that it may be possible to move at once to address the problem. However, we have not yet developed the methodology to describe some more complex interventions adequately. When this happens, priority should be given to intervention descriptions.

Many of the interventions described can be applied in both "regular" and "special" settings. The limiting conditions appear to be adequate training of teachers in the use of specific interventions and, once training is provided, availability of incentives and support for their application. Zabel (1988) expressed a similar view.

The point that we possess information that can be applied to good effect in mainstream situations assumes greater importance when we consider the evidence for the maintenance and generalization of effects. Desirable behavior changes obtained in carefully controlled "special" situations often fail to generalize easily to other environments. Nelson and Rutherford (1988) summarize research which demonstrates that it is possible to program for generalization. However, it is difficult and expensive. While it may not be less expensive to train regular teachers in the use of "special" interventions useful with behaviorally disordered students and to support them in their application, it may prove more efficient if the generalization problem is thus bypassed.

When Zabel (1988) reviewed the recommendations made for training regular as well as special teachers, he found that therapeutic management of disturbed/disturbing behavior is given little attention in the training of regular teachers, while many special teachers who are prepared to work effectively with the social and emotional behavior of behaviorally disordered students are not able to manage the full academic program needed by their students. Trainers clearly have more knowledge than they are transmitting to teachers in service or in training. Calling for longer periods of preservice training, as the Holmes Group (1986) has recently done, may be part of an answer, but it is noteworthy that the Holmes Group called for a required fifth year for teachers in training. The result of their proposal might well be even less time for instruction in and experience with behavior management skills. To date, the solutions proposed do not deal very realistically with the fundamental imbalance in the equation: What incentive is there for teachers to enter or remain in a profession where more is being demanded in preparation and practice, while other professions require equivalent or less investment in preparation? A society would like to have many things for its children, but gifts will be few. In general, we will receive in direct measure to what we invest.

Educators should be supported in undertaking research to determine the conditions under which more behaviorally disordered students can be accommodated in mainstream situations. Attention must also be given to an investigation of the teaching skills critical for providing appropriate therapeutic education to students who must be served in more restrictive settings. Yet positive outcomes from both these lines of investigation will have the same limited impact that successful model programs have had in the past if society does not provide the resources to continue them. Leaders in both regular and special education have an obligation to speak out on this issue.

COOPERATIVE INTERFACE

Better coordination of services and resources from all agencies concerned with the welfare of behaviorally disordered students would help manage the general funding problem. Huntze (1988) found in her review that, while a number of promising models for interagency cooperation exist, most have only a limited empirical foundation. Unlike some of the other areas mentioned, we are not failing to apply knowledge that has already been gathered—we simply do not know for certain what will or will not work in practice. Huntze proposed that there may be some knowledge in this area based on experience at the grass-roots level, but it has not been gathered and disseminated. This seems to be an area where systematic study is overdue.

A FINAL COMMENT

No one ever said that providing for appropriate education for all students in our society would be an easy task. The gulf between the ideal and the reality may seem especially wide to educators concerned with meeting the special needs associated with behavioral and emotional problems. In terms of the size of the challenge, we may not have gone very far, but we are able to point out some lines of investigation and practice which can be expanded and others which seem bogged down by critical methodological problems or have led to a dead end. Given limited resources, we need to make wise choices for investing in them.

References

Board of Education of the Hendrick Hudson Central School District v. Amy Rowley et al., 102 S. Ct. 3034 (1982).

Bower, E. M. (1982). Defining emotional disturbance: Public policy and research. *Psychology in the Schools*, **19**, 55–60.

Carpenter, R. L., & Apter, S. J. (1988). Research integration of cognitive-emotional interventions for behaviorally disordered children and youth. In M. C. Wang, M. C. Reynolds, & H. J. Walberg (Eds.), *Handbook of special education: Research and practice: Vol. 2. Mildly handicapped conditions* (pp. 155–169). Oxford, England: Pergamon Press.

Evertson, C., Hawley, W., & Zlotnick, M. (1984). *The Characteristics of effective teacher preparation programs: A review of research.* Nashville, TN: Vanderbilt University, Peabody Center for Effective Teaching.

Grosenick, J. K., Huntze, S. L., Kochan, B., Peterson, R. L., Robertshaw, C. S., & Wood, F. H. (1982). *National needs analysis in behavior disorders: Psychotherapy as a related service.* Columbia, MO: University of Missouri, Department of Special Education.

Hershberger, A. M. (1981). *A study to determine the effectiveness of local interagency agreements and identify their costs.* Final report. Menlo Park, CA: SRI International.

Holmes Group (1986). Tomorrow's teachers: A report of the Holmes Group. East Lansing, MI: The Holmes Group.

Huntze, S. L. (1988). Cooperative interface of schools and other child care systems for the behaviorally disordered. In M. C. Wang, M. C. Reynolds, & H. J. Walberg (Eds.), *Handbook of special education: Research and practice: Vol. 2. Mildly handicapped conditions* (pp. 195–217). Oxford, England: Pergamon Press.

Johnson, D. W., & Johnson, R. (1975). *Learning together and alone: Cooperation, competition, and individualization.* Englewood Cliffs, NJ: Prentice-Hall.

Johnson, R. T., & Johnson, D. W. (1983). Effects of cooperative, competitive, and individualistic learning experiences on social development. *Exceptional Children*, **49**, 323–329.

Midwest Regional Resource Center Task Force. (1979). *Interagency collaboration on full services for handicapped children and youth. Vol. I: A guide to state planning and development.* Washington, DC: Office of Special Education, Learning Resource Branch.

Montgomery, P. A., & Von Fleet, D. S. (1978). Evaluation of behavioral and academic changes through the re-ed process. *Behavioral Disorders*, **3**, 136–146.

Nelson, C. M., & Rutherford, R. B., Jr. (1988). Behavioral interventions with behaviorally disordered students. In M. C. Wang, M. C. Reynods, & H. J. Walberg (Eds.), *Handbook of special education: Research and practice: Vol. 2. Mildly handicapped conditions* (pp. 125–153). Oxford, England: Pergamon Press.

Shores, R. E., Roberts, M., & Nelson, C. M. (1976). An empirical model for the development of competencies of teachers of children with behavior disorders. *Behavioral Disorders*, **1**, 123–132.

Smith, C. R., Wood, F. H., & Grimes J. (1988). Issues in the identification and placement of behaviorally disordered students. In M. C. Wang, M. C. Reynolds, & H. J. Walberg (Eds.), *Handbook of special education: Research and practice: Vol. 2. Mildly handicapped conditions* (pp. 95-123). Oxford, England: Pergamon Press.

Special Section on Teacher Education. (1985, Summer.) *The Wingspread Journal*. Racine, WI: Johnson Foundation.

Tallmadge, G. K., Gamel, N. N., Munson, R. G., & Hanley, T. V. (1985). *Special study on terminology: Comprehensive review and evaluation report*. (Contract No. 300-84-0144). Washington, DC: U.S. Department of Education.

Wood, F. H., Smith, C. R., & Grimes, J. (Eds.). (1985). *The Iowa assessment model in behavioral disorders: A training manual*. Des Moines, IA: Iowa Department of Public Instruction.

Zabel, R. H. (1988). Preparation of teachers for behaviorally disordered students: A review of literature. In M. C. Wang, M. C. Reynolds, & H. J. Walberg (Eds.), *Handbook of special education: Research and practice: Vol. 2. Mildly handicapped conditions* (pp. 171–193). Oxford, England: Pergamon Press.

Learning Disability*

BARBARA K. KEOGH

University of California

In its brief but somewhat turbulent history, the field of learning disability has captured the interest of clinicians and researchers alike. The literature is filled with studies of learning disability, and a variety of intervention programs have been implemented. The topic has also generated a number of controversies, and continues to be characterized by conceptual and operational inconsistencies and confusions. These disagreements have in some cases led to increased understanding of learning disability and to improved services; in other cases they have resulted in slowed progress and roadblocks to services. Assuredly there has been progress, but a number of aspects of learning disability are still ambiguous and need careful and comprehensive study.

This chapter reviews selected aspects of learning disability as revealed through five basic questions and the many specific subquestions they generate: How do conceptual approaches affect research and practice within the field? Can conceptually and empirically discrete subgroups within learning disabilities be identified? What are the long-term consequences or outcomes of learning disabilities? What are the links between interventions and learning disabilities? What are the social and affective correlates and consequences of learning disabilities? Each question leads to comprehensive discussion of the "state of the art" on that topic, considering future directions and specific recommendations for policy, practice, and research. Taken as a whole, this chapter provides a solid description of the current status of learning disability and points the way to needed changes. It draws heavily on the contributions of various authors, but the generalizations merely skim the surface of these very substantive contributions.

* Preparation of this chapter was supported in part by a NICHD Program Grant to the Sociobehavioral Research Group, Mental Retardation Research Center, the University of California, Los Angeles.

Conceptualization and Classification

Prevalence figures summarized in the *Sixth Annual Report to Congress* (1984) on the implementation of Public Law 94–142 illustrate the major impact of learning disabilities on both special and regular educational systems. In 1982–83 there were 4,298,327 identified handicapped pupils ages 3–21; 1,745,871, or almost 41% of them, were classified learning disabled. It is estimated the learning disabled pupils represent almost 4% of all school children nationally. A detailed analysis of prevalence figures found in the 1984 *Annual Report* is interesting for two reasons. First, there are dramatic differences in numbers of learning disabled pupils across states and territories. For example, 64% of all handicapped children in Hawaii were classified as learning disabled; the comparable figure for Alabama was 26%. Second, on a national level the number of learning disabled pupils has more than doubled in less than 10 years, growing from 797,213 in 1976–77 to 1,745,871 in 1982–83. During the same period the number of identified speech impaired and mentally retarded pupils decreased, and there was only a modest increase in numbers of pupils identified as emotionally disturbed. Clearly the number of learning disabled pupils strains both human and fiscal resources. Further, there continue to be ambiguities and controversies about what learning disability "really" is and what should be done about it. Lack of a clear and consensual theory about learning disability has resulted in continuing definitional problems and in different operational procedures when implementing programs. It is not surprising, then, that there are such dramatic differences in incidence and prevalence of learning disabilities in different locations and in different time periods. Some of the influences which contribute to these inconsistencies deserve brief discussion.

Influences on Identification as Learning Disabled

First, learning disability is considered the proper and legitimate concern of many disciplines or professions, (e.g., neurology, psychiatry, psychology, education, ophthalmology, optometry, and occupational therapy, to name just a few). Different professionals focus on somewhat different aspects of problems in development, so that there are varying opinions about etiology, how and when to identify or diagnose, the importance of particular symptoms, treatment approach and emphasis, and professional roles and responsibilities. Some children will be considered learning disabled by all these professionals, but different professional orientations lead to real differences in numbers identified and in characteristics of those identified, a kind of "eye of the beholder" effect.

Second, although a discrepancy between aptitude and achievement is a widely accepted criterion of learning disability (Keogh & Hall, 1984; Reynolds et al. 1984–85; Shepard, 1980), there is considerable variation in how the discrepancy is operationalized. Federal regulations for implementation of PL 94–142 do not specify a particular formula; rather, states have developed their own formulae, and differences in formulae lead to differences in numbers identified. A number of authors (Cone & Wilson, 1981; Reynolds et al. 1984–85; Shepard, 1980) have analyzed various methods of quantifying the aptitude-achievement discrepancy. Commonly used methods include grade level deviations, expectancy formulae, standard score comparisons, and regression analyses. Although regression-discrepancy formulae appear soundest methodologically, all have limitations. The number of pupils identified as learning disabled varies according to the formula and method used. For example, Forness, Sinclair, and Guthrie (1983) classified 92 hospitalized pupils with eight different (but commonly used) formulae. Numbers of pupils classified as learning disabled ranged from 10.9% to 37% depending on the formula; only seven children were identified as learning disabled by all. Epps, Ysseldyke, and Algozzine (1983) reported similar findings when they classified regular education school-identified learning disabled pupils according to 14 different discrepancy formulae. No formula identified all learning disabled pupils correctly, and all formulae identified some non-learning disabled children as learning disabled. Overall, the percent of correct identification ranged from 5% to 69%, according to the formula used. It seems fair to conclude that, in part at least, prevalence is related to how the intuitively appealing notion of discrepancy is operationalized.

A third source of influence on prevalence is closely tied to the discrepancy issue but relates specifically to measurement. Many decisions about learning disability identification are made using technically inadequate tests. Based on a study of learning disability model programs, Thurlow and Ysseldyke (1979) found that only 9 of 30 commonly used instruments for learning disability identification met criteria of adequate norms, reliability, and validity. Their findings have been supported by others (Berk, 1984; Reynolds et al., 1984–85; Shepard, 1983; Shepard & Smith, 1983). The problem of measurement is further compounded by the limited knowledge and skill of professionals who use diagnostic tests. Many professionals do not have a clear understanding of normal variability, the psychometric limitations of tests, or how to interpret summary quantified scores. Thus, both the technical adequacy of tests used in identification and the competence of the professionals who use them affect the numbers and characteristics of those identified as learning disabled (Shepard, 1983).

Finally, there is increasing documentation of the effects of "institutional constraints" on referral, identification, and placement of special education pupils (Christenson, Ysseldyke, & Algozzine, 1982; Hocutt, Cox, & Pelosi, 1984; Mehan, Meihls, Hertweck, & Crowdes, 1981; Shepard & Smith, 1981). Federal and state legislation and regulations, school district policies, organizational arrangements within schools, amount and availability of space, number and quality of professional personnel, the nature of other special education programs or alternative resources, attitudes about special education, and decision-making routines are all institutional influences which must be taken into account when considering prevalence. Decisions about special education classification are not based exclusively on characteristics of pupils. Rather, such decisions are made within the context of complex and changing organizational structures. Thus, both individual and institutional characteristics must be considered if we are to understand the expression and the prevalence of learning disability.

Taken as a whole, then, professional differences, methods of operationalizing the aptitude-achievement discrepancy, measurement problems, and a variety of institutional constraints all affect who and how many are identified as learning disabled. One consequence is that pupil counts within categories of mild handicaps (mild mental retardation, emotional disturbance, behavior disorders, and learning disabilities) are confounded. Learning disability programs serve pupils with many different problem conditions (Keogh, Major-Kingsley, Omori-Gordon, & Reid, 1982; Norman & Zigmond, 1980; Torgesen & Dice, 1980). Further, many learning disability-like pupils are found in other special education classifications or are served in regular education programs (Ysseldyke, Algozzine, Richey, & Graden, 1982), and many learning disability programs provide services for generally low achieving students (Warner, Schumaker, Alley, & Deshler, 1980; Ysseldyke, Algozzine, Shinn, & McGue, 1982). Given the range of influences on classification, it should not surprise us that there is limited generalization across studies or programs. Both research and program evaluation efforts are threatened by sample heterogeneity, partly because of different or inconsistent definitional criteria, and partly because of the almost exclusive reliance on system-identified subjects for research samples (cf. Keogh & MacMillan, 1983; MacMillan, Meyers, & Morrison, 1980).

The Need for Classification

It is likely that both program developers and researchers in learning disability will continue to grapple with heterogeneity and diversity. In a sense this is valuable, as it provides a number of perspectives on the problem. Unfortunately, however, differences in perspectives have too often led to continuing and sometimes acrimonious arguments about "the definition." The argument has centered around efforts to find a single definition which could encompass the many facets of learning disabilities. Rather than one learning disability, we are realistically dealing with a number of learning disabilities. Thus, a multi-definitional or multisyndrome approach, along with a classification system or taxonomy to organize the types of learning disabilities, is necessary. Such an approach could bring logic and organization to the diversity within the broad learning disability rubric without sacrificing the rich array of differences.

The need for a classification system is not unique to learning disability, of course, as taxonomies or typologies are important in all scientific fields. They organize content, order attributes, determine group membership, and direct research and practice. Taxonomies bring order to a field through the identification of groups of classes which have certain common attributes or properties. The necessary and sufficient properties for membership define a class. Bailey (1973) suggested that some classes are monothetic: possession of a particular attribute assures class membership; a particular characteristic is both necessary and sufficient. In contrast, in polythetic classes no single attribute is necessary or sufficient for membership; rather, membership is determined by multiple, shared characteristics. Polythetic groupings are common in the social sciences, monothetic ones in the natural sciences. Most polythetic classification systems are derived empirically, from descriptions of individuals. While not as conceptually clean as monothetic groupings, polythetic categories reflect the complexities of clinical fields and allow recognition of consistencies of shared characteristics. A given individual in a group may not have all of the attributes which define the class, but may share some of the attributes.

The idea of a multidefinitional, polythetic approach fits the learning disability field well. Abundant clinical description documents that not all learning disabled individuals exhibit all learning disabilities symptoms. Not all have attentional, visual perceptual, short-term memory, or auditory sequencing problems. However, many learning disabled individuals have some of these characteristics. Most notably, what they have in common is some (usually broadly defined) discrepancy between presumed aptitude and achievement of expected level of performance, and one or more of a long list of specific characteristics or symptoms. The presence of a discrepancy alone does not identify an individual as learning disabled, nor is it a valid criterion for classification, as the discrepancy may be due to many causes other than learning disabilities. As noted by Reynolds et al. (1984–85), the discrepancy is a necessary but not sufficient indicator of learning disabilities. It merely establishes a pool of eligible individuals whose problems require further differentiation. Individuals in any identified eligibility pool will evidence a range of personal characteristics and problems, some of which they will share. Understanding learning disability requires specification of the probability of occurrence or expression of particular characteristics as well as description of the patterns of relationships among them.

Identification of the frequency and pattern of shared attributes would allow delineation of coherent subtypes of learning disabilities. A next step would be determination of the nature of the relationships and organization among them. Some groupings will likely be subordinate to others. A taxonomy or organizational system would bring order to the wide array of conditions and attributes which characterize learning disabilities and would move us beyond the continuing argument about "the" definition. It would also allow a more powerful test of child-treatment interactions. From both conceptual and applied perspectives, then, a multidefinitional, shared attribute approach to learning disabilities is promising. Efforts to formulate markers for describing learning disabled samples (Keogh et al. 1982) or the selection of rationally defined subgroups (Torgesen, 1982) are steps in this direction. Delineation of consistent subgroups within learning disabilities provides another approach.

Subtype Research

McKinney (1984, 1988) argued persuasively that a "single syndrome" theory is inadequate to explain the heterogeneity which characterizes groups of learning disabled individuals selected under present definitional criteria. He noted that a considerable volume of work, including earlier etiology-based subtypes, attests to the variation within learning disabilities. Most current subtyping work falls generally into two categories which relate to the approaches taken to classify subjects. Clinical-inferential studies yield typologies which are based on researchers' a priori impressions of the problem. Empirically based typologies, on the other hand, rely on multivariate statistical techniques to identify coherent subtypes. Although there is considerable variation in specifics within each approach, each deserves brief overview.

Clinical-Inferential Classification

Subtypes identified within the clinical-inferential tradition reflect an investigator's conceptualization of learning disability (McKinney, 1998). For example, one might assume that learning disability is a visual, auditory, or mixed condition; or that learning disabled children will evidence particular psychological or neurological symptoms. In such approaches subtype classification is often made on the basis of performance on tests which presumably reflect selected aspects of underlying psychological or neurological functioning (cf. Rourke, 1975, 1985). An example of this approach includes the studies of Mattis, French, & Rapin (1975) who used a priori decision rules to delineate three subtypes: language disorder, articulation graphomotor discoordination, and visual-perceptual disorder. The subtype work of Boder (1973) and Denckla (1972) are also examples.

As noted by McKinney (1988), although the clinical-inferential approaches have a good deal of intuitive appeal and are consistent with clinical practices, they have a number of limitations in interpretation. The first relates to subject selection and sample composition. Most samples have been restricted to preselected or system-identified subjects, and thus may reflect bias related to referral and diagnosis. Sample attributes (ethnicity, social class) may have further limited generalization to other groups. As few studies have included appropriate "normal" comparison groups, the question of the idiosyncratic nature of the findings with learning disabled individuals cannot be answered. Second, the studies have been limited by questions of adequacy of measures and by questionable reliability and validity of classification procedures, (i.e., by obscure or uncertain decision rules). Third, few studies have provided evidence of external validity of subtypes, although it is reasonable that systematic differences among subtypes might be associated with other subject characteristics, (e.g., sex, age, and a range of demographics). Taken as a whole, McKinney suggested that, ". . . the value of the literature on the clinical-inferential classification of learning disabilities subtypes for special education seems to rest primarily on its heuristic merit in stimulating more objective research and assisting in the clinical interpretation of results from more rigorous studies" (1988, p 261).

Empirical Classification

Empirical classification techniques, in contrast to clinical-inferential ones, attempt to identify homogenous subgroups according to statistically determined similarities and differences. The goal in these procedures is to find individuals who are similar to each other in certain attributes or measures, but who differ from individuals assigned to different subtypes. Two primary techniques are commonly used: the Q-factor analysis and cluster analysis.

Conceptually similar to more traditional factor analysis, the Q technique identifies correlations among subjects, and among tests, thus, it yields groups of similar individuals rather than groups of similar tests. Studies by Doehring and his colleagues (Doehring & Hoshko, 1977; Doehring, Hoshko, & Bryans, 1979) and the work of Rourke and his associates (Rourke, 1975, 1978; Rourke & Finlayson, 1978) are illustrative of the *Q* technique.

Cluster analytic techniques have also been used in a number of individual studies, and as noted by McKinney (1988), have been central in several major programs of research. For detailed findings, the reader is referred to the work of Satz (Morris, Blashfield, & Satz, 1981; Satz & Fletcher, 1980; Satz & Morris, 1981), Lyon (Lyon, Stewart, & Freedman, 1982, Lyon & Watson, 1981; Lyon, Watson, Reitta, Porch, & Rhodes, 1981), and to the Carolina Longitudinal Study (McKinney & Feagans, 1984, McKinney & Speece, 1983; Speece, McKinney, & Appelbaum, 1985). These investigators have applied somewhat different clustering techniques to samples which include both learning disabled and normal achievers, and have included children across a broad age range. Despite some specific differences in numbers and types of clusters, there are commonalities in the findings which deserve attention. The different research groups have identified specific perceptual, linguistic, and/or auditory and mixed perceptual/linguistic subgroups. Overall the findings argue against a single syndrome definition of learning disability ; they also suggest that learning disabled groups do not organize themselves "neatly" within perceptual and linguistic domains. Consistent with the *Q*-factor findings, many of the cluster studies have identified a subgroup of children who do not evidence deficits on the measures used in the studies. It is uncertain whether this is a function of the measures used or of under-achievement associated with poor pedagogy, limited experience, or low motivation.

Taken as a whole, the cluster work to date is encouraging. There are a number of consistencies across research programs, and the majority of the findings are conceptually interpretable and fit with clinical evidence. It is possible that further studies using this approach will identify patterns or subtypes which take into account attentional disorders, memory deficits, or particular information-processing subtypes. Findings from subtype research may provide powerful directions for settling the definitional controversy which has plagued the learning disability field. Findings may also provide the basis for a classification system or taxonomy of learning disabilities and may lead to better understanding of long-term outcomes and of intervention-pupil links.

McKinney (1988) noted, however, that there are still problems which limit application. Many of the cluster approaches have used clinic or preidentified special education children; thus, questions of subject generalization remain. As with other empirical or clinical-inferential approaches, the nature of the sampling affects the findings. Preselected samples, especially without normal comparison groups, may yield idiosyncratic results. A second point concerns the question of stability of subtypes over time. From a developmental perspective it is reasonable that subtype organization may change, and that maturation, experience, and particular instructional or remedial efforts will affect subtype placement. The nature of this changing membership, or the stability of subtype classificaton, is important if we are to understand the expression of learning disabilities in various age and developmental periods. Further, the meaningfulness of the empirically derived clusters is dependent on external validation. Yet there is relatively little evidence which provides setting and behavioral generalization. Finally, the educational or treatment relevance of the subtype findings is still uncertain, a point of particular importance in the studies using neuropsychological measures. From an educational perspective the practical implications of subtype research ultimately relate to its ability to direct remediation.

Long-term Consequences and Outcomes

In his comprehensive review of longitudinal studies, Kavale (1988) noted that there are a number of commonly held beliefs about the long-term consequences of learning disabilities: Academic problems persist, emotional problems develop, delinquency is probable, and vocational choices are limited to low-status positions. Kavale suggested that while there is some tentative and fragmented evidence to support these beliefs, they have also been challenged; and considerable evidence argues against accepting them as firm generalizations. Inconsistencies in the findings about outcomes relate to differences in research methodologies, to sample or subject attributes, to the variables and measures chosen as indices of outcome, and to the intervening experiences of learning disabled individuals over time. There are also serious interpretive limitations to many longitudinal findings as correlations between measures do not allow inferences about cause. Thus, the social and effective stresses often found to be associated with learning disabilities may be either consequences or causes of the learning problems.

Difficulties in interpreting the research literature also relate to the lack of an agreed-upon conceptual definition of learning disabilities, as longitudinal studies are frequently focused on children with reading disabilities, hyperactivity, and/or minimal brain dysfunction. As demonstrated by Kavale in his 1988 review, the outcomes for these conditions may be somewhat negative. Because these problem conditions often interact with learning disabilities, they may confound the study of learning disability itself, and they may contribute in tandem to the often-reported negative findings in the long-term studies of learning disability (cf. Ackerman, Dykman, & Peters, 1977; Eaves & Crichton, 1974–75). An examination of studies in which learning disability was separated from other problem conditions may shed light on the long-term consequences of learning disability itself.

Longitudinal Studies of Learning Disability

Kavale suggested that when learning disability is separated from other problems, (e.g., hyperactivity), the long-term picture is somewhat more optimistic. Lehtinen-Rogan and Hartman (1976) studied 91 private school learning disabled children as adults. Over two-thirds had completed high school, and over one-third had graduated from college; over half were independent of their parents, and 70% were employed. On the negative side many reported low self-esteem and social isolation problems. Warner et al. (1980) compared a group of learning disabled children as adults with a group of non-learning disabled adults. Few differences emerged, although the former learning disabled subjects held jobs with lower social status, were less involved socially, and were "less satisfied" with their lives. Similar findings were reported by Major-Kingsley (1982) in her follow-up study of 40 learning disabled boys as young adults. Although similar to a non-learning disabled comparison group in many ways, the learning disabled adults expressed more feelings of low self-esteem and reported continuing problems with academic subjects, especially reading. However, a majority of the learning disabled subjects had completed high school, and many were in posthigh-school educational programs.

The literature from learning disability follow-up studies is not all positive, however. Focusing specifically on school, Koppitz (1971) reported a five-year follow-up study of 177 learning disabled children in which only 24% were found to be in regular classes; the majority of children continued to have serious academic and behavioral problems. Her findings were consistent with those of Hinton and Knights (1971) and with Ackerman et al. (1977), who found that learning disabled pupils identified in grade school were seriously deficient in basic skills at age 14. From this brief sampling of the published research literature reviewed by Kavale (1988), it is apparent that the long-term outcomes of learning disabilities are still uncertain. Differences in findings are related to sample characteristics, to age at assessment and follow up, to the social class and family backgrounds of identified learning disabled pupils, and to the nature and intensity of the interventions experienced.

Two major points which emerged in Kavale's extensive review deserve particular note: First, academic problems are relatively persistent, but usually become less severe over time. On the average, learning disabled children, compared to their non-learning disabled peers, make slower academic progress, are apt to repeat one or more grades in school, and may continue to have problems in specific psychological functions, (e.g, auditory processing). Second, many learning disabled individuals continue to have related problems of self-esteem and social adequacy. Despite seemingly satisfactory vocational accomplishments and independent living capabilities, learning disabled young adults may be at heightened risk for subsequent affective and social difficulties.

To be emphasized is that long-term outcomes are related to learning disabled children's social, family, and educational experiences. Like their peers, learning disabled children do not live in isolation, and like other children, they are powerfully affected by those around them. Major longitudinal studies, such as those conducted by Nichols and Chen (1981) and Werner and Smith (1982), demonstrated clearly the impact of socioeconomic status and family environments on children's academic and social development. These influences may be particularly powerful for young learning disabled children who are more vulnerable than their peers. Prognosis and long-term outcomes, thus, are related to the social and economic conditions of the family, to the adequacy of schooling, and to the availability and appropriateness of support services. Given the complexity of the interactions between learning disabled children and their worlds, it is not surprising that the research on outcomes yields inconsistent findings. It is clear, however, that further comprehensive longitudinal work is necessary in order to identify the nature of these interactions. From a practical view it is also clear that services for learning disabled individuals may need to go beyond a traditional educational definition in both content and timing of services.

Intervention

From the standpoint of human values it might be argued that the vast research enterprise in the learning disability field has one major goal: To improve the quality of services for learning disabled individuals. Improved and effective services obviously require better understanding of learning disability and its expression, as well as increased understanding of curriculum content and instructional practices. The conceptual ambiguities about learning disability, referred to in other sections of this chapter, are especially pertinent when interventions in learning disability are considered. Even cursory examination of the intervention literature identifies a range of approaches and practices which reflect differences in views on the nature of learning disabilities and on what can and should be done to change it. In his major review of intervention in learning disabilities, Lloyd (1986) organized interventions into three major approaches: medical, indirect, and instructional. This organizational system is helpful as it ties intervention to conceptualization and makes the intervenor's views of learning disability explicit.

Medical and medically oriented interventions are based on assumptions of some biological or organic basis of learning disability. Learning disability is frequently associated with consideration of hyperactivity, hyperkinesis, or minimal brain dysfunction. In this view the locus of the problem is in the child and is thought to be amenable to change through biochemical intervention, (e.g., medication or diet). Closely related, but from a somewhat different perspective, indirect approaches are based on the assumption that learning disability is caused by some underlying psychological or cognitive-processing problem. Intervention focuses on remediation of the presumed process deficit through a variety of educational, psychological, and physical techniques. Examples of such interventions include perceptual motor training, vision training, and psycholinguistic training. Instruction approaches, in contrast to both medical and indirect interventions, focus directly on particular skill deficits which are thought to be related to the material or tasks to be learned. Although a variety of particular techniques are included in the direct instructional approaches, they have in common an emphasis on mastery of specific, content-based skills.

Medical and indirect approaches are based on assumptions that changes in presumed underlying deficits will result in improved learning and achievement. Extensive literature has addressed the effectiveness of both medical and indirect approaches (cf. Adelman & Compas, 1977; Kavale, 1982; Kavale & Forness, 1985; Sprague, 1977; Whalen & Henker, 1976). Overall, the findings might best be characterized as equivocal. Most approaches are effective with some learning disabled children but not with others; most approaches yield improved performance in some domains but not in others; most approaches bring about changes in the process targeted but do not necessarily affect academic performance. Based on the evidence to date, generalizations about effectiveness of these interventions for learning disabilities are limited.

In contrast to the medical and indirect interventions, instructional approaches focus specifically on behavior and academic performance. For the most part these approaches have been developed within the behavioral, task analytic tradition, although in recent efforts they have been somewhat broadened. Examples are the work of Semel and Wiig (1981) and Pascarella and Pflaum (1981), who applied cognitive-psycholinguistic content to direct instruction programs. Another broader approach found under the instructional umbrella is cognitive-behavior modification (CBM). Emerging from earlier work by Mahoney (1974) and Meichenbaum (1977), CBM techniques were applied to problems of learning disabled individuals with some success (Lloyd, Hallahan, Kosiewicz, & Kneedler, 1982; Lloyd, Saltzman, & Kauffman, 1981). As noted by Lloyd (1988), the bulk of the direct instruction work has incorporated behavioral techniques, and has demonstrated improved performance in a variety of academic tasks (reading, arithmetic, spelling) and in attending, speaking, and listening skills. These educationally based approaches are especially relevant to the academic problems of learning disabled children, and have resulted in a growing instructional technology. Lloyd's (1988) review demonstrated that effective instruction in academic skills is possible and reasonable and that such learning does not have to be "piecemeal or overly specific." Certainly the findings of these instructional approaches are encouraging, especially if learning disability is conceptualized as an academic learning problem. However, there is less evidence to support the effectiveness of direct instruction when applied to other learning disability related problems, (e.g., social adjustment or self-concept). These are serious considerations given the many affective and social correlates of learning disability.

Taken as a whole, questions of intervention effectiveness continue to be troublesome for advocates of medical, indirect, and instructional approaches. It may be that specific interventions interact uniquely with different expressions of learning disability: an aptitude-by-treatment interaction (ATI) notion. If ATIs are viable in the planning of interventions for learning disabled pupils, then the need for a taxonomy of learning disabilities becomes even more important. Said differently, subtyping may provide the basis for more powerful selection of interventions. As our understanding of the variations within learning disabilities increases, the implications for intervention may emerge more clearly.

The other side of the coin has to do with the nature of programs. Lloyd (1988) identified several major issues which must be dealt with if we are to advance our understanding of intervention with learning disabled individuals. The first deals with the question of generality or generalization, and is expressed in several ways. How applicable is an intervention across individuals? How well do specific skills or strategies generalize within a given child? How effectively do skills transfer across situations? How robustly are treatment effects maintained? These are issues which confront all treatment proponents. Unfortunately, in many cases they have not been tested empirically. Thus, the generalization of many intervention approaches is unknown.

Another intervention issue Lloyd identified has to do with the impact of mediating variables on program effectiveness. How do individual differences in children's self-views, their attributional styles, or their cognitive characteristics affect their responses to intervention? How do program differences interact with pupils' learning styles? Closely related, how do pupils' active or passive roles in the intervention process affect learning? These are important questions which must be considered when implementing and testing interventions.

The questions are not specific to learning disability as they are commonly faced by program developers and evaluators in most fields. They are, however, particularly critical in a field which lacks conceptual clarity and where there is little solid theory to guide practice. Careful and comprehensive evaluation of program practices is a high priority for

future work. Optimistically, such efforts should lead to greater understanding of individual differences among learning disabled children, to
more precise delineation of components of intervention, and to inclusion
of a broader range of outcome indices. Of particular concern are considerations of interventions that address social problems of learning disabled children. Some of these issues are addressed in the following
section.

Social Aspects of Learning Disability

Social competence is a critical domain of human development, and
indeed may be particularly important for learning disabled children who
have problems in other areas. Yet until relatively recently, the major
emphasis in learning disability research and intervention has been on
academic deficits and correlates. As Gresham (1988) emphasized in his
comprehensive paper, the identification and remediation of social skills
problems is a critical aspect of an "appropriate" education and carries
important diagnostic and intervention implications. Yet the conceptualization of social competence is somewhat ambiguous, and diagnostic and
assessment techniques are only beginning to be developed. In Gresham's
formulation, personal competence is composed of three subdomains:
academic competence, social competence, and physical competence.
One or all may be involved in learning disability. Gresham suggested
further that social competence has at least two subcomponents: adaptive
behavior and social skills. A considerable literature argues for the
importance of these subdomains or components, and increasing numbers of intervention programs are designed to improve learning disabled
children's adaptive and social skill deficiencies (cf. Bryan, 1982; Cartledge & Milburn, 1980; Gresham, 1981; Hops, 1983; La Greca & Mesibov, 1979). To date, however, generalizations about intervention
effectiveness are limited by differences in research designs and strategies, in variations among subjects, in inconsistent operational measures, and in the nature of the definitions of social competence used
to guide the studies. There is considerable agreement, however, that
learning disabled children as a group are low in peer-assessed sociometric status; that they are also low in academic self-esteem; and that they
exhibit deficits in interpersonal-, self- and task-related behaviors. There
is some, albeit inconsistent, support for the notion that they are poor in
social perception, and that they are low in general self-concept or self-
esteem.

In an effort to gain better understanding of the social problems of
children, Gresham (1988) categorized social skill problems into four
groups: skill deficits, performance deficits, self-contol/skill deficits, and
self-control/performance deficits. These distinctions provide useful

direction for assessment, diagnosis, and intervention. The grouping also untangles two aspects of social skills problems: the knowledge about how to perform, and the affective or emotional arousal responses. In Gresham's view the social problems of learning disabled children relate more to self-control skills and self-control deficits than to direct skill and performance deficiencies. Such an analysis is consistent with a number of motivational perspectives which are relevant to learning disabled pupils (cf. Bandura, 1977; Dweck & Goetz, 1978; Harter, 1978).

Gresham emphasized that the social problems of learning disabled individuals cannot be viewed in isolation. A contextual or "ecological" behavioral approach may be particularly useful in understanding the social behaviors and social problems of learning disabled children, as this perspective takes into account both setting events and individual characteristics. As an example, teachers' expectations, standards, and tolerances are seen as affecting the frequency and nature of their interactions with particular children. As many learning disabled pupils exhibit behaviors which are inconsistent with teachers' views of "model behaviors," many may be viewed as deviant or troublesome and assumed to have social problems. Thus, adults' views may be important influences on referral and evaluation as well as on intervention. Given the importance of social competence in interpersonal relations, and given the number of programs aimed at developing social competence, it is clear that more refined conceptual and operational definitions are needed to direct both research and intervention. As suggested by Gresham (1988), it is also necessary to evaluate interventions relative to their social validity.

Social Validity of Intervention

Social validity refers to the social context in which interventions are implemented, thereby forcing consideration of the appropriateness of goals, of practices, and of outcomes. Gresham (1988), borrowing from earlier work of Wolf (1978), suggested that social validity requires consideration of the significance of the goals of intervention, the social acceptability of the practices or procedures used to achieve these goals, and the social importance of the outcomes. Social significance, one aspect of social validity, reflects individual or subjective values; and it may differ for parents, teachers, and children. Parents and teachers (or special education and regular education teachers) may hold different views as to the value and appropriateness of particular placements and programs for learning disabled children. Parents and teachers may define different goals and emphasize different outcomes. These differences may lead to disagreement about referral, placement, and intervention.

A second level of social validity refers to the social acceptability of an intervention. To put it directly: Do the ends justify the means? For example, concern about the acceptability of practices has been voiced about programs using aversive control techniques. Yet in general the content of social competence interventions has received relatively limited scrutiny. It is not known if selection into a social skills training program has possible negative effects on children's self-perceptions. The impact of research using sociometric techniques is also uncertain.

Finally, a third aspect of social validation refers to the social importance of the outcomes or the long-term effects of social skills interventions. Does the intervention help the learning disabled child in his or her life outside the program? Certainly social competence and social acceptance are important and valued goals. Yet the impact of social training programs is relatively unknown and generalization of effects is often not documented. A number of investigators have demonstrated that it is possible to teach a variety of specific skills. At issue is the value of these skills in the "real world" of learning disabled children's social experiences.

Generalizations and Recommendations

Although the topics in this chapter differ in focus and content, two powerful generalizations emerge as a whole. First, there is explicit acknowledgment of the diversity of characteristics which define and describe learning disabilities. Identified learning disabled individuals evidence a wide range of educational, behavioral, social, and motivational characteristics. We should expect variance on all of these attributes within any group of learning disabled pupils. Thus, it is not possible to talk about a "typical" learning disabled child, and the search for a single prototype is likely a fruitless one. Rather, there is increasing consensus that a more productive route in understanding learning disability and how to deal with it is to recognize and order the diversity within a theoretically and empirically sound organizational system. By bringing order to the variations among learning disabled pupils, it will be possible to test therapeutic and intervention practices with more precision.

A second generalization relates to the state of our knowledge. We have learned a good deal about learning disability over the last 20 years, and we have made progress in setting up a structure within which to provide services. Yet it is clear from the content of these reviews that our knowledge is rudimentary and our understanding of learning disability is limited; thus, our practices are still relatively unrefined and mostly of unknown effectiveness. This generalization about the state of our knowledge could be interpreted as expressing a kind of pessimism. On the contrary, recognition of the limits of our understanding point the direction for future efforts. The state-of-the-art papers discussed in this chapter have answered few questions about learning disability but they have identified a number of important questions which may lead to those answers. The recommendations which follow are based on the consensus which emerged within the five papers (i.e., Gresham, 1988; Kavale, 1988, Keogh, 1988; Lloyd, 1988; McKinney, 1988). They are directed at three levels: practice, research, and policy.

Practice

Recommendation One. The focus of educational services in learning disability should be shifted from assessment and diagnosis to instruction and pedagogy. This recommendation is based on a growing literature which challenges the reliability and validity of many techniques used in identification and diagnosis, and which underscores the heterogeneity of individuals subsumed under the learning disability rubric. The emphasis on fine-grained diagnosis has not necessarily led to appropriate and differentiated educational interventions and is questionable until there is evidence which links diagnosis to intervention. The focus of educational services might more productively be directed toward improving pedagogy for pupils within a broadly defined special educational category, learning disability.

Recommendation Two. Major efforts should be directed toward improving the level of professional services provided for pupils with learning disabilities. Evidence from a number of independent sources documents the limitations of psychological and educational practices in the learning disability field. Classroom teachers, school psychologists, and school administrators too often make important decisions about pupils on the basis of poorly conceptualized theory and imprecise or incorrect procedures. The level of services is directly tied to the quality of preparation of professionals who deliver services. Thus, pre- and inservice training should be high priorities in planning and support.

Recommendation Three. School districts and other agencies providing services to learning disabled pupils should be encouraged to conduct systematic evaluations of program practices and intervention effects. In particular, it is recommended that evaluation efforts be directed to determining the comparative effectiveness of different program orientations, and to identify the relative importance of specific program components or practices. Because of the definitional ambiguity of learning disability, and because so many disciplines are represented in the field, there are markedly different perspectives on remediation. The result is a vast array of programs and practices. To date, there are few data which allow comparisons among perspectives or which document the relative effectiveness of various components or practices. Yet both clinial and financial considerations dictate the need for more powerful tests of program impact. Inherent in this recommendation is the assumption that improved knowledge about program impact will lead to more effective services for learning disabled pupils.

Research

Recommendation One. Priority should be given to research focused on the development and testing of a comprehensive classification system or taxonomy of learning disabilities, with effort to include research directed at the specification of conceptually and empirically sound subgroups within the broad learning disability classification. As consistently demonstrated in the research and practice literatures, there is not a single prototype of a learning disabled pupil. Rather, there is overwhelming consensus that individuals within the learning disability category differ in educational, intellectual, motivational, and social attributes. It is not surprising that program impact varies, and that numbers and characteristics of identified learning disabled pupils differ geographically and over time. The delineation of soundly based subtypes and their organization into a logical system or taxonomy will improve understanding of learning disability; it will also allow the specification of learning disability-intervention links. From both theoretical and practical perspectives the need for conceptual organization is clear.

Recommendation Two. The study of learning disability and the evaluation of program impact should be carried out using cross-categorical designs. The first research recommendation emphasized variability within the learning disability category. This recommendation addresses directly questions of similarities and differences across categories of mildly handicapped pupils, especially those classified as slow learners, mentally retarded, emotionally disturbed, or as socially or behaviorally disordered. Learning disability must be understood in relation to these similar but presumably different conditions. Understanding learning disability relative to these conditions will help clarify the nature of learning disability and may lead to more effective interventions.

Recommendation Three. Support should be provided for comprehensive, longitudinal study of learning disability. The expression of learning disability varies over time and is embedded in a developmental framework. Thus, to understand learning disability it is necessary to study it using longitudinal strategies. To date, the natural course of learning disability has not been well described nor have the influences on the development of learning disability been documented. Longitudinal studies will provide information related to early identification, prevention, remedial services, and long-term needs, and will yield insights which cannot be obtained with single, short-term studies. It should be emphasized that real understanding of learning disability and its consequences requires commitment to its study over time.

Policy

Recommendation One. The federal government should develop a long-range and comprehensive plan for research and program support in learning disability. A coherent policy necessarily requires considering the expertise of a number of relevant disciplines and providing consistent support over time. Research programs are productive when guided by sound and agreed-upon goals or priorities and when there is stability of support. Effective research and services for learning disabled pupils require comprehensive planning and effective mechanisms for review and monitoring of activities. Vigorous federal leadership is imperative in planning and implementation.

Recommendation Two. The guidelines and regulations related to PL 94–142 should be reviewed and evaluated by an appropriate group representing consumers of services, professionals involved in the delivery of services and in research, and local, state, and federal officials responsible for policy. Differences in numbers of learning disabled pupils receiving services, the range of services, and the content and quality of services suggest inconsistencies and problems in the implementation of PL 94–142. Thus, educational opportunities for learning disabled pupils are related to geographic location, age, and social class. The time is right for a serious and comprehensive evaluation of the strengths and weaknesses in its implementation.

Recommendation Three. Federal policy in learning disability should be developed to take into account the need for both "basic" and "applied" research. This recommendation suggests the need for at least partial separation of the study of basic processes from concerns for the delivery of services to learning disabled pupils. The present confounding of service needs with the study of the learning disability condition has limited understanding of both. The importance of research which does not have immediate application but which leads to fundamental understanding is well documented in other fields. Insight into learning disability and its many expressions calls for research at both theoretical and applied levels. This does not imply that the two strands of investigation will remain forever separate. Rather, it argues that clearer understanding of the problem will benefit application.

Conclusions

The recommendations proposed are general, yet give a range of specifics in practice, research, and policy (e.g., school psychologists need more training in interpreting test results; researchers need to be more aware of subject or sampling confounds; and policymakers need better understanding of system effects on learning disability). The learning disability field has made progress since the passing of PL 94–142, and we do know more than previously. We are still far from understanding the learning disabilities condition(s), however, and there is a clear need for systematic programs of research and evaluation. In this authors view, the critical issue which underlines both research and practice relates to the conceptualization of learning disability. We have struggled unsuccessfully for years to find "the definition." But the many expressions of learning disabilities do not fit a single definition. The range of conditions, causes, and characteristics of learning disabilities is broad. Our task is to identify commonalities and regularities which have clinical and educational relevance. It we take a constructionist perspective on learning disability, our task is to construct logical, comprehensive, and useful definitions which are empirically testable. Our constructions will likely not lead to a single definition which describes the learning disabled pupil. Rather our constructions will reflect the diversity captured within the learning disability rubric. We need to think in terms of learning disabilities rather than a single learning disability. A shared attributes notion may allow us to build a coherent and comprehensive conceptual system which can direct effective practice.

References

Ackerman, P. T., Dykman, R. A., & Peters, J. E. (1977). Teenage status of hyperactive and nonhyperactive learning disabled boys. *American Journal of Orthopsychiatry*, **47**(4), 577–596.

Adelman, H. S., & Compas, B. E. (1977). Stimulant drugs and learning problems: *Journal of Special Education*, **11**, 377–416.

Bailey, K. D. (1973). Monothetic and polythetic typologies and their relation to conceptualization, measurement, and scaling. *American Sociological Review*, **38**(1), 18–33.

Bandura, A. (1977). Self-efficacy: Toward a unifying theory of behavioral change. *Psychological Review*, **84**(2), 191–215.

Berk, R. A. (1984). An evaluation of procedures for computing an ability-achievement discrepancy score. *Journal of Learning Disabilities*, **17**(5), 262–266.

Boder, E. (1973). Development dyslexia: A diagnostic approach based on three atypical reading-spelling patterns. *Developmental Medicine and Child Neurology*, **15**(5), 663–687.

Bryan, T. (1962). Social skills of learning disabled children and youth: An overview. *Learning Disability Quarterly*, **5**(4), 332–333.

Cartledge, G., & Milburn, J. F. (Eds.). (1980). *Teaching social skills to children: Innovative approaches*. New York: Pergamon Press.

Christenson, S., Ysseldyke, J., & Algozzine, B. (1982). Institutional constraints and external pressures influencing referral decisions. *Psychology in the Schools*, **19**(3), 341–345.

Cone, T. E., & Wilson, L. R. (1981). Quantifying a severe discrepancy: A critical analysis. *Learning Disability Quarterly*, **4**(4), 359–371.

Denckla, M. B. (1972). Clinical syndromes in learning disabilities: The case for "splitting" vs. "lumping." *Journal of Learning Disabilities*, **5**(7), 401–406.

Doehring, D. G., Hoshko, I. M. (1977). Classification of reading problems by Q-technique of factor analysis. *Cortex*, **13**(3), 281–294.

Doehring, D. G., Hoshko, I. M. & Bryans, B. N. (1979). Statistical classification of children with reading problems. *Journal of Clinical Neuropsychology*, **1**(1), 5–16.

Dweck, C. S., & Goetz, T. E. (1978). Attributions and learned helplessness. In J. H. Harvey, W. Ickes, & R. F. Kidd (Eds.). *New directions in attribution research* (Vol. 2, pp. 158–179). Hillsdale, N.J.: Erlbaum Associates.

Eaves, L. C., & Crichton, J. U. (1974–75). A five-year follow-up of children with minimal brain dysfunction. *Academic Therapy*, **10**(2), 173–180.

Epps, S., Ysseldyke, J. E., & Algozzine, B. (1983). Impact of different definitions of learning disabilities on the number of students identified. *Journal of Psychoeducational Assessment*, **1**(4), 341–352.

Forness, S. R., Sinclair, E., & Guthrie, D. (1983). Learning disability discrepancy formulas: Their use in actual practice. *Learning Disability Quarterly*, **6**(2), 107–114.

Gresham, F. M. (1981). Social skills training with handicapped children: A review. *Review of Educational Research*, **51**(1), 139–176.

Gresham, F. M. (1988). Social competence and motivational characteristics of learning disabled students. In M. Wang, M. Reynolds, & H. Walberg (Eds.), *Handbook of special education: Research and practice: Vol. 2. Mildly handicapped conditions* (pp. 283–302). Oxford, England: Pergamon Press.

Harter, S. (1978). Effectance motivation reconsidered: Toward a developmental model. *Human Development*, **21**(1), 34–64.

Hinton, G. G., & Knights, R. M. (1971). Children with learning problems: Academic history, academic prediction, and adjustment three years after assessment. *Exceptional Children*, **37**(1), 513–519.

Hocutt, A. M., Cox, J. L., & Pelosi, J. (1984). *An exploration of issues regarding the identification and placement of LD, MR, and ED students*. A policy-oriented study of special education's service delivery system. (RTI Report N. RT1/2076–06/01ES). Washington, DC: Department of Education.

Hops, H. (1983). Children's social competence and skill: Current research practices and future directions. *Behavior Therapy*, **14**(1), 3–16.

Kavale, K. A. (1982). Meta-analysis of the relationship between visual and perceptual skills and reading achievement. *Journal of Learning Disabilities*. **15**(1), 42–51.

Kavale, K. A. (1988). The long-term consequences of learning disabilities. In M. Wang, M. Reynolds, & H. Walberg (Eds.), *Handbook of special education: Research and practice: Vol. 2. Mildly handicapped conditions* (pp. 303–344). Oxford, England: Pergamon Press.

Kavale, K. A., & Forness, S. R. (1985). *The science of learning disabilities*. San Diego, CA: College-Hill Press.

Keogh, B. K. (1988). Learning Disabilities: Diversity in search of order. In M. Wang, M. Reynolds, & H. Walberg (Eds.). *Handbook of special education: Research and practice: Vol. 2. Mildly handicapped conditions* (pp. 225–251). Oxford, England: Pergamon Press.

Keogh, B. K., & Hall, R. J. (1984). Cognitive training with learning-disabled pupils. In A. W. Meyers, & W. E. Craighead (Eds.), *Cognitive behavior therapy with children*. New York: Plenum Press.

Keogh, B. K., & MacMillan, D. L. (1983). The logic of sample selection: Who represents what? *Exceptional Education Quarterly*, **4**(3), 84–96.

Keogh, B. K., Major-Kingsley, S., Omori-Gordon, H., & Reid, H. P. (1982). *A system of marker variables for the field of learning disabilities*. Syracuse, NY: Syracuse University Press.

Koppitz, E. M. (1971). *Children with learning disabilities: A five year follow-up study.* New York: Grune & Stratton.

LaGreca, A. M., & Mesibov, G. B. (1979). Social skills intervention with learning disabled children: Selecting and implementing training. *Journal of Clinical Child Psychology,* **8**(3), 234–241.

Lehtinen-Rogan, L., & Hartman, L. D. (1976). *A follow-up study of learning disabled children as adults.* Final Report. Washington, DC: Department Health, Education, and Welfare (Bureau of Education for the Handicapped). (ERIC Document Reproduction Service No. ED 163728).

Lloyd, J. W. (1988). Direct academic interventions in learning disability. In M. Wang, M. Reynolds, & H. Walberg (Eds.), *Handbook of special education: Research and practice: Vol. 2. Mildly handicapped conditions* (pp. 345–366). Oxford, England: Pergamon Press.

Lloyd, J. W., Hallahan, D. P., Kosiewicz, M. M., & Kneedler, R. D. (1982). Reactive effects of self-assessment and self-recording on attention to task and academic productivity. *Learning Disability Quarterly,* **5**, 216–227.

Lloyd, J., Saltzman, N. J. & Kauffman, J. M. (1981). Pridicatable generalization in academic learning as a result of preskills and strategy training. *Learning Disability Quarterly,* **4**, 203–216.

Lyon, R., Stewart, N., & Freedman, D. (1982). Neuropsychological characteristics of empirically derived subgroups of learning disabled readers. *Journal of Clinical Neuropsychology,* **4**(4), 343–365.

Lyon, R., & Watson, B. (1981). Empirically derived subgroups of learning disabled readers: Diagnostic characteristics. *Journal of Learning Disabilities,* **14**(5), 256–261.

Lyon, R., Watson, B., Reitta, S., Porch, B., & Rhodes, J. (1981). Selected linguistic and perceptual abilities of empirically derived subgroups of learning disabled readers. *Journal of School Psychology,* **19**(2), 152–166.

MacMillan, D. L., Meyers, C. E., & Morrison, G. M. (1980). System-identification of mildly mentally retarded children: Implications for interpreting and conducting research. *American Journal of Mental Deficiency,* **85**(2), 108–115.

Mahoney, M. J. (1974). *Cognition and behavior modification.* Cambridge, MA: Ballinger.

Major-Kinglsey, S. (1982) *Learning disabled boys as young adults: Achievement, adjustment and aspirations.* Upublished doctoral dissertation, University of California, Los Angeles.

Mattis, S., French, J. H., & Rapin, I. (1975). Dyslexia in children and young adults: Three independent neuropsychological syndromes. *Developmental Medicine and Child Neurology,* **17**(2), 150–163.

McKinney, J. D. (1984). The search for subtypes of specific learning disability. *Annual Review of Learning Disabilities,* **2**, 19–26.

McKinney, J. D. (1988). Research in conceptually and empirically derived subtypes of specific learning disabilities. In M. Wang, M. Reynolds, & H. Walberg (Eds.) *Handbook of special education: Research and practice: Vol. 2. Mildly handicapped conditions* (pp. 253–281). Oxford, England: Pergamon Press.

McKinney, J. D., & Feagans, L. (1984). Academic and behavioral characteristics of learning disabled children and average achievers: Longitudinal studies. *Learning Disability Quarterly,* **7**(3), 251–265.

McKinney, J. D., & Speece, D. L. (1983). Classroom behavior and the academic progress of learning disabled students. *Journal of Applied Developmental Psychology,* **4**(2), 149–161.

Mehan, H., Meihls, J. L., Hertweck, A., & Crowdes, M. S. (1981). Identifying handicapped students. In S. B. Bacharach (Ed.), *Organizational behavior in schools and school districts* (pp. 381–428). New York: Praeger.

Meichenbaum, D. (1977). *Cognitive-behavior modification: An integrative approach.* New York: Plenum Press.

Morris, R., Blashfield, R., & Satz, P. (1981). Neuropsychology and cluster analysis: Potentials and problems. *Journal of Clinical Neuropsychology,* **3**(1), 79–99.

Nichols, P. L., & Chen, T. C. (1981). *Minimal brain dysfunction: A prospective study.* Hillsdale, NJ: Erlbaum.

Norman, C. A., Jr., & Zigmond, N. (1980). Characteristics of children labeled and served as learning disabled in school systems affiliated with Child Service Demonstration Centers. *Journal of Learning Disabilities,* **13**(9), 542–547.

Pascarella, E. T., & Pflaum, S. W. (1981). The interaction of children's attribution and level of control over error correction in reading instruction. *Journal of Educational Psychology*, **73**, 533–540.

Reynolds, C. R., Berk, R. A., Boodoo, G. M., Cox, J., Gutkin, T. B., Mann, L., Page, E. B., & Willson, V. C. (1984–85). *Critical measurement issues in learning disabilities*. Report of the Work Group on Measurement Issues in the Assessment of Learning Disabilities. Washington, DC: U.S. Department of Education, Program in Special Education.

Rourke, B. P. (1975). Brain-behavior relationships in children with learning disablities. *American Psychologist*, **30**, 911–920.

Rourke, B. P. (1978). Neuropsychological research on reading retardation. A review. In A. L. Benton & D. Pearl (Eds.), *Dyslexia: An appraisal of current knowledge*. New York: Oxford University Press.

Rourke, B. P. (Ed.) (1985). *Neuropsychology of learning disabilities: Essentials of subtype analysis*. New York: Guilford.

Rourke, B. P., & Finlayson, M. A. (1978). Neuropsychological significance of variations in patterns of academic performance: Verbal and visual-spatial abilities. *Journal of Abnormal Child Psychology*, **3**(2) 62–66.

Satz, P., & Fletcher, J. (1980). Minimal brain dysfunctions: An appraisal of research concepts and methods. In H. E. Rie & E. D. Rie (Eds.), *Handbook of minimal brain dysfunctions: A critical review*. New York: Wiley.

Satz, P., & Morris, R. (1961). Learning disability subtypes: A review. In F. J. Pirozzola & M. C. Wittrock (Eds.), *Neuropsychological and cognitive processes in reading*. New York: Academic Press.

Semel, E. M., & Wiig, E. H. (1981). Semel Auditory Processing Program: Training effects among children with language-learning disabilities. *Journal of Learning Disabilities*, **14**, 192–197.

Shepard, L. (1980). An evaluation of the regression discrepancy method for identifying children with learning disabilities. *Journal of Special Education*, **14**(1), 79–91.

Shepard, L. A. (1983). The role of measurement in educational policy: Lessons from the identification of learning disabilities. *Educational Measurement: Issues and Practice*, **2**(3), 4–8.

Shepard, L. A., & Smith, M. L. (1981). *The identification, assessment, placement, and remediation of perceptual communication disordered children in Colorado*. Boulder, CO: Laboratory of Educational Research, University of Colorado.

Shepard, L. A., & Smith, M. L. (1983). An evaluation of identification of learning disabled students in Colorado. *Learning Disability Quarterly*, **6**(2), 115–127.

Sixth Annual Report to Congress on the Implementation of Public Law 94–142: The Education for All Handicapped Children Act. (1984). Office of Special Education, U.S. Department of Education.

Speece, D. L., McKinney, J. D., & Applebaum, M. I. (1985). Classification and validation of behavioral subtypes of learning- disabled children. *Journal of Educational Psychology*, **77**(1), 67–77.

Sprague, R. L. (1977). Psychopharmaco therapy in children. In M. F. McMillan & S. Henao (Eds.), *Child psychiatry: Treatment and research*. New York: Brunner/Mazel.

Thurlow, M. L., & Ysseldyke, J. E. (1979). Current assessment and decision-making practices in model LD programs. *Learning Disability Quarterly*, **2**(4), 15–24.

Torgesen, J. K. (1982). The use of rationally defined subgroups in research on learning disabilities. In J. P. Das, R. F. Mulcahy, & A. E. Wall (Eds.). *Theory and research in learning disabilities*. New York: Plenum Press.

Torgesen, J. K., & Dice, C. (1980). Characteristics of research on learning disabilities. *Journal of Learning Disabilities*, **13**(9), 531–535.

Warner, M. M., Schumaker, J. R., Alley, G. R., & Deshler, D. D. (1980). Learning disabled adolescents in the public school: Are they different from other low achievers? *Exceptional Education Quarterly*, **1**(2), 27–36.

Werner, E. E., & Smith, R. S. (1982). *Vulnerable, but invincible: A longitudinal study of resilient children and youth*. New York: McGraw-Hill.

Whalen, C. K., & Henker, B. (1976). Psychostimulants and children: A review and analysis. *Psychological Bulletin*, **83**, 1113–1130.

Wolf, M. M. (1978). Social validity: The case for subjective measurement or How applied behavior analysis is finding its heart. *Journal of Applied Behavior Analysis*, **11**(2), 203–214.

Ysseldyke, J. E., Algozzine, B., Richey, L., & Graden, J. (1982). Declaring students eligible for learning disability services: Why bother with the data? *Learning Disability Quarterly*, **5**(1), 37–44.

Ysseldyke, J. E., Algozzine, B., Shinn, M. R., & McGue, M. (1982). Similarities and differences between low achievers and students classified learning disabled. *Journal of Special Education*, **16**(1), 73–85.

The Education of Deaf Children and Youth

JOSEPH E. FISCHGRUND*

Headmaster, Pennsylvania School for the Deaf
Philadelphia, Pennsylvania

In 1965, The Advisory Committee in the Education of the Deaf, established by the Secretary of Health, Education, and Welfare, issued the now famous Babbidge Report (1965) which brought about sweeping changes in the educational and rehabilitative systems for deaf individuals. Twenty years later, with the passage of the Education of the Deaf Act of 1986, the United States Congress established the Commission on the Education of the Deaf. The charge to this commission was to take the same kind of look at the education of deaf children and the rehabilitation of deaf adults as did the previous Babbidge Report.

What is important here is that clearly there was a perceived need once again to undertake a critical study of the education of deaf students and the rehabilitation services available for deaf adults. This need resulted from an apparent dissatisfaction among deaf individuals, service providers, and policy makers with current services and the ways they were being delivered.

This need further led to a significant amount of research in the education of deaf children and youth over the past decade. In order to grasp the progress made through a number of specific endeavors, this chapter will summarize five research topics and their implications. These five topics are as follows:

1. English language development
2. Speech and hearing for communication
3. Environments and strategies for learning and teaching
4. Academic development and preparation for work
5. Intellectual, personal and social development

* The author wishes to express his appreciation to Dr. E. Ross Stuckless for both his guidance and his substantive contribution to this chapter.

English Language Development

Many researchers agree that the teaching of English language to deaf students is a paramount yet extremely difficult task. Stuckless (1989) wrote:

> The acquisition of language is a critical element in a deaf student's education, both for active participation in society and as a requisite for success in academic content areas. However, . . . literacy in English remains beyond the grasp of many, if not most, deaf students (p.1).

This section will review reading, writing, and instructional approaches as they relate to the acquisition of English language.

Reading

One significant problem regarding English language development is the acquisition of reading as a secondary English language skill. Numerous studies exist using several measures of reading which indicate the pervasive severity of the problem for most deaf students. A number of studies have also examined more discrete aspects of reading (e.g., the understanding of multiple meanings in vocabulary and figurative language, such as the use of idioms and metaphors), consistently showing deaf students outperformed by hearing students. For example, most older adolescent deaf students derive less useful information from the syntax of a sentence than do eight-year-old students with hearing (Quigley, Wilbur, Power, Montanelli, & Steinkamp, 1976). Several studies of discourse analysis with deaf students have indicated the influence of top-down theories of reading which emphasize the importance of what the reader brings to the task of reading rather than the reader's linguistic weaknesses, and a growing body of knowledge from studies involving hearing readers supports an interactive view involving both top-down and bottom-up strategies (Quigley & Paul, 1989).

There are great ambiguities in the form of uncontrolled variables in a number of studies on reader-based variables, beginning with modes of communication used with and by the deaf student. For example, while two studies revealed the use of simultaneous communication (now Total Communication) that seemed to lead to a higher reading performance than oral approaches alone, other research (Geers, Moog, & Schick, 1984) appears to have demonstrated just the opposite.

While Quigley and Paul (1989) could not identify any research directly assessing the effects of American Sign Language (ASL) on English language development, they did find a number of studies conducted in the 1960s which compared the English language performance of deaf children with signing deaf parents to deaf children with hearing parents. These studies consistently showed the former group of deaf students performing better than the latter. However, factors like parental acceptance could not be controlled, and manual communication alone, in any form, is not the exclusive determinant of how well a deaf child learns to read.

Few studies have been conducted on the effects of oral education where the subjects are profoundly deaf and exposed primarily to an oral approach. The demonstrated successes have mostly arisen in conjunction with variables such as a high socioeconomic level environment, and there is a call for more well-documented research in this area.

Clearly, there is no research evidence at this point to indicate that communication methodology can be tied to achievement in English language development, particularly reading. Recent studies of literacy indicate that when literacy is seen as a holistic process it is clearly the quality of communication about texts, through texts, and in texts that is the fundamental issue in the acquisition of literacy. This suggests that professionals in the education of deaf children and youth might spend far less time discussing mode of communication and far more time discussing quality of communication as it relates to literacy.

A phonological or speech-based recording strategy is used by most hearing persons to facilitate the processing of print into meaning. Although numerous studies have shown that most deaf students use a nonspeech-based code to mediate between print and meaning, fairly recent research has shown extensive use of "inner" speech by some deaf students, even among those whose speech is rated as unintelligible. In addition, at least two studies have concluded that most good deaf readers use primarily a speech-based code rather than visual or sign codes to mediate print.

Written Language

A high correlation exists between variables associated with reading and those associated with writing. Research on the written language of deaf students reveals the same depressed performance level as with reading comprehension. Though there is some evidence that closely links reading and writing at the sentential level, in many cases the written language problems of deaf students might be better examined on an intersentential level, as through discourse analysis, than on a sentential or intrasentential level. One researcher concluded that too much instructional emphasis is given to aiding the deaf student's understanding of single sentence structure, and not enough to understanding a sentence within a broader pragmatic context (Quigley & Paul, 1989).

This latter point needs to be expanded. Research is needed not just on written language at the intersentential level but at even larger levels.

For example, more research is needed on the relationship of how children tell stories through their primary mode of communication, how they might read and interpret stories, and how they might construct stories. The child's construction of the text is the fundamental issue in writing, and is only now being addressed in this field. In particular, the effects of the "writing process" approach, which maintains as a basic premise that all children have stories to tell, and which is currently being widely utilized in general and special education, needs greater attention and study.

Little or no change has taken place in the mastery of English by deaf students over a 40-year period. Support for various instructional approaches to reading and writing are more polemic than empirical, and little is really known about the effectiveness of various instructional practices and materials in this critical area (Quigley & Paul, 1989).

Research on Instruction

Quigley and Paul also reviewed the two general approaches taken to language instruction: natural and structured, but indicated that no data presently exist which give major weight to one approach over the other. Most educational programs use some type of symbol system to teach English to deaf students, ranging from systems like the Fitzgerald Key and various sentence patterns, to symbols based on transformational grammar. The use of "metalinguistic" systems has never been adequately evaluated, thus indicating yet another gap in the research.

The scarcity of information based on the research reviewed in this section on methodology indicates one of the most serious problems faced by educators of deaf children and youth: We really do not know what works in language, reading, and writing instruction. Not only is research needed within the context of schools and programs which educate deaf children, such as the research on the use of metalinguistic systems noted above, but research is needed which brings in validated instructional practices from regular education settings. Quigley and Paul, for example, cited no "time on task studies" as they relate to the acquisition of reading and writing skills by deaf students, yet the research literature in the acquisition of reading and writing skills by hearing students is abundant with research of this type. Recent research in language education has focused on "the language of the classroom," while it is clear that most research in the education of deaf children and youth has focused on the language productions of the children themselves. It is suggested here that educators of deaf children and youth who are committed to the fundamental proposition that literacy is a primary goal in each classroom, step back from the historical pattern of research narrowly focused in the area of deafness. Instead, they should look to new sources, particularly those outside of the education of deaf children and youth, for approaches to the evaluation and understanding of instructional practices.

Speech and Hearing for Communication

On the importance of speech development in the deaf child, Stuckless (1989) noted:

> A relatively small proportion of pre-lingually deaf students acquire what can be considered intelligible speech and probably do not profit as they might from appropriate amplification. . . . There should be no question that the effort to develop the deaf child's potential for oral/aural communication is a legitimate and necessary educational responsibility regardless of prevailing mode of communication or type of school placement (p.1).

In order to explore this area the following topics will be addressed: the audibility of speech, auditory training and speech reading, and research on speech development.

Audibility of Speech

One of the most important first steps in improving the speech communication skills of the hearing-impaired child is notably improving the audibility of the speech signal (Levitt, 1989). For the severely and profoundly hearing-impaired child, it is essential to utilize available residual hearing as efficiently as possible, which generally means frequency dependent amplification, by placing the amplification of speech at the most comfortable level for the child at all frequencies. Levitt (1989) cited the work of his colleagues which indicates what can be achieved in speech and auditory skills under conducive conditions.

Research shows that children with hearing losses in the 80–100 dB puretone range are likely to have great difficulty with segmental contrasts in speech. Many of these children are presently enrolled in schools for the deaf. Levitt cited work he and several associates had done which indicated that among those with this hearing loss who have been successfully mainstreamed, many had a fair degree of hearing at the level of 400° Hz and above, which is generally not taken into account by the usual puretone average.

Three areas of investigation are necessary to improve the auditory potential of hearing-impaired children: (a) identifying the causes of the differences in perceptual performance by children within identical degrees of hearing impairment, (b) teaching the child to learn to discriminate sounds and to recognize sounds in context, and (c) improving the acoustic amplification systems (Levitt, 1989).

Auditory Training and Speechreading

Literature related to auditory training and speech development indicates that the speech signal appears highly redundant, and identifying these redundancies and putting them to use is a key to success in training. These redundancies can be presented auditorily, visually, or contextually. Levitt devoted considerable attention to describing and classifying a number of well-documented auditory training programs and materials. Two limitations to some of these programs are, first, that some are geared to a particular subset of the population and not applicable to the broad range of children who may be in the teachers' care; and second, that teachers are required to develop many of their own materials. He also identified a number of speech training programs in which auditory training plays a major part, and pointed out that a common element in these programs is that each systematically trains and tests auditory ability as the child moves along through the curriculum.

While auditory training techniques have been altered considerably by technical advances in amplification, speechreading training has changed very little over the years. Analytic and synthetic approaches continue to be used, with the mix depending largely on the viewpoint of the clinician. Most speechreading programs and materials are designed for hearing-impaired adults and older students with well-developed language skills, and while the general principles may apply to young children, the materials often do not. Since speechreading correlates higher with language than does any other communication skill, it is particularly important that speechreading materials be commensurate with the child's language level.

Research on Speech Development

Levitt (1989) presented a well-documented description of error patterns in the speech of hearing-impaired children. While major differences exist from child to child in speech intelligibility, major similarities typify their speech. There are common segmental and suprasegmental errors, all of which reduce the intelligibility of the child's speech, and there are several speech training approaches and programs that address these concerns. Three basic components in effective speech training programs are a structured curriculum, a curriculum-based evaluation instrument, and teaching materials appropriate to the child's level of language development. However, two hazards in teaching speech are: (a) too much effort being expended on teaching segmental features and not enough on suprasegmental features, and (b) the tendency to concentrate on those aspects of speech which are easiest to teach, but which may be of only secondary importance to the overall intelligibility (Levitt, 1989).

A series of longitudinal studies of hearing-impaired children in which Levitt and several colleagues engaged indicated some of the more salient findings relative to speech development. Not unexpectedly, speech intelligibility was found to be largely a function of hearing loss. Among the numerous correlates, several other factors stood out. As can be expected, children whose onset of deafness was postlingual had far better speech than those whose deafness was prelingual. Children with behavioral and/or emotional problems and children whose home language is other than English also fell below the general level. In addition, Levitt and his associates observed better speech intelligibility among children who had the benefit of early education (prior to age three), and among children with U-shaped audiograms. By-and-large, mainstreamed children had more intelligible speech than those in schools for the deaf, but most also had considerably more residual hearing.

Levitt also found a small proportion of profoundly deaf children with quite intelligible speech. These children provide convincing evidence that it is indeed possible for profoundly deaf children to acquire intelligible speech. They also reflect the need to study such children in relation to children at the other end of the speech intelligibility scale in order to identify factors contributing to success or the lack of it in speech development.

Considerable attention has been devoted to technological advances which hold promise for major developments in sensory aids. One controversial area today is the use of single channel and multichannel cochlear prostheses with hearing-impaired children, and some strong reservations against their use with young children are cited. However, advances in technology are likely to be infused into the classroom and to have substantial effects on the teaching and the learning of oral/aural communication skills.

The information Levitt provides is important to educators of deaf children and youth. First, his analysis of theoretical studies of the speech signal and its perception, as well as this analysis of training materials, are most insightful. It points again to the necessity of developing, to the best possible advantage, each child's exploitable residual hearing. The fact that residual hearing provides the fundamental basis for speech production is too often ignored in speech training programs for deaf and hearing-impaired children.

While he cited extensive research in the area of speech production and speech perception, Levitt's insightful analysis of this rather narrow field itself ironically points out a greater need. It is quite clear that speech must motivate the hearing-impaired child for it to be developed and, more importantly, meaningfully utilized. Once again, educators of the deaf should turn to related fields such as discourse analysis, speech act theory and more contextually based systems of analysis to look at how, when, and why profoundly deaf children utilize their speech and hearing abilities. It is only when speech is placed in the overall context of communicative development and social interaction that educators will be able to break through oral/aural communicative barriers.

Environments and Strategies for Learning and Teaching

In introducing the research on Environments and Strategies for Learning and Teaching, Stuckless (1989) wrote:

> Two major movements have dominated the education of deaf students for more than a decade. The first movement is toward the broad adoption of "Total Communication" within educational programs for deaf students at all educational levels. . . . The second movement is in the direction of mainstreaming (p.1).

This latter topic is particularly sensitive among educators and policy makers in all sectors, and there is a great need to bring more objectivity to school placement decisions and examine closely the levels and kinds of support services deaf students require in various educational environments. To approach this section of the chapter, it is first necessary to see how changing demographics influence the population of deaf children. Then the current state of mainstreaming, Total Communication, and technology and media will be presented.

Changing Demographics

Changing demographics illustrate the present decline in the school-age population of deaf children. This is due primarily to the fact that victims of the 1959–65 rubella epidemic have now passed through the school system, and the success of the rubella immunization program, which has now almost eradicated rubella as a cause of childhood deafness (Lowenbraun & Thompson, 1989).

However, Silverman (1987) noted an important demographic trend where not long ago "the ratio of students in state residential schools to students in other environments was about 70:30. . .[now] those numbers are just about reversed" (p. 351). This tremendous swing away from placements in residential progams is an overriding concern in any discussion of environments and strategies for teaching and learning. Additionally, recent demographic studies also indicate that approximately 30% of all deaf students in programs for deaf and hearing-impaired individuals are either of racial, linguistic, or ethnic minority status. These three issues—the leaving of the rubella population from school settings, the swing away from residential and center school placements, and the increasing number of minority deaf students—are the three most important demographically driven policy issues faced by educators of the deaf today.

Mainstreaming

Research has shed little light on what constitutes "least restrictive environment," but there are a number of studies on the general topic. Several studies and reviews of studies have indicated the influence of school placement on social, emotional, and/or academic development. One such review of seven studies has suggested overall academic advantages to mainstream placements and disadvantages relative to social and emotional growth. Another study has concluded that physical integration does not necessarily promote either the use of oral language or social interaction (Lowenbraun & Thompson, 1989).

A limited amount of literature is concerned with predictors of success in mainstreamed programs, but it is not really conclusive, in part because of different interpretations or inadequate descriptions of mainstream programs. No studies have been found in which the effects of using an interpreter or tutor on mainstreaming success were examined.

An extensive literature search and an analysis of the few existing studies that address least restrictive environment have clearly shown that there is great need to investigate what the concept of least restrictive environment means to the profoundly deaf child (Lowenbraun & Thompson, 1989). Currently, approaches which present what is called a continuum, but is really a hierarchy, encourage the perception that special school placements are inherently more restrictive than regular school placements. There is, however, no objective evidence to support such a view, only expressions of opinion and belief. Research which can elucidate the rather complex issues involved in determining what is in fact the least restrictive environment for profoundly deaf children is much needed.

Total Communication

Another important area of discussion deals with Total Communication. While tracing the history and presenting several definitions of Total Communication, Lowenbraun and Thompson (1989) acknowledged that the concept of Total Communication extends to a variety of manual communication systems, and it is difficult to identify what really constitutes Total Communication except by self-report. Various surveys point clearly to the increased use of Total Communication programs for deaf students over the past decade or more. There are also several studies which question how well Total Communication is used in many classes, especially in regard to English as represented by the signs used in school and at home.

Lowenbraun and Thompson reviewed a number of studies in which signs have been used with young deaf children in the family, and several studies comparing learning under Total Communication with learning under other modes. While results of these studies are not conclusive, they do tend to give credence to the simultaneous use of speech and signs for instruction.

As noted in the comments on English language development, it is clear that the field of the education of deaf children and youth has spent far too much time concerning itself with mode of communication rather than quality of education. The paucity of studies which relate learning to communication mode or style is yet another example of this lack of objective scrutiny. A suggestion here is that educators of the deaf look beyond the modality issues to the real issues of quality educational programming and effective teaching and learning. Brownley (1987) suggested that quality education for deaf children happens when a school emphasizes (a) accountability for learning, (b) objective assessment, (c) multi-disciplinary team work, (d) program options implemented with integrity, and (e) compatibility with family systems.

Other formulations of what constitutes effective teaching and learning in general education are to be found in the work of Lezotte and Bancroft (1985) and others who are involved in what is generally termed the effective schools, effective teaching, or school improvement movement. Once again, educators of the deaf need to move beyond their own particular narrow concerns toward the broad issues under discussion in general education if true quality in education is to be established. In addition, concerns about least restrictive environment should be discussed in the context of effective and/or quality educational practices, rather than in the political, social, and institutional context in which they are now being discussed.

Technology and Media

The final subtopic reviewed in this section is the application of technology and media in education. Two surveys have suggested that most programs for deaf students are reasonably well supplied with media equipment and microcomputers, but not much is known about how often and how effectively they are used. More to the point, little, if any, compelling evidence suggests that the use of media with deaf students over the past two decades or more has materially increased learning.

Once again the field of the education of deaf children and youth functions as a hypothesis in search of data. Symposia are held, computers are purchased, previous equipment gets sent to storerooms, and the latest advertisement arrives in the mail. However, there is little research data to support the theory that the technology we have available has yet to make a significant or demonstrable difference in the education of deaf children and youth. The state of practice in the area of technology, if measured by purchase orders and numbers of units of equipment, is clearly far ahead of the knowledge base which should support such practices.

Academic Development and Preparation for Work

A fourth major concern for educators of deaf children and youth is the area of transition to either postsecondary education or to the world of work. For example, testimony by the Commission on Education of the Deaf (1988) indicated that if intensive specialized training does not become available, a 70% rate of labor force nonparticipation or unemployment could be predicted for deaf individuals as technological advances reduce the number and kinds of jobs they have traditionally filled. In addition, the Commission also reported, "About 60% of all deaf high school students who graduate or drop out are not able to benefit from postsecondary education," (p. 69) and thus go into the labor market in semiskilled or unskilled jobs or remain unemployed. These rather depressing figures underscore the importance of research integration in the area of transition. This section will review how various educational subject areas are influencing the futures of deaf students. It will also discuss preparation for work through career education.

Education in Various Subject Areas

Lang (1989) focused on preparation for transition at the secondary level with particular emphasis on the content areas of science, mathematics, and social studies. He tied work done in these areas with deaf students to the general literature in each area. On the subject of science education, for example, he dealt primarily with the application of science curricula and materials to deaf students, and he presented evaluations of the curricula with hearing, and, where available, with deaf students.

Lang was able to identify numerous curricula originally designed for elementary level hearing children that have since been applied at the elementary level with deaf children, but at the secondary level, science teachers of the deaf have been slower to apply such curricula. Part of this reticence at the secondary level may be due to the fact that many of the materials were originally developed with the science-oriented student in mind. Also, the reading levels of many of these materials make understanding difficult for most deaf students.

In addition, Lang reported on numerous national surveys of science teachers and science education programs for deaf students, including a recent study in which he was a principal investigator. This study included representation from schools for the deaf and mainstream programs at the elementary, junior high, and secondary levels. A main observation from this study was that few science teachers working with hearing-impaired students have had adequate preparation in science education. Three-fourths had no degree in science education, and one-half of this number had never taken even one science education course in college. Relatively few had an undergraduate major in the sciences. Lang cited literature which underscores the poor preparation of many science teachers working with nonhandicapped students, and suggests that the problem is even more serious among teachers of deaf students.

A high proportion of hearing-impaired students are being taught science in inadequate classroom facilities and with inadequate equipment. Among almost 500 teachers surveyed, one-half felt that their students were not being adequately prepared for college-level science and technology courses. More critically, these teachers felt that their students were not being prepared to function well in today's technological society because they lack a sufficient understanding of science.

As with science, there is a dearth of literature in mathematics education of the hearing impaired. This may be due to the great emphasis placed on the development of language skills, to the near exclusion of other academic areas in the literature (Lang, 1989). In fact, the emphasis given to language instruction in the content curricular areas may have negative effects on the achievement of deaf students in the academic realm.

Survey literature exists from which inferences are drawn for mathematics education similar to those for science education—frequent neglect of curricula and inadequate preparation of teachers in mathematics and mathematics education.

A review of education in social studies shows that virtually no research pertaining specifically to hearing-impaired students has been published. Some concern is expressed that social studies instruction makes considerable use of printed materials. Often these pose problems for the hearing-impaired student, although it is suggested that hearing-impaired students are not unique in this regard.

Lang devoted a section of his research review of the classroom assessment of hearing-impaired students, obviously of considerable importance in overall assessment of academic development and vital for tailoring instruction to hearing-impaired students. The language of tests and test formats relative to this student population indicated that there is a paucity of research and virtually no norms for hearing-impaired students across standardized tests in science, mathematics, and social studies.

Preparation for Work

Literature on career education and preparation of the hearing-impaired student for work has addressed current concepts concerning career education and its infusion into general curriculum. Results have been reported from several studies based on interviews and other assessments of hearing-impaired students. This general area is now receiving considerable attention, boosted in large part by the relatively recent proliferation of opportunities for hearing-impaired students to continue their education beyond the secondary level, particularly in career-oriented areas.

Lang's conclusions and recommendations are worth heeding. He noted:

> We should determine how best to continue the momentum gained during the last decade with disadvantaged students in helping hearing-impaired students in terms of policies and resources. . . . We can learn from the findings on policy-making and national assessments of the general population over the past decade as we prepare to develop new policies in the education of hearing impaired students. . . . If research on the various components of the school curriculum described in this report could be woven into the fabric of the school program, great strides would be made in enhancing the academic development and preparation of hearing-impaired students for the workforce (p. 89).

Cognitive, Personal, and Social Development of Deaf Children and Adolescents

Greenberg and Kusche (1989) have done perhaps the most extensive work available in the area of cognitive, personal, and social development of deaf children and adolescents. They emphasized the difficulty in drawing generalizations across most of the studies they reviewed because of the problem associated with cohort differences. In the past, researchers have neglected to provide enough information about subject characteristics and environmental circumstances to permit appropriate interpretation. Other changes have occurred (e.g., communication methods used with deaf children and changes in educational environments as a function of mainstreaming) which make it difficult to generalize many older research findings to today's deaf children. The findings of Greenberg and Kusche are organized under the following topics: intelligence and achievement, information processing, social and personality development, and familial adaptations to deafness.

Intelligence and Achievement

Following these observations, Greenberg and Kusche presented a review of research literature concerning the intelligence of hearing-impaired children and various subgroups within this population. They also reported on educational achievement characteristics, but observed a relatively low correlation between the two. This is due to the fact that the learning capacities of hearing-impaired children are generally measured nonverbally, whereas most achievement has a high verbal component.

Information Processing

In the area of information processing the cognitive development of hearing-impaired persons can be best understood in terms of different processing skills being more useful in handling some types of information than others. This is illustrated through the example of verbal processing skills which are crucial to reading, but possibly detrimental to some creative arts. It is impossible to show different patterns of information-processing skills among hearing-impaired students rather than among normally hearing students, and it is suggested that this may be a more productive line of inquiry than the consideration of general intelligence.

Using an information-processing model, Greenberg and Kusche carefully reviewed the research literature on perception, cognitive style, categorization, rule learning, Piagetian tasks, complex reasoning and problem-solving skills, and memory. After a thorough review of the literature, Greenberg and Kusche concluded:

> An extensive amount of data suggests that deaf children rely heavily upon visual-spatial perception and processing strategies and show strength in the area of holistic, simultaneous visual processing. Weaknesses, on the other hand, involve areas in which verbal sequential and/or abstract propositional processing are necessary for optimal performance (pp. 108–109).

They also noted, "There seems to be much variation within the deaf population, however, and as noted earlier, we know little about the current cohort being educated today" (p. 109).

As in all of the previous studies discussed in this chapter, the issue of language acquisition and development comes to the forefront in this topic area as well. Greenberg and Kusche concluded, "The literature clearly indicates that various types of specialized training in educational intervention programs specifically designed for deaf children (and various subtypes of deaf children) are needed" (p. 109).

Social and Personality Development

A second subtopic is social and personality development and the literature on behavioral disorders, social maturity, and personality development. Numerous studies of social-cognitive ability have been reported on. The literature on social and personality development features teacher–peer interaction taking place in mainstream settings. This suggests that mainstreaming may be more successful in secondary education, when the child is more mature. In order for social interaction to take place at the elementary level, mainstreaming must be modified (Greenberg & Kusche, 1989). These conclusions give some credence to the concerns expressed by many deaf individuals and educators of the deaf that young deaf children in mainstream settings are often at a social, communicative disadvantage. At the same time, the findings indicate that success may be possible in the elementary years if careful attention is paid to the nature of the interactions, the quality of the environment, and the commitment that program implementors and designers have to the fundamental issue of social and communicative interaction in the classroom rather than to simply a generalized concept of integration.

Familial Adaptations to Deafness

A final subtopic in this area is the family's adaptation to deafness. A number of concrete examples of research in this area have been converted into practice. Various curricula have been developed and subsequently evaluated with demonstrated gains. There have also been family-focused early intervention programs and cognitively oriented intervention programs, such as the programs now underway with hearing-impaired students as a result of Feuerstein's work in Israel. The most important point here, according to Greenberg and Kusche, is that their "review of family development is unanimous in affirming the critical nature of optimal early and continued communication experience for personal development" (p. 114).

In conclusion, there is a tremendous gap in the research literature concerning the school-age deaf child and the family. At the time of Greenberg and Kusche's research review, no reports were published on the quality of parent or family interaction with the deaf child beyond the pre-school years. There is little information available on coping strategies for parents of deaf children, and how these strategies affect the lives of both parent and child. This gap in our knowledge base has identified not only an area in need of research but a critical issue for educators of deaf children and youth. All current formulations of quality in education or effective school practices indicate the importance of the home–school relationship. Until educators of deaf children and youth are able to learn more about how school-age deaf children interact in their homes and communities, and how those homes and communities interact with the school and other institutions in our society, real success in the educational process will continue to elude us.

Summary and Conclusion

Taken together, the five research topics reviewed in this chapter present a tremendous wealth of data related to the education of deaf children and youth. While it is difficult to point out specific recommendations, several major trends do emerge.

First, many practices in the field of the education of deaf children and youth are far ahead of the research and knowledge base that should support them. For the most part, these practices grow out of individual experience and/or philosophical position. While many of these practices may in fact have validity, it is impossible at this juncture in time to distinguish those which do and those which do not.

Secondly, the field of the education of deaf children and youth has spent far too much time narrowly examining itself and far too little time examining generally acknowledged trends and practices in the field of general education. This tendency to focus only on the nature of deafness and the deaf learner, rather than on the general issues of teaching and learning, has been to the detriment of the field.

Third, far too much time has also been spent in the examination of philosophical positions such as the manual/oral controversy or, currently, the mainstream versus center school placement controversy. The various reviews of the literature make it most clear that the examination of the education of deaf children and youth through the lens of these particular controversies has been most unproductive.

Related to the above discussion, the real issues of quality and effectiveness in education have yet to be examined in the field of education of deaf children and youth, except in a very few instances. Brownley (1987) in his landmark presentation to the Conference of Educational Administrators Serving the Deaf notes the following:

> Quality educational programming for deaf children does not currently exist, nor will it exist in the year 2000, if the criteria for quality focuses only on fancy facilities and equipment, glossy public relations or rhetoric attempting to prove which educational option is best for deaf children. Quality education is happening and will happen where school programs of any design make a commitment to pursue the following principles:
>
> 1. Development and support of strong local leadership including school administrators, teachers, parents and community leaders.
> 2. Objective ongoing assessment involving multi-disciplinary teams of individuals who are committed to the goal of student progress;
> 3. Comprehensive standards for programs and services including high expectations for academic achievement and social/emotional growth for all students;

4. Competent and qualified professional staff who share a commitment to a common mission and who continue to grow professionally;
5. Involvement of parents and other communities in meaningful partnerships with school personnel;
6. Openness to share knowledge and resources with other school programs as well as an open-mindedness to consider innovations developed by other educators. (p. 340)

Finally, as Brownley's conclusions summarized in a most striking manner:

Quality education for deaf children happens when each child's unique needs are identified objectively and placement decisions are made and continued based upon evidence of success both academically and emotionally. Standards for quality programming must be raised. Collaboration between various options will ensure that no gaps need to exist. Sharing of our knowledge will ensure a continuously growing competency in providing a quality education to deaf children. People make a difference. People working together make a positive difference (p. 343).

References

Babbidge, H. (1965). *Report of the advisory committee on the education of the deaf.* Washington, DC: Department of Health, Education, and Welfare.

Brownley, J. (1987). Quality education for all deaf children: An achievable goal. *American Annals of the Deaf,* **132**(5), 340–343.

Commission on the Education of the Deaf (1988). *Toward equality: Education of the deaf.* Washington, DC: Government Printing Office.

Education of the Deaf Act (1986). P L 99–271 (August 4, 1986). U.S. Congress.

Feuerstein, R. (1980), *Instrumental enrichment.* Baltimore: University Park Press.

Geers, A. E., Moog, J. S., & Schick, B. (1984). Acquisition of spoken and signed English by profoundly deaf children. *Journal of Speech and Hearing Disorders,* **49**, 378–388.

Greenberg, M. T., & Kusche, C. A. (1989). Cognitive, personal and social development of deaf children and adolescents. In M. C. Wang, M. C. Reynolds, & H. J. Walberg (Eds.), *Handbook of special education: Research and practice: Vol. 3. Low incidence conditions* (pp. 95–129). Oxford, England: Pergamon Press.

Lang, H. G. (1989). Academic development and preparation for work. In M. C. Wang, M. C. Reynolds, & H. J. Walberg (Eds.), *Handbook of special education: Research and practice: Vol. 3. Low incidence conditions* (pp. 71–93). Oxford, England: Pergamon Press.

Levitt, H. G. (1989). Speech and hearing in communications. In M. C. Wang, M. C. Reynolds, & H. J. Walberg (Eds.), *Handbook of special education: Research and practice: Vol. 3. Low incidence conditions* (pp. 23–45). Oxford, England: Pergamon Press.

Lezotte, L. W., & Bancroft, B. A. (1985). Growing use of the effective schools model for school improvement. *Educational Leadership,* **42**(6), 23–27.

Lowenbraun, S., & Thompson, P. V. (1989). Environments and strategies for learning and teaching. In M. C. Wang, M. C. Reynolds, & H. J. Walberg (Eds.), *Handbook of special education: Research and practice: Vol. 3. Low incidence conditions* (pp. 47–69). Oxford, England: Pergamon Press.

Quigley, S. P., & Paul, P. V. (1989). English language development. In M. C. Wang, M. C. Reynolds, & H. J. Walberg (Eds.), *Handbook of special education: Research and practice: Vol. 3. Low incidence conditions* (pp. 3–21). Oxford, England: Pergamon Press.

Quigley, S. P., Wilbur, R., Power, D., Montanelli, D., & Steinkamp, M. (1976). Syntactic structures in the language of deaf children (Final Rep.) Champaign, IL: University of Illinois, Institute for Child Behavior and Development. (ERIC Document Reproduction Service No. ED 119 447).

Silverman, S. R. (1987). Laying the groundwork for the future of education of the deaf. *American Annals of the Deaf,* **132**(5), 351–353.

Stuckless, E. R. (1989). Education of deaf children and youth: Introduction. In M. C. Wang, M. C. Reynolds, & H. J. Walberg (Eds.), *Handbook of special education: Research and practice: Vol. 3. Low incidence conditions* (pp. 1–2). Oxford, England: Pergamon Press.

Education of Visually Handicapped Children and Youth

GERALDINE T. SCHOLL

University of Michigan

Over the years reviews of research related to the education of visually handicapped children and youth have appeared in the literature. Common threads run through these reviews: research was characterized as limited (Ashcroft, 1959; Meyerson, 1953), fragmented (Nolan, 1963, 1969), in need of an integrated and cooperative research effort (Ingram, 1941; Nolan, 1963, 1969; Tisdall, 1968; Umsted, 1975), lacking in longitudinal studies (Graham, 1960; Meyerson, 1953; Umsted, 1975), and in need of an interdisciplinary approach (Nolan, 1969; Umsted, 1975). The low prevalence and heterogeneity of the population were frequently cited as sources of difficulty in conducting research on this population and reasons for the disappointing quality of the research.

Current research in this field continues to be limited both in quantity and quality. Visually handicapped and deaf-blind children and youth are low prevalence groups, the two lowest in number among those being served under PL 94–142 and PL 89–313 (DE-OSERS-SEP, 1984). The diverse characteristics and widely scattered geographical distribution of these low prevalence populations, coupled with the small number of personnel needed to serve them, complicate the preparation of personnel, all aspects of educational programming, including curriculum development, and the conduct of research.

The difficulty of conducting research discourages many from studying this population. Further, the small number of professional personnel in the field results in fewer people who are interested in and qualified to conduct research. As a result, there is a sense of isolation among these professionals and limited communication with those outside this special area. Evidence of this isolation is found in the small number of articles related

161

to visually handicapped children and youth in special education journals which cover all areas of handicap.

Areas of needed research have consistently been identified in reviews over the years. For purposes of this chapter, five areas were selected: the demographic characteristics of the visually handicapped population; their developmental characteristics; the high prevalence of multiple handicaps among the population; their assessment needs; and the current status of computer technology that could facilitate the education and ultimate adult adjustment of persons who are visually handicapped. It is important to determine what is known, what needs to be known, and what could be accomplished with a coordinated and concerted program of research in each of these areas. Such a synthesis and integration is basic to the development of an agenda for future research, and ultimately to the improvement of educational practices. In the sections that follow, current issues are identified for each of the five areas and recommendations presented for future research.

National Estimates of Prevalence and Demographics of Children with Visual Impairments

The category of visual impairments shares with other categories of exceptionality many problems concerning prevalence and demographics. This topic is discussed in the following section according to findings by Kirchner (1989). First, there is little consistency in descriptions of vision problems and their importance for educational planning in terms of variation or severity—for example, pathology (the active stage of disease or trauma), impairment (residual defects in an organ or body part after the active stage of pathology), disability (limitations in functioning in relation to specific tasks), and handicap (limitations in performance of major social roles). Each of these four concepts must be considered to describe variations among children and to suggest appropriate educational programs for individuals.

Second, as with other categories of exceptionality, there is the problem of definition. For many years, the field of visual impairment was tied to the legal definition of blindness, which has two weaknesses: it is not useful for identifying educational needs, and it does not account for how an individual uses vision, namely, functional vision. States vary in their eligibility requirements for programs and services designed for this group, some using a legal definition, others a visual acuity cut-off, and still others a functional definition. Thus, a child may be eligible for services in one state but not in another.

Third, there is little consistency in the terminology used to label this population in the literature or in practice: blind, visually handicapped, visually impaired, visually limited, low vision, and so on. Each state, program, educator, or researcher uses one or more of these terms with slight variations in meaning.

Finally, the issue of definition is further complicated by the low prevalence of visual impairments and the ease with which children with severe visual impairments can be overlooked, together with the high prevalence of other disabilities within this population where the visual impairment may not be the primary educationally handicapping condition.

Coupled with the absence of an accepted definition is the lack of an accurate determination of numbers, because statistical sources of data use different definitions. There are several sources for data, such as the Health Examination Survey and Health Interview Survey of the National Center for Health Statistics; the U.S. Bureau of the Census; the U.S. Social Security Administration; the U.S. Office of Special Education; the American Printing House for the Blind; and the Model Reporting Area; but each has limitations for educational purposes. The lack of an accurate database complicates effective long-range planning by local school districts charged with educating individual students, by colleges/universities for preparing an adequate number of personnel, and by state leaders for meeting personnel training needs.

Finally, there is an absence of data on characteristics of the visually impaired population. Little is known about variables that have relevance for educational programming, such as causes of the impairment, degree of vision, and age and type of onset. There is a severe lack of information about other educationally relevant characteristics, such as racial and ethnic composition, socioeconomic status, geographical distribution, and prevalence of other exceptionalities. This lack of information leaves gaps in knowledge about how this population should be described and what educational plans should be designed and implemented to serve students more efficiently.

Over the years there have been recommendations to remedy some of the deficiencies described above. For example, the 1930 White House Conference on Child Health and Protection stated, "Since there is so much uncertainty as to the number of blind children who are now without educational advantages to which they are entitled, it is suggested that a census of the blind (be) sponsored by the Federal Census Bureau. . . ." (WHCCHAP, 1931, p. 271). Relative to this continuing need, broad recommendations can be made (Kirchner, 1989):

1. Federal agencies currently collecting data on children with visual impairments need to engage in collaborative planning through the Sub-Committee on Vision within the Federal Interagency Committee on Handicapped Research.

2. Methodological studies should be undertaken to improve the measurement of concepts of visual impairment, disability, and handicap; to seek innovative methods of sampling low-prevalence populations; and to explore alternatives to gathering data from interview surveys.

3. In order to conduct a postcensus disabilities survey, more questions aimed at a broader range of handicapped people need to be included in the decennial census.

Implications of Visual Impairments for Child Development

A critical area in need of research-based knowledge is the developmental characteristics of visually handicapped children and youth. Warren (1989) presents relevant information on this topic. Many questions remain unanswered about how these children and youth are similar to and different from their nonvisually handicapped peers. An assumption is usually made that they are more alike than different, and educators typically advise parents and teachers in mainstreamed programs to treat the visually handicapped child like any other child. Whether this is appropriate advice is not known. Warren's (1984) extensive review of the current state of knowledge concerning the growth and development of young visually handicapped children furnished the base for this subsequent overview (Warren, 1989).

There is sufficient research data to support the notion that the sensory capabilities (other than vision) of the child with a visual impairment are not more keen than those of the sighted; however, attentive capabilities may be developed to a greater degree. In some areas, such as sound localization and tactual form perception, differences in favor of the visually handicapped population have been noted, with later blinded children showing superior performance to those impaired earlier in life. While lags in motor performance have been noted, particularly in young blind children, programs of early intervention directed toward encouraging movement activities can reduce these lags. Early training programs and increased use of residual vision have shown improvements in posture and mobility. The establishment of strong, early, social interpersonal ties and the development of self-confidence seem to be critically important in developing mobility skills.

Because vision is such an important source of information about the world and provides the mechanism for effective integration of information from other sensory modalities, absence of vision may contribute to lags in cognitive development. Training programs have been successful in reducing the lags noted in certain aspects of cognitive development, but further research is needed to find efficient ways of helping visually handicapped children reach their maximum. An enriched experiential background contributes not only to the cognitive development but also the language development of the visually handicapped child.

Also, when compared with their normal peers, social developmental lags have been noted in visually handicapped children. However, any residual vision, as well as loss of vision later in life, seems to contribute to reducing the impact of the lags. In addition, the environment and the emotional adjustment of the parents appear to be critical to the child's social development.

There are several recommendations that evolve from a review of developmental issues (Warren, 1989):

1. There is a need for longitudinal research. Most of the available studies are cross-sectional and cannot take into account experiential factors over a long period of time.
2. Studies should be directed toward the variations relative to vision loss, such as age of onset, degree of residual vision, and the impact of other impairments on development.
3. It appears that the environment, which provides the experiential background for the child, is an important factor in growth and development. Studies are needed to determine how the environment can be structured in order to optimize development in all areas.
4. Adequate funding and cooperative efforts among the limited number of researchers in this field should be encouraged in order to have a more integrated research program.

Research Issues in Educating Visually Handicapped Persons with Multiple Impairments

Visually handicapped persons share with the general population a similar prevalence of various exceptionalities: giftedness, all ranges of mental retardation, emotional disturbances, learning disabilities, physical disabilities, speech and language problems, and other deviations. The focus here is on those visually handicapped children and youth with severe multiple impairments, as discussed by Hammer (1989).

Many handicapped children with multiple impairments were born prematurely and are alive today as a result of recent advances in neonatal care and treatment. The range of problems in this population is extensive; they present so many variations in levels of function and behavior that it is not possible to place them in a single category. To meet the educational needs of this group effectively, there must be a count of their numbers, a description of their characteristics, and a determination of the most effective educational placements for them. Many children with visual impairments are found in other programs, particularly those for students with severe mental retardation. Placement of visually handicapped students in these settings frequently is based on the mistaken assumption that mental retardation is their primary disability. The role of vision in limiting a child's experience and thus retarding learning is not recognized by many educators.

An adequate count and description of visually handicapped/multiply handicapped students requires that a multiaxial diagnostic system be developed that can provide standard diagnostic, clinical, and research data on this diverse population. The American Psychiatric Association's *Diagnostic and Statistical Manual of Mental Disorders (DSM-III)*, although it has some flaws, might provide a model for this purpose.

Personnel must be prepared to meet the complex education and training needs of this diverse group. Of critical importance in preparation programs is training in how to be effective advocates for these pupils. To prepare such personnel may require modifications in current teacher preparation programs, as well as attitudinal changes among administrators about the role and responsibilities of teachers needed for this group. Finally, all professionals concerned with the welfare of visually impaired children must recognize the role of vision in learning and the impact visual loss has on programming for their education.

Another critical need for the visually handicapped/multiply handicapped population is assessment procedures that can be used to place them in an appropriate educational setting and to plan and implement an individualized education program that will maximize their abilities. Most currently used instruments tend to highlight the disability rather than identify abilities. Personnel concerned with these pupils must have information about abilities from the assessment in order to build on what the child can do rather than what he or she cannot do. While there are several instruments available for use with multiply handicapped pupils, some do not adequately take into account the role of vision loss in the development process. Psychologists, therefore, must frequently modify content and procedures in order to assess the abilities of a particular child. Following an assessment, the broad range of services needed for the education of each child must be determined and obtained.

Based on the information in this section, the following recommendations are suggested (Hammer, 1989):

1. Case findings must be undertaken to identify students in other programs, particularly the multiply handicapped, who may have vision losses that are interfering with their appropriate education.
2. Personnel preparation programs must be designed to address the needs of visually handicapped/multiply handicapped pupils. Meeting state certification requirements does not guarantee appropriate preparation for teachers of this group.

3. Researchers skilled in statistics and research design for studies of small N groups must be recruited to study the diverse needs of the visually handicapped/multiply handicapped population.

Assessment of Blind and Visually Handicapped Children and Youth

Issues in the assessment of blind and visually handicapped children and youth are related to the preceding sections on development and the visually handicapped/multiply handicapped population, and they are elaborated upon here according to Scholl and Theodorou (1989). Appropriate assessment precedures cannot be identified without the knowledge base from these two areas. To determine the best setting for the individual child and to plan an appropriate individualized educational program, an assessment must include a broad range of developmental variables, including cognitive (language, mental, and achievement); psychomotor (including mobility); affective (social, emotional, and self-concept); and visual (case history, medical, and functional).

The use of standardized instruments to assess educational need for handicapped groups is increasingly questioned in the literature, particularly in light of the differences in their development and experiential backgrounds when compared with nonhandicapped children. The gaps in knowledge about the patterns of growth and development of visually handicapped children (discussed in a preceding section) call into question the use of standardized instruments with this populaton. PL 94–142 requires that students be assessed on instruments that have been validated for the specific purpose for which they are used and that instruments be standardized on a population having the same characteristics as the pupils being assessed. However, this is not reasonable when applied to the visually handicapped population for several reasons: (a) there are relatively few instruments designed specifically for and standardized on this population, (b) the application of results from other tests using norms derived from the nonhandicapped population is questionable, (c) modification in administration and scoring because of visual impairment invalidates the test results when using regular norms, and (d) few psychologists are sufficiently familiar with developmental characteristics and the impact of vision loss on learning to arrive at an accurate interpretation of test results when regular standardized instruments are employed. These issues are even more critical when such instruments are used for special groups (e.g., multiply handicapped children and infants).

In light of the above problems, there is a trend toward the use of informal, nontest approaches to assessment, particularly with visually handicapped and visually handicapped/multiply handicapped students. Basic to the use of such techniques is the identification of specific questions or problem areas that require assessment. A clear definition of the reason for assessment by parent and/or teacher will then help determine the kind of tool or procedure that will answer the questions. Techniques for such assessments include observation in all the settings where the child functions; interviews with parents, teachers, the child, and other relevant adults in the child's life; checklists of behavioral functioning and characteristics; and trial teaching to determine useful teaching and learning approaches. While such measures do not yield quantitative data, the qualitative data they provide are useful for educational programming.

The following recommendations are relevant in light of the above (Scholl & Theodorou, 1989):

1. People who have contact with visually handicapped students in any aspect of the assessment process should receive sufficient preservice and/or inservice instruction to help them function more effectively with this population. Such people include school psychologists, regular and special education teachers (including teachers of the visually handicapped), parents, administrators, and other support personnel.

2. A national research plan should be developed to seek answers to the questions, problems, and issues regarding assessment. Such a plan should include the collection and dissemination of longitudinal data.

3. To increase communication within and outside the field, personnel involved in research, education, and training of visually handicapped children and youth should disseminate their findings and experiences to personnel outside of their field (e.g., other special educators, regular educators, and members of other disciplines).

Implications of the Research and Development of Modern Technology on the Education of Blind and Visually Handicapped Students

Recent advances in technology have changed the lives of all people, including those who are handicapped. In some areas, modern technology is enhancing the educational and employment opportunities for visually handicapped individuals. The following section reviews this particular topic as discussed by Scadden (1989).

The two areas of daily life that are most adversely affected by limited vision, independent travel and access to the printed word, are being improved by some of the current advances in technology. However, in order to insure that the visually handicapped population will not be left behind in future technological advances, all currently available and future technology must be made accessible to them. Barriers to full utilization of technology include the high cost of adapting available technology for use by a low-prevalence population, inadequacy of objective evaluative data concerning new technology, and lack of available instruction and training programs for personnel involved in the education and training of visually handicapped individuals.

Developments in electronic sensory aids have the potential to provide information about the environment to blind and visually impaired persons. However, the current travel aids present some difficulties in being put to use by blind persons. Cost is a significant factor, but the current state of the art is another. Many of these aids provide minimal additional environmental information, normal environmental sounds tend to be masked during their use, and cosmetically they are not desirable. Numerous developments improve activities of daily living, such as thermometers, pressure gauges, calculators, scales, and other tools that can supply data through spoken output.

Technology related to computer access has made significant advances through the development of voice, large print, and braille output. In addition, the Optacon, paperless braille, and electronic braille provide greater independent access to the printed word than previously. An increasing number of regular school programs include the computer as a teaching and learning tool. Specialized output adaptations for computers used in regular classrooms must be made available to visually handicapped students if they are to have equal opportunities for education. Similarly, adaptations to computer technology in the workplace are available, and they can increase the employment opportunities for blind and visually handicapped persons if needed modifications are provided and if personnel are trained to help the visually handicapped person make use of the technology.

In order to provide equal access to technology in both school and work, the following recommendations are offered (Scadden, 1989):

1. Future technological research and development must consider the needs of the visually handicapped population and provide adaptations that will give them equal access. In addition, a system for evaluation of both hardware and software for use by visually handicapped individuals should be developed.
2. Educators and rehabilitation counselors should explore new technology to determine how educational programs and work opportunities can be developed from its use.
3. Preparation programs for all personnel working with visually handicapped students should include information about technology, and, in particular, provide information on ways to keep abreast of new developments.

References

American Psychiatric Association (1980). *Diagnostic and Statistical Manual of Mental Disorders: DSM-III* (3rd ed.). Washington, DC: Author.

Ashcroft, S. C. (1959). The blind and partially seeing. *Review of Educational Research*, **29**(5), 519–28.

Department of Education, Office of Special Education and Rehabilitative Services, Special Education Programs. (1984). *Sixth annual report to Congress on the implementation of Public Law 94–142: The Education for All Handicapped Children Act*. Washington, DC: Author.

Graham, M. D. (1960). *Social research on blindness: Present status and future potentials*. New York: American Foundation for the Blind.

Hammer, E. K. (1989). Research issues in educating visually handicapped persons with multiple impairments. In M. C. Wang, M. C. Reynolds, & H. J. Walberg (Eds.), *Handbook of special education: Research and practice: Vol. 3. Low incidence conditions* (pp. 173–188). Oxford, England: Pergamon Press.

Ingram, C. P. (1941). The visually handicapped, the delicate, and the crippled. *Review of Educational Research*, **11**(3), 315–29.

Kirchner, C. (1989). National estimates of prevalence and demographics of children with severe visual loss. In M. C. Wang, M. C. Reynolds, & H. J. Walberg (Eds.), *Handbook of special education: Research and practice: Vol. 3. Low incidence conditions* (pp. 135–153). Oxford, England: Pergamon Press.

Meyerson, L. (1953). The visually handicapped. *Review of Educational Research*, **23**(5), 476–91.

Nolan, C. Y. (1963). The visually impaired. In S. A. Kirk, & B. B. Weiner (Eds,), *Behavioral research on exceptional children* (pp. 115–154). Washington, DC: Council for Exceptional Children.

Nolan, C. Y. (1969). Research in education of the blind. In M. H. Goldbery, & J. R. Swinton (Eds.), *Blindness research: The expanding frontiers* (pp. 240–9). University Park, PA: Pennsylvania State University.

Scadden, L. A. (1989). Implications of the research and development of modern technology on the education of blind and visually handicapped students. In M. C. Wang, M. C. Reynolds, & H. J. Walberg (Eds.), *Handbook of special education: Research and practice: Vol. 3. Low incidence conditions* (pp. 203–220). Oxford, England: Pergamon Press.

Scholl, G. T., & Theodorou, E. (1989). Assessment of blind and visually handicapped children and youth. In M. C. Wang, M. C. Reynolds, & H. J. Walberg (Eds.), *Handbook of special education: Research and practice: Vol. 3. Low incidence conditions* (pp. 189–202). Oxford, England: Pergamon Press.

Tisdall, W. J. (1968). The visually impaired. In G. O. Johnson & H. D. Blank (Eds.), *Exceptional children research review* (pp. 110–134). Washington, DC: Council for Exceptional Children.

Umsted, R. C. (1975). Children with visual handicaps. In J. J. Gallagher (Ed.), *The application of child development research to exceptional children* (pp. 333–45). Reston, VA: Council for Exceptional Children.

Warren, D. H. (1984). *Blindness and early childhood development* (2nd ed.). New York: American Foundation for the Blind.

Warren, D. H. (1989). Implications of visual impairments for child development. In M. C. Wang, M. C. Reynolds, & H. J. Walberg (Eds.), *Handbook of special education: Research and practice: Vol. 3. Low incidence conditions* (pp. 155–172). Oxford, England: Pergamon Press.

White House Conference on Child Health and Protection. (1931). The blind and partially seeing. In C. S. Berry (Chairman), *Report of the Committee on Special Classes*. (Special education: The handicapped and the gifted, pp. 113–274). New York: The Century Co.

Handicapped Infants

VERNA HART

University of Pittsburgh

Research with handicapped infants is itself in its infancy. There is a lack of well-controlled studies of identified handicapped infants and a sparsity of well-designed, consistent intervention programs. Furthermore, little discrepancy exists between the state of the art and the state of practice when discussing many aspects of educating handicapped infants.

Although studies have been carried out with small samples of handicapped infants, there has not been a systematic approach with identification, referral, service, and evaluation of intervention with the very young handicapped population. Various factors have contributed to this limitation. There is difficulty in identifying early those infants in need of special services; the majority of infants who are in need of intervention are not visibly identified during the initial hospital stay. There is also a lack of well-defined predictors to determine which at-risk children will need special education and which will demonstrate plasticity of the brain, maturation, or other growth factors and not require early intervention. Even if children are identified as needing special help, assessing them is difficult because of a lack of comprehensive assessment instruments that have been standardized on handicapped infants. Not only does a need for such instrumentation exist, but there also is a need for more basic research as a means for developing such assessment tools. These might help in determining whether the developmental sequence for infants with varying types of handicapping conditions is specific to each designated handicapping condition.

Another factor has been the absence, in most states, of legislation enabling individual school districts to use their educational funds for young handicapped children. Without a mandate to serve them and a lack of funds if there were such a desire, most early intervention has been left to a hit-and-miss approach carried out by a myriad of professionals (i.e., medical doctors, public health nurses, physical and occupational therapists, nurse practitioners, educators, child development specialists, developmental psychologists, and others). The programs usually have been small and often implemented independently according to the specific interests of interveners and without well-conceived cooperation and coordination with other agencies. Public Law 99–457, passed by the U.S. Congress in 1986, requires special education for handicapped children aged three to five (by the 1990–91 school year), and it has created incentives for special programs down to infancy. Prior to the passage of this law, most states, although they have spent many public dollars on children who later were diagnosed as handicapped, have had no systematic state-wide procedure for early identification, referral, and intervention.

Although both public and private providers have been involved for a number of years in work with handicapped infants, (e.g., those serving young cerebral palsied and Down's syndrome children), the research basis for the service delivery models and techniques as well for intervention for such infants is extremely limited. Personnel beginning new programs have few resources for data-based information in designing them. There is a lack of well-designed data-based information regarding intervention with specific types of handicaps. Most programs take information that has been researched with normal babies or with a specific type of handicap and use it for all of the children they serve.

An additional problem has been the lack of agreement among professionals as to the children who should be served and the most appropriate time to enroll them. Some think that all children who are at risk for any type of developmental delay, no matter what the cause, should be served, while others believe that only those who already evidence a delay should be enrolled in a program. The lack of financial resources has prevented full-scale investigations of which medical and at-risk factors will eventually lead to handicapping conditions. Lack of agreement regarding the children to be helped has usually resulted in their being served according to the interests of the investigators: Physicians have frequently followed only those children who have shown some type of medical problem, while educators and psychologists have studied those who demonstrate various types of developmental delays. Thus, services have tended to be fragmented according to the interests of the investigators. They have not fully addressed the factors that prevent children from developing to their maximum, nor have they addressed the most effective way to ameliorate these factors.

There is also a lack of agreement as to the preparation of personnel for serving handicapped infants. In many programs this problem has meant hiring someone with interest but without formal training and previous experience in this type of work. There has been no systematic study of the type of personnel most appropriate for this task or for the training needed.

All of the above factors are considered in this chapter. The most critical areas identified include issues dealing with early identification and referral of handicapped infants, problems with their assessment, the efficacy of early intervention, parental interaction and work with families, and personnel preparation.

Identification and Referral of Handicapped Infants

Scott and Carran (1989) reported on the state of the art in identification and referral of both handicapped and at-risk infants. They urged an interdisciplinary effort by medical and behavioral professionals to develop effective and predictive infant screening devices, to create and implement effective risk registers, and to produce a comprehensive computer tracking system to follow the infants.

Identification and referral mechanisms for handicapped infants have changed over the past decade because of a change in that population. While obvious handicapping conditions caused by genetic, familial, or physical etiologies are still being identified and the babies referred for evaluation, there is now interest in the cause of milder handicapping conditions that might not be apparent at birth.

Premature infants of lower and lower birth weights are surviving. Although statistics vary from setting to setting and often reflect the availability of technology and sophistication of staff in neonatology, 85% of infants weighing between 1,000 and 1,500 grams (2.2 and 3.3 pounds) now survive. The survival rate of those weighing less than 1,000 grams has doubled during the last decade and is now about 40% (Ross, 1983). However, many of the children who survive their premature births will have handicapping conditions.

Low birth weight children, those who weigh below 2,500 grams (5.5 pounds), comprise 90% of the neonatal intensive care unit (NICU) population. Nearly 250,000 such children are born each year in the United States. However, when considering the total numbers of infants born, those below 2,500 grams comprise only 6% of the total births (National Center for Health Statistics, 1984). Of the 94% of the babies delivered who go through the normal newborn nursery, Smith and Simons (1975) suggested that approximately 0.1% will have developmental problems detected before the age of one year. However, the low birth weight group has a larger percentage of children who present handicapped conditions.

Data from the Collaborative Perinatal Study and others suggested that low birth weight (LBW) children (weighing from 1,500 to 2,500 grams) have a two-and-one-half times greater chance of needing special education services than the normal birth weight group (Broman, Nichols, and Kennedy, 1975; Wiener, 1968). Although the majority of the LBW infants develop normally (Cohen, Sigman, Parmalee, and Beckwith, 1982; Yu, Orgill, Bajuk, and Astbury, 1984), many investigations have shown high prevalence of later neurological, intellectual, or behavioral problems in them (Arias and Tomich, 1982; Drillien, Thompson, and Burgoyne, 1980; Fitzhardinge and Steven, 1972; Lubchenco, Delivoria-Papadopoulos & Searls, 1972; Lubchenco *et al.* 1963). The very low birth weight (VLBW) infants, those weighing less than 1,500 grams (3.3 pounds), have as great or even greater incidence of disabilities. Because the numbers of VLBW infants who have survived have been followed longitudinally only long enough to reach school age (not enough to obtain a long-term incidence figure), the percentage showing handicaps is not known, although shorter-term figures report a range from 7% to as high as 30%, with a 20% average for those weighing less than 1,000 grams (Horwood, Boyle, Torrance, and Sinclair, 1982; Scott & Masi, 1979; Siegel, *et al.* 1982). Thus, infants are surviving, but not without a cost to the immature organism.

If one considers the above information, it becomes apparent that identification is a major problem. There are no well-identified predictors to determine which of the children who go through the normal nursery will need early intervention. Scott and Masi (1979) reported 13% of the children as handicapped enough to be referred for special educational services at some time during their school years. Although the incidence of handicapping conditions is smaller in this group (normal births), there are nine times the number of children who go through the normal nursery as compared to the NICU. The majority of handicapped children come from this group of supposedly normal birth children. An early means to find these minimally handicapped children who are not identified in their initial hospital stay and to intervene with them is necessary. Currently, there are no means to identify the psycho-educational problems in the nursery. Many normal birth infants will develop problems later due to experiential factors. It is necessary to find a way to indentify these factors as well. Because we lack resources to serve all of the children who have been treated in an NICU or who graduate from a normal nursery but come from high-risk homes, better follow-up methods must be developed and predictors must be verified.

Scott and Carran based their proposal to identify and refer handicapped infants on five theoretical perspectives: (a) the problems are more easily remediated early in their course before they are well-established, (b) early development is often critically important, (c) intervention can modify development, (d) failure to identify problems early results in an accumulated developmental lag, and (e) increased survival rates lead to a greater number of infants who are at risk for handicapping conditions.

Using these perspectives, they advocated an epidemiological framework in which a multiple risk factor model would be developed. A risk register would record congenital or family history information, events that might produce a handicapping condition, and any psychosocial problems. It would be valuable as an indicator for determining which infants and children need longitudinal follow-up and periodic developmental evaluation.

A comprehensive computerized tracking system would be developed with both medical and educational factors considered. Both endogenous and exogenous factors would be included, with varying degrees of prevention sought; and screening services would be comprehensive in nature.

To carry this out, it would be necessary both to identify and quantify risk factors. Such identification and quantification would allow primary prevention by minimizing risks; secondary prevention by reducing, eliminating, or curing the identified risk factors; or tertiary prevention by bringing the handicapped children to their maximum potential.

To implement their plan, the authors make the following recommendations: (a) personnel should be trained to see that early child health and special education cannot be separated; (b) parents and professionals should join forces; (c) professionals should recognize that multiple risks are involved in the etiology of early childhood handicaps; and (d) major research efforts are needed on the efficacy of computerized tracking of infants at risk in order to look at patterns of predictors for handicapped infants as well as those at risk, and to carry out longitudinal studies to look at multiple causes or risks and how they combine to form handicapping conditions.

Infant Assessment

Once the children are identified, they must be assessed to ascertain their intervention needs. Infant assessment is not new; many tests currently in use have been used for years. New instruments continue to be developed because of dissatisfaction with the old. However, some of the same criticisms can be leveled against the new as with the old.

In their review of infant assessment, Sheehan and Klein (1989), stated these purposes for assessment: (a) to describe patterns of infant development and behavior; (b) to screen children and to identify those in need of further, extensive assessment; (c) to aid in decisions about referral for further treatment; (d) to predict the future developmental status of individuals; (e) to aid in theory development and validation regarding infant development; (f) to facilitate instructional planning and to set short- and long-term goals for interventions; (g) to facilitate evaluation of infant progress; and (h) to capture salient features of the environment without culturally negative influences.

Sheehan and Klein estimated that 300 infant assessment tools are available across the country with variable, if not suspect, psychometric quality and validity. The authors noted that two major weaknesses exist with our current devices and the ways they are used: Results obtained by testing infants' development have limited generalizability and such poor predictive validity that they rarely account for greater than 10% of the variation that is seen in later childhood performance (although the relationship is greater with those children who are severely impaired from birth); and most infant assessment tools fail to provide clear guidance as to the most efficacious intervention for the children involved.

Sheehan and Klein noted that three of the most used infant tests—the Bayley Scales, the Gesell Schedules, and Cattell—have the same bulk of items but with changes in arrangement, and they are theoretically based on a maturationist theory which runs counter to the present goals of early intervention. Several factors have promoted their continued use: (a) they present a common language of communication among professionals regarding infant performance and development, (b) they meet the need for standardized measures in establishing psychoeducational intervention programs, (c) they meet the criteria from funding sources for accountability as documented by standardized measurements, and (d) they are readily available.

Throughout their work Sheehan and Klein have pointed out the importance of studying interaction patterns when working with handicapped infants. They discussed the mother–child interaction as a basis for identification, program planning, and program evaluation. A high degree of sensitivity is needed to assess this accurately, and evaluators need to be sensitive to cultural differences and their implications.

Efficacy of Early Intervention

Many studies have been conducted to determine the value of early interventions. Depending on the variables chosen for scrutiny, the results have varied. Dunst, Snyder, and Mankinen (1989) addressed this problem and concluded that the conflicting results are obtained by focusing on an ecologically restricted view of the goals and purposes of early intervention, mainly child progress. Instead, they advocated a very broad perspective of the purposes of early intervention, including direct and indirect impact not only upon the child but upon the parents and family.

With this perspective in mind and in order to rule out competing explanations for observed effects, Dunst *et al.* (1989) set forth a theoretical framework for studying the effects of early intervention and then scrutinized 105 studies from that perspective. The children in the studies were divided into four nonmutually exclusive groups: (a) those at risk due to environmental factors, such as poor conditions of rearing and low socioeconomic status (SES); (b) those at risk because of biological factors, such as cerebral palsy, sensory impairments, spina bifida, genetic disorders, and brain damage; (c) those at risk due to medically related factors, such as prematurity and low birth weight; and (d) those at risk due to family or systemic factors, such as teenage mothers, retarded parents, and parental alcohol and drug abuse.

They noted that interventions with these groups have varied in focus: supplemental enrichment for the conditions of rearing; enhancement of a wide array of developmental and behavioral competencies for the biologically impaired; supplemental sensory stimulation to facilitate responses to animate and inanimate environments in the medically related group; and interventions oriented to parent and family functioning in the group with nonoptimal parenting skills. They also categorized the types of intervention into four groups: (a) cognitive, (b) behavioral, (c) sensory stimulation, and (d) medical, physical, or occupational therapy. Most of the interventions reported within the studies were combinations of these types.

Dunst *et al.* proposed the following paradigm for discerning the effects of intervention: $B=f(I,S,F,C,O,X)$. In this paradigm, the dependent or outcome variable (B) changes as a function (f) of the intervention which includes variables of I (early intervention characteristics, such as age of entry, intensity of involvement, degree of parent involvement, etc.); S (social support characteristics, such as size of network, degree of helpfulness, reciprocity, etc.); F (family characteristics, of SES, age, parental attitudes, etc.); C (child characteristics, such as age, level of retardation, temperament, etc.); O (other explanatory variables, such as policy decisions, competency level of the intervener, etc.); and X (the set of competing characteristics that pose threats to internal validity). Manipulation of the variables on the right side of the equation should affect the level, magnitude, value, etc., of B. The authors proposed that efficacy should be considered along a continuum and not treated as an either-or notion.

In their critique of efficacy studies in early intervention, the major criterion for inclusion was that interventions began between birth and three years of age for the majority of children in the programs. Dunst *et al.* then classified the studies into one of three categories of causal inference: low, low to moderate, and moderate to high. These categories are based on the degree of specificity of early intervention-related variables (age of entry, length of involvement, degree or type of parental involvement, theoretical bases, etc.); assessment of impact of other forms of support (extent to which other types of formal and informal "interventions" are assessed in terms of their contributions to changes in the dependent measures); adequacy of control of family and child characteristics (adequate descriptive information) and the inclusion of tests of conditional relationships (between child, family, and intervention-related variables); control and assessment of threats to internal validity (degree to which competing explanations might account for changes in the dependent measure); the ecological relevance of the dependent measures; and the degree of dependence between the independent and dependent variables. Two of the authors rated all 105 studies, with interrater agreement on the above six factors of 89%, 96%, 90%, 96%, 95%, and 89%.

The three causal inference categories were further separated into 14 groups, and the studies were roughly ordered on a continuum from low to high causal inference. A brief description of the analyses used to assign them to the separate groups and causal categories follows.

Low Causal

Group 1. These studies rated the lowest on the six study dimensions espoused by the authors. They all used pre-experimental pretest-posttest designs. While a number of the studies included only biologically at-risk children (Bagnato & Neisworth, 1980; Ford, 1978; Jelinek & Flamboe, 1979; Rottman, 1979; Safford, Gregg, Schneider, & Sewell, 1976; Wiedar & Hicks, 1970; Wolery & Dyk, 1985; Zeitlin, 1981), several others included both biologically and environmentally at-risk children (Huntinger, 1978; Kaplan & Atkins, 1978; Shearer & Shearer, 1972); and one study included biologically, environmentally, and medically at-risk children (Nielsen, Collings, Meisel, Lowry, Engh, & Johnson, 1975). The major conclusion was that the children in these programs generally showed statistically significant developmental progress, but the relationships between specific aspects of the early intervention and the observed changes were not directly discernable.

Group 2. These studies used pre-experimental nonequivalent groups posttest-only designs. Comparison groups (not established by random procedures) were used in some observations. Four of the studies (Hanson & Schwartz, 1978; Hayden & Dmitriev, 1975; Hayden & Haring, 1977; Zausmer, Pueschel, & Shea 1972) included Down's syndrome children, while subjects in the fifth one (Adelson & Fraiberg, 1974) were visually impaired. The major conclusion was that participants generally demonstrated rates and patterns of development that showed some advantage over nonparticipants (comparison groups), but the factors related to group differences were not directly discernable.

Group 3. Several attempts were made in this group of studies to assess the manner in which outcomes differed as a function of other variables, thus increasing the types of causal inferences that could be made. Pre-experimental pretest-posttest designs were used. Down's Syndrome infants were included in two of the studies (Clunies-Ross, 1979; Mahoney & Snow, 1983), biologically and medically at-risk infants in a third study (Bagnato & Neisworth, 1985), and both biologically and environmentally at-risk infants in the remaining studies (Bailey & Bricker, 1985; Barna, Bidder, Gray, Clements, & Gardner, 1980; Bricker & Sheehan, 1981; Goodman, Cecil, & Barker, 1984; Gordon, 1977; Hewitt, Newcombe & Bidder, 1983; Macy, Solomon, Schoen, & Galey, 1983; Shapiro, Gordon, & Neiditch, 1977). The conclusions reached were that the children receiving special interventions generally showed statistically significant developmental progress, and that progress can be expected to vary as a function of diagnosis and degree of severity, but the extent to which specific factors were associated with the observed changes was not directly discernable.

Low to Moderate Causal

Group 4. Studies in the low to moderate causal inference category generally permitted stronger statements to be made about cause-effect relationships. These studies examined some of the factors related to significant changes in child functioning. The studies included children biologically at risk (Bricker & Dow, 1980; Simeonsson & Huntington, 1981), children environmentally at risk (Murray, 1977), and children both biologically and environmentally at risk (Brassell, 1974, 1977). The major conclusion was that the amount of progress shown by the participants was affected by their age at the time of intervention, length of involvement, and factors of nonintervention child and family characteristics, thus suggesting that degree of efficacy was differentially influenced by a number of variables.

Group 5. The studies in this group used quasi-experimental nonequivalent control group designs wherein pretest similarities in the experimental and control groups were explicitly tested or differences between the groups were statistically controlled. Treatment groups and control groups were compared to establish the effects of interventions. The studies included Down's syndrome infants (Brinkworth, 1973, 1975; Connolly & Russell, 1976; Cunningham, Aumonier, & Sloper, 1982; Ludlow & Allen, 1979; Piper & Pless, 1980), biologically at-risk autistic children (Lovaas, 1982), heterogeneously formed groups of biologically and environmentally at-risk children (Brassell & Dunst, 1978; Dunst, Vance, & Gallagher, 1983; Peniston, 1972), and medically at-risk infants

(Leib, Benfield, & Guidubaldi, 1980). The major conclusion was that the children in experimental groups demonstrated greater progress than those in control groups, but the exact nature of the causal factors was not directly discernable.

Group 6. Each of the studies in this group used matched group designs, with subjects in the experimental and control groups equated on family and/or child characteristics prior to the treatment. Subjects included biologically at-risk infants (Aronson & Fallstrom, 1977; Bidder, Bryant, & Gray, 1975; Carlsen, 1975; Chee, Kreutzberg, & Clark, 1978; Harris, 1981; Ottenbacher, Short, & Watson, 1981; Sandow & Clarke, 1978; Sandow, Clarke, Cox, & Stewart, 1981; Sellick & Over, 1980) and medically at-risk infants (Bromwich & Parmelee, 1979). The authors concluded that the amount of progress made by the experimental subjects was greater than that for the control subjects but only in instances where the treatment was broad-based and comprehensive in nature.

Group 7. All studies in this group used true experimental designs with biologically impaired preschoolers randomly assigned to treatment and control conditions. Subjects included children with Down's syndrome (Kantner, Clark, Allen & Chase, 1976), children with cerebral palsy (Scherzer, Mike, & Ilson, 1976; Wright & Nicholson, 1973), and children with nonspecified handicapping conditions (Kelly, 1982; Sandler, Coren, and Thurman, 1983). The major conclusion was that the experimental subjects generally showed greater improvements in their rates of development than the controls, and that the differences between groups were attributable to the interventions, although the dimension of the treatments accounting for the differences was primarily mediational rather than causal in nature.

Group 8. This group was comprised of meta-analyses of previously conducted studies. Studies included biologically, medically, and environmentally at-risk infants and employed pre-experimental, quasi-experimental, and to a small degree, true experimental designs. Ottenbacher and Peterson (1985) included 38 studies, Snyder and Sheehan (1985) 8, White (1984) and White and Casto (1985) 162, and White, Mastropieri & Casto (1985) the 21 Handicapped Children's Early Education Program projects that had been judged as exemplary. It was concluded that certain variables, such as program type, degree of structure, and intensity of treatment were important factors in the amount of progress shown by children. However, results were often confounded by design characteristics of the research.

Group 9. This group employed variations of quasi-experimental non-equivalent group designs to investigate the extent to which different conditions of rearing affect child development for environmentally at-risk infants (Hunt, 1976, 1980; Paraskevopoulos & Hunt, 1971) and biologically impaired infants (Bayley, Rhodes, Gooch & Marcus 1971; Dunst, in press; Stedman & Eichorn, 1964). The major conclusion was that conditions of rearing as well as different types of learning experiences within settings accelerated rates of sensorimotor and intellectual development, and the infants' rates of development were significantly enhanced as a function of both participation in early intervention and positive rearing conditions.

Moderate to High Causal

Group 10. Greater degrees of causal inference are possible in the final group of studies. Direct causal inferences were specific aims of the investigators of the Group X studies in their investigations of environmentally at-risk children (Eisenstadt & Powell, 1980; Gutelius & Kirsch, 1975) and environmentally and biologically at-risk children (Dunst & Leet, 1985; Maisto & German, 1979, 1981). Also of interest was the manner in which different mediating variables affected aspects of child and family functioning. The authors concluded that age of entry; social support (e.g., adequacy of family resources) and informal support; and family characteristics (e.g., locus of control, SES, education level, and commitment to the intervention and child progress) affected child, parent, and family functioning.

Group 11. This group used quasi-experimental designs wherein subjects were their own controls for establishing the efficacy of the interventions. The studies included biologically at-risk infants (Barrera *et al.*, 1976; Dunst, 1974; Horton, 1971) or biologically and environmentally at-risk children (Brassell & Dunst, 1975a, 1975b; Huntinger, 1978). The authors' major conclusion was that the amount of participant progress appeared directly related to the particular types of learning experiences provided and was significantly greater in those domains as compared with developmental changes in domains for which there were no specifically targeted interventions.

Group 12. The purpose of these studies was to determine the extent to which different types of social support affected child, parent, and family functioning in households with preschool children. Studies included medically at-risk children (Crnic, Friedrich, & Greenberg, 1983; Crnic, Greenberg, Ragosin, Robinson & Basham, 1983), biologically and environmentally at-risk children (Dunst & Trivette, 1984;

Dunst, Trivette & Cross, in press), and children with nonspecific handicapping conditions (Vadasy, Fewell, Meyer & Greenberg, 1985). The authors concluded that social support had positive mediational influences on child, parent, and family functioning beyond that attributable to other explanatory variables.

Group 13. All of these studies used single-subject research designs to determine the extent to which operant conditioning procedures were useful. Studies included biologically at-risk infants (Brinker & Lewis, 1982; Cyrulik-Jacobs, Shapira, & Jones, 1975; Dunst, Cushing & Vance, 1985; Friedlander, McCarthy & Soferenko, 1967; Glenn, 1983; Hanson, 1985; Laub & Dunst, 1974; Utley, Duncan, Strain, & Scanlon, 1983; Watson, 1972), environmentally at-risk infants (Moran & Whitman, 1985; Ramey, Hieger, & Klisz, 1972; Ramey, Starr, Pallas, Whitten, & Reed, 1976), medically at-risk infants (Solkoff & Cotton, 1975), and heterogeneously formed groups of infants (LeLaurin, 1985). The authors concluded that behavioral change was facilitated quite rapidly in instances where operant conditioning procedures were employed as a form of early intervention.

Group 14. These studies used both experimental and control groups to assess the effects of early intervention with environmentally at-risk infants and older preschoolers (Garber & Heber, 1981; Lazar & Darlington, 1982; Ramey & Haskins, 1981; Ramey, Bryant, Sparling, & Wasik, 1985) and medically and environmentally at-risk infants (Cappleman, Thompson, DeRemer-Sullivan, King, & Sturm, 1982; Field, Widmayer, Stringer, & Ignatoff, 1980). The major conclusion drawn was that participation in an early intervention program for these children produced both immediate and long-term effects which appeared directly and specifically related to the intervention. However, the exact nature of which aspects produced the effects was not always discernable.

General Conclusions

In summing up their major conclusions, Dunst *et al.* (1989) stated that the large majority of children who participate in early intervention programs make developmental progress and manifest behavior change across time, but the specific interventions responsible for the changes are difficult to ascertain; most convincing evidence regarding early intervention efficacy comes from studies of environmentally at-risk infants but there still is not enough evidence from biologically at-risk infants; cognitively and behaviorally oriented programs tend to produce the greatest effects, although those findings may be confounded by the longer intervention periods often used in such programs; variables, such as age of entry and intensity and duration of treatment, emerge as important covariates of program effectiveness; early and long-term interventions have greater effect; formal and informal support have strong mediational effects in parent and family functioning and to a lesser degree in child functioning; rates of progress differ considerably as a function of severity of impairment, with more severely impaired infants making smaller gains; entry level performance is one of the best indicators of the amount of progress a child is likely to make, with higher functioning children likely to make more progress; child progress is likely to be influenced by child characteristics, including behavioral problems, temperament, and degree of motivation; parent and family characteristics are likely to influence child progress. It is noteworthy that studies of biologically at-risk children most often have used child progress almost exclusively for documenting program effectiveness, whereas environmentally at-risk studies have used broader-based measures of child, parent, and family functioning. The authors also noted that little evidence supports therapeutic-type interventions by means of physical and occupational therapy, although this finding may be confounded with the short term of treatment in many of the relevant studies.

To ensure that practice is in keeping with the state of the art, the authors offered a series of questions, based upon research findings, to bridge the gap between program policy and program practice. Their recommendations were then to incorporate the positive answers into program plans and implementation.

1. Does the program have a philosophy about children and families that guides the development, implementation, and evaluation of program practices?
2. Does the program explicitly identify the components of its interventions and the manner in which the treatment variables are expected to "cause" changes in the outcome measure(s)?
3. Does the program view its efforts within the broader contexts of the family and community, and the manner in which child-level and family-level interventions will impact upon child, parent, family, and community functioning?
4. Does the program, and its activities, take a positive stance toward children and families and focus on building strengths rather than only correcting deficits?
5. Does the program tailor its activities to the individualized needs of family members rather than "fit" the children and their parents to predetermined activities?
6. Is the program realistic in terms of expectations for changes in child performance resulting from the interventions?

7. Does the program take these factors (diagnosis, severity of impairment, age of entry, intensity and duration of treatment) into consideration in terms of expectations established for determining program effectiveness?
8. Does the program take into consideration existing time demands on the family members before asking them to assume additional responsibilities as part of participation in the intervention program?
9. Does the program provide or facilitate adequate provisions of support in order to maintain and enhance personal and familial well-being?
10. Do the activities of the program support, empower, and strengthen families as part of their participation?
11. Does the program measure the impact of its services on the child, parents, and family in order to discern the broad-based effects of early intervention efforts? (Dunst *et al.*, 1989, pp. 287–88)

Families of Young Handicapped Children

Whether the presence of a handicapped child causes increased failed marriages is a controversial topic and one that is difficult to verify because of the methodological problems involved in studying the issue. Gallagher and Bristol (1989) reported studies in which such breakdowns appear more likely to occur in families where there are personal or financial difficulties before the birth of the child, the child is conceived premaritally, care of the child is not a shared value, or the demands of the child are greater than the resources that the family and community can accommodate.

To determine why some families succeed in coping with stress and others do not, the authors proposed a Double ABCX Model (McCubbin and Patterson, 1981; McCubbin, Sussman & Patterson, 1983). In this model, the A factors would consider characteristics of the stressor event and the severity of the handicap. The B factors would consider the family's internal crisis-meeting resources, family cohesion, and social support. Psychological and social resources, both formal and informal and particularly that from the family, and their relationship to successful adaptation would be studied. Incorporated into this are the facts that some kinds of services for some families increase stress, that active coping strategies seem more effective than passive receipt of support, and that the more strategies available, the greater their utility. The C factors would include the family definition of the stressor (e.g., any tendency towards externalization of blame for the handicap). This area includes ideology or subjective beliefs. Lastly, the X factors are those that contribute to prevention or precipitation of a family crisis. Thus, this model incorporates the multiple dimensions of intervention that all of the authors have espoused.

Gallagher and Bristol (1989) also discussed the efficacy of family intervention. Like Dunst *et al.* (1989), they pointed out the many methodological problems with the efficacy studies. They noted that studies generally have reported positive findings in child performance, parent knowledge, skills and satisfaction, and program success. Parent intervention focusing on feelings, counseling, or therapy were not effective for the majority of families studied. They also reported that father support groups reduced stress and that respite care is a greater benefit to families with recently disabled children than to families with children having had long-term disabilities.

Gallagher and Bristol concluded with recommendations to inservice personnel to build greater sophistication in program evaluation, to make available a menu of services to meet the great diversity of family needs and resources, to seek conceptual frameworks from social scientists to help organize family programs more effectively, to study families from a longitudinal perspective, to study family patterns other than the nuclear middle-class, and to include working with families from a multidisciplinary or transdisciplinary approach as an integral part of personnel preparation. Upgrading the skills of current professors and inservice training for those currently in the field is necessary, as well as preservice programs for those about to enter it. These recommendations require additional resources from funding agencies and long-term support for research, instrument development, leadership training, inservice training, and dissemination.

Personnel Preparation

The need for qualified professionals to serve handicapped infants and their families is evident. Bricker and Slentz (1989) addressed this issue from several perspectives. They summarized the contemporary view of early intervention as follows: early experience is important, subsequent experience is also important, enriched early experiences do not protect the child from subsequent poor environments, and a deprived early environment does not have to doom the child to retardation or maladaptive functioning if corrective action is taken. Thus, early experience is seen as but one link in the chain of growth and development.

The survival of at-risk infants has added to the problems of early intervention. Added to the ethical issues involved in saving and maintaining severely impaired newborns, with the cost increasing to astronomical proportions, are questions of the type of care and stimulation that will maximize the biological and psychological growth in at-risk children.

Bricker and Slentz believe programs may be developing for the infants without the necessary preplanning in terms of curriculum content and evaluation, and without adequately prepared personnel. Their concerns are particularly relevant at this time because of the broad implications of Public Law 99–457. They observed inadequate guidelines (or debated interpretation of them), underfunding, the unavailability of adequately trained personnel, and the wide variety of agencies and personnel serving the infants. They noted that children from birth through age two have a need for different models of service delivery; a need for greater individual attention, especially for the more severely impaired; and greater family involvement than is necessary for the three- to five-year-olds.

The authors discussed the need for personnel prepared to deliver all of the services required by the infants. In their review of literature they found few references to document the optimal program to prepare such individuals. Choosing not to address related disciplines, the authors focused on educators and their preparation. They looked at the trends of states across the country during the past few years in terms of mandating services to handicapped infants, setting up guidelines to implement them, and requiring specific certification for educators serving them. Their aggregate data, obtained prior to the impact of the Preschool Planning Grants in effect when PL 99–142 became law, revealed that 18% of the 57 states/territories had no mandated services for the birth to five age group, 35% mandated services for only four- and five-year-olds, 22% mandated then for two- to five-year-olds, and an additional 21% mandated services for children in the age group from birth to five years. They also cited 1983 figures showing 18 states requiring preschool certification, and 12 having no certification in operation or under development at that time. These figures, then, gave some indication of the amount of planning and implementation that must be undertaken to carry out the mandates of PL 99–457.

Of particular interest to the authors was the seeming contradiction within some of the states. Some states mandated services, required certification, and provided guidelines for serving the children, while others mandated services and provided guidelines but did not require special teacher certification. Others mandated services and required certification but provided no guidelines. Still others had certification requirements and guidelines but no mandate to serve, while others mandated services only. There were also states that had no mandate, guidelines, or certification requirements, although the surveys with later dates showed a trend toward mandates, certification, and guidelines. Data on the impact of the state preschool planning grants in this area were not available at the time of the authors' review.

Preservice training efforts cited in the literature were also addressed by Bricker and Slentz, showing a range of required courses from a single course to a calendar year or more of training; categorical and noncategorical emphases; a focus from direct interventionists to consultants, or both; and targeted populations that ranged from specific handicapping conditions to the at-risk population. Content seemed to be hybrid, with normal child development and ecological and interdisciplinary foci. Students were noted as being trained by educators (some but not all special educators), psychologists, social workers, or combinations of these. Although the programs had different content, targeted recipients, and focus, a number of commonalities were cited: competency-based programs, clinically-based models with strong practicum or field placement requirements, and close supervision of students in these placements.

Because so few studies dealt with the development of professionals to work with handicapped infants, the authors undertook a study to determine current practices in the field. A 22-item questionnaire was sent to the personnel preparation programs funded by the U.S. Department of Education Office of Special Education Rehabilitative Services (OSERS), as well as to the participants who had attended a conference addressing early childhood special education personnel preparation in September, 1984. Of the 131 questionnaires mailed, 65 were returned. Only 43 of the returns were judged appropriate for inclusion in the study. Thus, Bricker and Slentz suggested a cautious interpretation of the findings.

Responses came from six states in the East, nine in the Midwest, eight in the West, and nine in the South. Some states were represented by more than one school: California (5); Illinois and Pennsylvania (3); and Connecticut, District of Columbia, Louisiana, Massachusetts, Minnesota, and Wisconsin (2). Seventy-four percent of the programs reported funding from OSERS. Two-thirds of the respondents held multiple roles in the programs with the most frequent consisting of teaching, supervising, and advising. Seventy-two percent of the programs were located in special education departments. Preservice programs targeted all levels, from associate to postdoctoral, with 90% at the master's level. Training included an inservice emphasis in almost half of the programs.

Respondents were asked to agree or disagree with four general position statements: (a) that the birth to age three group requires information and skills different from the three to five age group, and training programs should reflect these differences; (b) that the primary focus of the intervention for infants should be the primary caregiver and family members and training programs should reflect this emphasis; (c) that training programs should require extensive practical experience; and (d) that intervention with the infants and families requires coordination of many disciplines and agencies. Although the majority of the respondents agreed overwhelmingly with the statements, the information about their program content contrasted with their questionnaire responses. Only 12% reported a specialized infant focus. Most reported a combined birth to five-year-old approach. Emphasis in 95% of the programs was on handicapped children, with both handicapped and at-risk children dealt with in 16%, and a normal component added in 51% of the programs. a great variance was noted in the number of hours required in early childhood special education by the different programs, with a range from six to 63 hours at the bachelor's level. Master's programs reported less variance and a mean of 21 hours in the area of emphasis.

Respondents reported a variety of general and specialized roles for which they were preparing their students, including in descending order: classroom teacher, parent educator, team collaborator, infant specialist, facilitator/consultant, program developer, advocate, and program evaluator. Most programs were preparing their candidates for more than one role. Also, most of these programs required their students to fulfill competencies to meet the roles; and 95% followed them after graduation, reporting 81% employed in their specialty area.

After reviewing the literature and the results of their study, Bricker and Slentz identified several issues that they believe must be addressed. The first of these is the necessity for training personnel specifically to work with infants, with particular competencies, content, practica, instructional formats, team collaboration, and instructional settings addressed to infants. The second is a focus on the primary caregivers, mainly parents. The third issue is the need for greater maturity and professonal judgment when working with infants and their families outside of the typical school structure. Bricker and Slentz questioned whether undergraduate trainees who may have very few practicum hours of experience have the maturity and professional judgment to meet the needs of the family.

They also pointed out the necessity for greater coordination of efforts with other disciplines and agencies than is necessary with other age groups. Until the passage of PL 99–457, there had been no federal mandate to serve the birth to three population. Because of a lack of direction, states have developed a variety of approaches, often using uncoordinated and splintered responsibilities of mental health, public health, education, and private agency support to meet the needs of the very young handicapped population. The variety of agencies dealing with infant intervention, as well as the need for numerous professionals because of the severity of the problems manifested by the handicapped infants, require the coordination of inputs from many sources. All of these multiple inputs must be coordinated into a single cohesive plan of action for the infants and their families. Training programs must allow the opportunity to develop the skills to do this.

Bricker and Slentz further discussed the issue of whether the interventionist should be a generalist, knowledgeable in a number of areas and able to coordinate input from a variety of professionals into a cohesive and practical intervention plan, or whether the interventionist should be a specialist in education who functions on a team with other specialists, such as physical and occupational therapists, all having specific areas of expertise. Factors weighing on the decision as to the type of professional to be trained include the necessity to prepare personnel for small towns and rural areas where there may be few professionals to work as a team, the question of territoriality of professionals with distinct areas of expertise, and the low-incidence groups that require specialized training.

Bricker and Slentz offered three recommendations concerning research. The first is that appropriate federal agencies associated with research establish the study of personnel preparation as a priority area. The second is to encourage and support research directed towards solving some of the difficult design and methodology problems associated with studying personnel preparation, and the third is for consistent longitudinal funding for such efforts.

References

Adelson, E., & Fraiberg, S. (1974). Gross motor development in infants blind from birth. *Child Development.* **45**, 114–126.

Arias, F., & Tomich, P. (1982). Etiology and outcome of low birth weight & preterm infants. *Obstetrics & Gynecology.* **60**(2), 277–281.

Aronson, M., & Fallstrom, K. (1977). Immediate and long-term effects of developmental training in children with Down's syndrome. *Developmental Medicine and Child Neurology.* **19**, 489–494.

Bagnato, S., & Neisworth, J. (1980). The intervention efficiency index: An approach to preschool program accountability. *Exceptional Children.* **46**, 264–269.

Bagnato, S. J., & Neisworth, J. T. (1985). Efficacy of interdisciplinary assessment and treatment for infants and preschoolers with congenital and acquired brain injury. *Analysis and Intervention in Developmental Disabilities.* **5**, 81–102.

Bailey, E., & Bricker, D. (1985). Evaluation of a three-year early intervention demonstration project. *Topics in Early Childhood Special Education.* **5**(2), 52–65.

Barna, S., Bidder, R., Gray, O., Clements, J., & Gardner, S. (1980) The progress of developmentally delayed children in a home-training scheme. *Child: Care, Health and Development.* **6**, 154–157.

Barrera, M., Routh, D. Parr, C., Johnson, N., Arendshorst, D., Goolsby, E., & Schroeder, S. (1976). Early intervention with biologically handicapped infants and young children; A Preliminary study with each child as his own control. In T. Tjossem (Ed.), *Intervention strategies for high risk infants and young children* (610–627). Baltimore: University Park Press.

Bayley, N., Rhodes, L., Gooch, B., & Marcus, M. (1971). Environmental factors in the development of institutionalized children. In S. Hellmuth (Ed.), *Exceptional Infant: Vol. 2. Studies in Subnormalities* (450–472). New York: Brunner/Mazel.

Bidder, R., Bryant, G., & Gray, D. (1975). Benefits to Down's Syndrome children through training their mothers. *Archives of Diseases in Childhood*, **50**, 383–386.

Brassel, W. (1974 June). *Early intervention with organically damaged and high-risk infants.* Paper presented at the meeting of the American Association on Mental Deficiency, Toronto, Canada.

Brassel, W. (1977). Intervention with handicapped infants: Correlates of progress. *Mental Retardation.* **15**, 18–22.

Brassel, W., & Dunst, C. (1975a). Cognitive intervention by parents of impaired infants. *Mental Retardation.* **13**, 42.

Brassel, W., Dunst, C. (1975b). Facilitating cognitive development in impaired infants. In C. Dunst (Ed.), *Trends in early intervention services: Methods, models, and evaluation* (pp. 142–153). Arlington, VA: Department of Human Resources.

Brassel, W., & Dunst, C. (1978). Fostering the object construct: Large scale intervention with handicapped infants. *American Journal of Mental Deficiency.* **82**, 507–510.

Bricker, D., & Dow, D. (1980). Early intervention with the young severely handicapped child. *Journal of the Association for the Severely Handicapped.* **5**, 130–142.

Bricker, D., & Sheehan, R. (1981). Effectiveness of an early intervention program as indexed by measures of child change. *Journal of the Division for Early Childhood.* **4**, 11–27.

Bricker, D., & Slentz, K. (1989). Personnel preparation: Handicapped infants. In M. C. Wang, M. C. Reynolds, & H. J. Walberg (Eds.), *Handbook of special education: Research and practice: Vol. 3. Low incidence conditions* (pp. 319–345). Oxford, England: Pergamon Press.

Brinker, R., & Lewis, M. (1982). Discovering the competent handicapped infant: A process approach to assessment and intervention. *Topics in Early Childhood Special Education.* **2**(2), 1–16.

Brinkworth, R. (1973). The unfinished child: Effects of early home training on the mongol infant. In A. D. Clarke (Eds.), *Mental retardation and behavioral research* (pp. 213–222). London: Churchill Livingstone.

Brinkworth, R. (1975). The unfinished child: Early treatment and training for the infant with Down's Syndrome. *Royal Society Health Journal.* **95**, 73–78.

Broman, S., Nichols, P., & Kennedy, W. (1975). *Preschool IQ: Prenatal and early developmental correlates.* New York: Wiley.

Bromwich, R., & Parmelee, A. (1979). An invention program for preterm infants. In T. Field (Ed.). *Infants born at risk* (pp. 389–411). New York: Spectrum.

Cappleman, M., Thompson, R., DeRemer-Sullivan, R., King, A., & Sturm, J. (1982). Effectiveness of a home-based intervention program with infants of adolescent mothers. *Child Psychiatry and Human Development*, **13**, 55–65.

Carlsen, P. (1975). Comparison of two occupational therapy approaches for treating the young cerebral-palsied child. *American Journal of Occupational Therapy.* **5**, 267–272.

Chee, F., Kreutzberg, J., & Clark, D. (1978). Semicircular canal stimulation in cerebral palsied children. *Physical Therapy.* **58**, 1071–1075.

Clunies-Ross, G. (1979). Accelerating the development of Down's syndrome infants and young children. *Journal of Special Education.* **13**, 169–177.

Cohen, S., Sigman, M., Parmalee, A., & Beckwith, L. (1982). Perinatal risk and developmental outcome in preterm infants. *Seminars in Perinatalogy.* **6**(4), 334–339.

Connolly, B., & Russell, F. (1976). Interdisciplinary early intervention program. *Physical Therapy.* **56**, 155–157.

Crnic, K., Friedrich, W., & Greenberg, M. (1983). Adaptation of families with mentally retarded children: A model of stress, coping, and family ecology. *American Journal of Mental Deficiency.* **88**, 125–138.

Crnic, K., Greenberg, M., Ragosin, A., Robinson, N., & Basham, R. (1983). Effects of stress and social support on mothers and premature and full-term infants. *Child Development.* **54**, 209, 217.

Cunningham, C., Aumonier, M., & Sloper, P. (1982). Health visitor support for families with Down's syndrome infants. *Child: Care, Health, and Development.* **8**, 1–19.

Cyrulik-Jacobs, A., Shapira, Y., & Jones, M. (1975). Application of an automatic operant response procedure to the study of auditory perception and processing ability of neurologically-impaired infants. In B. Friedlander, G. Sterritt, & G. Kirk (Eds.) *Exceptional infant: Vol. 3. Assessment and intervention* (pp. 109–123). New York: Brunner/Mazel.

Drillien, C., Thompson, A., & Burgoyne, K. (1980). Low birthweight children at early school age. A longitudinal study. *Developmental Medicine and Child Neurology*. 22, 26–47.

Dunst, C. (1974, June). *Patterns of cognitive skill acquisitions in developmentally delayed infants*. Paper presented at the meeting of the American Association on Mental Deficiency, Toronto.

Dunst, C. (in press). Sensorimotor development of Down's Syndrome infants. In D. Cichitti & L. Beeghly (Eds.), *Down's Syndrome: The developmental perspective*. Cambridge, MA: Harvard University Press.

Dunst, C., Cushing, P. & Vance, S. (1985). Response-contingent learning in profoundly handicapped infants: A social systems perspective. *Analysis and Intervention in Developmental Disabilities*. 5, 7–21.

Dunst, C., & Leet, H. (1985). *Family resource scale: Reliability and validity*. Unpublished manuscript, Western Carolina Center Family, Infant and Preschool Program, Morganton, NC.

Dunst, C. J., Snyder, S. W. & Mankinen, M. (1989). Efficacy of early intervention. In M. C. Wang, M. C. Reynolds, & H. J. Walberg (Eds.), *Handbook of special education: Research and practice: Vol. 3. Low incidence conditions* (pp. 259–294). Oxford, England: Pergamon Press.

Dunst, C. & Trivette, C. (1984, August). *Differential influences of social support on mentally retarded children and their families*. Paper presented at the meeting of the American Psychological Association, Toronto, Canada.

Dunst, C., Trivette, C., & Cross, A. (in press). Mediating influences of social support: Personal, family, and child outcomes. *American Journal of Mental Deficiency*.

Dunst, C. J., Vance, S. D., & Gallagher, S. L. (1983). *Differential efficacy of early intervention with handicapped infants*. Paper presented at the annual meeting of the council for Exceptional Children, Detroit.

Eisenstadt, J., & Powell, D. (1980). *Parent characteristics and the utilization of a parent-child program*. Unpublished manuscript, Purdue University, Department of Child Development and Family Studies, West Lafayette, IN.

Field, T., Widmayer, S., Stringer, S., & Ignatoff, E. (1980). Teenage, lower-class, black mothers and their preterm infants: An intervention and developmental follow-up. *Child Development*. 51, 426, 436.

Fitzhardinge, P., & Steven, E. (1972). The small for date infant II: Neurological and intellectual sequelae. *Pediatrics*, 50(1).

Ford, J. (1978). A multidisciplinary approach to early intervention strategies for the education of the developmentally handicapped 0–3 years old: A pilot study. *Australian Journal of Mental Retardation*. 5, 26–29.

Friedlander, B., McCarthy, J., & Soferenko, A. (1967). Automated psychological evaluation with severely retarded institutionalized infants. *American Journal of Mental Deficiency*. 71, 909–919.

Gallagher, J. J. & Bristol, M. (1989). Families of young handicapped children. In M. C. Wang, M. C. Reynolds, & H. J. Walberg (Eds.), *Handbook of special education: Research and practice: Vol. 3. Low incidence conditions* (pp. 295–317). Oxford, England: Pergamon Press.

Garber, H., & Heber, R. (1981). The efficacy of early intervention with family rehabilitation. In M. Begab, H. C. Haywood, & H. Garber, *Psychosocial influences in retarded performance: Vol. 2. Strategies for improving competence* (pp. 71–88). Baltimore: University Park Press.

Glenn, S. (1983). The application of an automated system for the assessment of profound mentally handicapped children. *International Journal of Rehabilitation Research*. 6(3), 358–360.

Goodman, J., Cecil, H., & Barker, W. (1984). Early intervention with retarded children: Some encouraging results. *Developmental Medicine and Child Neurology*. 26, 47–55.

Gordon, R. (1977). *Study of impact of early developmental program on multihandicapped young children and their families*. New York: New York University Medical Center Infant School Program. (ERIC Document Reproduction Service No. ED 149 563).

Gutelius, M., & Kirsch, A. (1975). Factors promoting success in infant education. *American Journal of Public Health*. **65**, 383–387.

Hanson, M. (1985). An analysis of the effects of early intervention services for infants and toddlers with moderate and severe handicaps. *Topics in Early Childhood Special Education*. **5**(2), 36–51.

Hanson, M., & Schwartz, R. (1978). Results of a longitudinal intervention program for Down's syndrome infants and their families. *Education and Training of the Mentally Retarded*. **13**, 403–407.

Harris, S. (1981). Effects of neurodevelopmental therapy on motor performance of infants with Down's syndrome. *Developmental Medicine and Child Neurology*. **23**, 477–483.

Hayden, A., & Dmitriev, V. (1975). The multidisciplinary preschool program for Down's syndrome children at the University of Washington Model Preschool Centre. In B. Friedlander, G. Sterritt, and G. Kirk (Eds.), *Exceptional infant: Vol. 3. Assessment and intervention* (pp. 193–221). New York: Brunner/Mazel.

Hayden, A., & Haring, N. (1977). The acceleration and maintenance of developmental gains in Down's Syndrome school-aged children. In P. Mittler (Ed.), *Research to practice in mental retardation: Vol. 1. Care and intervention* (pp. 129–141). Baltimore: University Park Press.

Hewitt, K., Newcombe, R., & Bidder, R. (1983). Profiles of skill gain in delayed infants and young children. *Child: Care, Health and Development*. **9**, 127–135.

Horton, K. (1971, July). *Early amplification and language learning*. Paper presented at the meeting of the Academy of Rehabilitative Audiology, Winter Park, CO.

Horwood, S., Boyle, M., Torrance, G., & Sinclair, J. (1982). Mortality & morbidity of 500- to 1,400- gram birth weight infants live-born to residents of a defined geographic region before and after neonatal intensive care. *Pediatrics*, **69**(5), 613–620.

Hunt, J. McV. (1976). The utility of ordinal scales inspired by Piaget's observation. *Merrill-Palmer Quarterly*. **22**, 31–45.

Hunt, J. McV. (1980). Implications of plasticity and hierachical achievements for the assessment of development and risk of mental retardation. In D. Sawin, R. Hawkins, L. Walker, & J. Penticuff (Eds.), *Exceptional infant: Vol. 4. Psychosocial risks in infant-environment transactions* (pp. 7–54). New York: Brunner/Mazel.

Huntinger, P. (1978). *Program performance report for handicapped children's early education program: Macomb 0–3 regional project*. Macomb, IL: Western Illinois University. (ERIC Document Reproduction Service No. ED 184–278).

Jelinek, J., & Flamboe, T. (1979). *The Wyoming infant stimulation program*. Laramie, WY: WISP Project. (ERIC Document Reproduction Service No. ED 171–090).

Kantmer, R., Clark, D., Allen, L, & Chase. M. (1976). Effects of vestibular stimulation on nystagmus response and motor performance in the developmentally delayed infant. *Physical Therapy*. **56**, 414–417.

Kaplan, M., & Atkins, J., (1978). *Model services for handicapped infants*. (ERIC Document Reproduction Service No. ED 175–174).

Kelly, J. (1982). Effects of intervention on caregiver-infant interaction when the infant is handicapped. *Journal of the Division for Early Childhood*. **5**, 53–63.

Laub, K. & Dunst, C. (1974, May). *Effects of non-imitative and imitative adult vocalizing on a developmentally delayed infant's rate of vocalization*. Paper presented at the meeting of the North Carolina Speech and Hearing Association, Durham.

Lazar, I., & Darlington, R. (1982). Lasting effects of early education: A report from the consortium for longitudinal studies, *Monographs of the Society for Research in Child Development*. **47**. (2–3, Serial No. 195).

Leib, S., Benfield, G., & Guidubaldi, J. (1980). Effects of early intervention and stimulation on the preterm infant. *Pediatrics*. **66**, 83–90.

LeLaurin, K. (1985). The experimental analysis of the effects of early intervention with normal, at-risk, and handicapped children under age three. *Analysis and Intervention in Developmental Disabilities*. **5**, 103–124.

Lovaas, O. (1982). *An overview of the young autism project.* Paper presented at the meeting of the American Psychological Association, Washington, DC.

Lubchenco, L., Delivoria-Papadopoulos, M., & Searls, D. (1972). Long-term follow up studies of prematurely born infants II: Influence of birthweight and gestational age on sequelae. *Journal of Pediatrics*, **80**, 509.

Lubchenco, L., Horner, F., Reid, L., Hix, I., Metcalf, D., Cohig, R., Elliot, H., Boung, M. (1963). Sequelae of premature birth. Evaluation of premature infants of low birthweights at ten years of age. *American Journal of Diseases of Children.* **106**, 101–115.

Ludlow, J., & Allen, L. (1979). The effects of early intervention and preschool stimulus on the development of the Down's syndrome Child. *Journal of Mental Deficiency Research.* **23**, 29–44.

Macy, D., Solomon, G., Schoen, M., & Galey, G. (1983). The DEBT project: Early intervention for handicapped children and their parents. *Exceptional Children.* **49**, 447–448.

Mahoney, G., & Snow, K. (1983). The relationship of sensorimotor functioning to children's response to early langugage training. *Mental Retardation.* **21**, 248–254.

Maisto, A., & German, M. (1979). Variables related to progress in a parent infant training program for high-risk infants. *Journal of Pediatric Psychology.* **4**, 409–419.

Maisto, A., & German, M. (1981). Maternal locus of control and developmental gain demonstrated by high risk infants: A longitudinal analysis. *Journal of Psychology.* **109**, 213–221.

McCubbin, H., & Patterson, J. (1981). *Systematic assessment of family stress, resources and coping.* St. Paul, MN: Family Stress Project, University of Minnesota.

McCubbin, H., Sussman, M. & Patterson, J. (1983). *Social stress and the family.* New York; Haworth Press.

Moran, D., & Whitman, T. (1985). The multiple effects of a play-oriented parent training program for mothers of developmentally delayed children. *Analysis and Intervention in Developmental Disabilities.* **5**, 47–70.

Murray, H. (1977). *Early intervention in the context of family characteristics.* Denver, CO: Education Commission of the States. (ERIC Document Reproduction Service No. Ed 145–956).

National Center for Health Statistics (September 1984). Advanced report of final natality statistics, 1982. *Monthly Vital Statistics Report.* **33**(6), Supp. DHHS Pub. No. (PHS) 84–1120. Public Health Service. Hyattsville, MD.

Nielsen, G., Collings, S., Meisel, J., Lowry, M., Engh, H., & Johnson, D. (1975). An intervention program for atypical infants. In B. Friedlander, G. Sterritt, & G. Kirk (Eds.) *Exceptional infant: Vol: 3. Assessment and intervention* (pp. 222–244). New York: Brunner/Mazel.

Ottenbacher, K., & Petersen, P. (1985). The efficacy of early intervention programs for children with organic impairment: A quantitative review. *Evaluation and Program Planning.* **8**, 135–146.

Ottenbacher, K., Short, M., & Watson, P. (1981). The effects of a clinically applied program of vestibular stimulation on the neuromotor performance of children with severe developmental disability. *Physical and Occupational Therapy in Pediatrics.* **1**(3), 1–11.

Paraskevopoulos, J., & Hunt, J. McV. (1971). Object construction and imitation under differing condition of rearing. *Journal of Genetic Psychology.* **119**, 301–321.

Peniston, E. (1972). An evaluation of the Portage Project. Unpublished manuscript, The Portage Project, Portage, WI. Data presented in Shearer, M., & Shearer, D. The Portage Project: A model for early childhood education. *Exceptional Children.* **26**, 210–217.

Piper, M., & Pless, I. (1980). Early intervention for infants with Down's Syndrome: A controlled trial. *Pediatrics.* **65**, 463–468.

Ramey, C., Bryant, D., Sparling, J., & Wasik, B. (1985). Project CARE: A comparison of two early intervention strategies to prevent retarded development. *Topics in Early Childhood Special Education.* **5**(2), 12–25.

Ramey, C. & Haskins, R. (1981). The causes and treatment of school failure: Insights from the Carolina Abecedarian Project. In M. Begab, C. Haywood, & H. Garder (Eds.), *Psychosocial Influences in Retarded Performance* (Vol. 2, pp. 89–112). Baltimore: University Park Press.

Ramey, C., Hieger, L., & Klisz, D. (1972). Synchronous reinforcement of vocal responses in failure-to-thrive infants. *Child Development.* **43**, 1449–1455.

Ramey, C., Starr, R., Pallas, J., Whitten, C., & Reed, V. (1976). Nutrition, response-contingent stimulation, and the maternal deprivation syndrome: Results of an early intervention program. *Merrill-Palmer Quarterly.* **12**, 32–44.

Ross, G. (1983). Mortality and morbidity in very low birth-weight infants. *Pediatric Annals.* **12**, 32–44.

Rottman, C. (1979). *Project Outreach for the infant program for visually impaired: Final performance report 1978–79.* Mason, MI: Ingham Intermediate School District. (ERIC Document Reproduction Service No. ED181–645.

Safford, P., Gregg, L., Schneider, G., & Sewell, J. (1976). A stimulation program for young sensory-impaired, multihandicapped children. *Education and training of the Mentally Retarded.* **11**, 12–17.

Sandler, A., Coren, A., Thurman, S. (1983). A training program for parents of handicapped preschool children: Effects upon mother, father, child. *Exceptional Children.* **49**, 355–358.

Sandow, S., & Clarke, A. (1978). Home intervention with parents of severely subnormal preschool children: An interim report. *Child: Care, Health and Development.* **4**, 29–39.

Sandow, S. A., Clarke, A. D. B., Cox, M. V., & Stewart, F. L. (1981). Home intervention with parents of severely subnormal pre-school children. A final report. *Child: Care, Health, & Development.* **7**, 135–144.

Scherzer, A., Mike, V., & Ilson, J. (1976). Physical therapy as a determinant of change in the cerebral palsied infant. *Pediatrics,* **58**, 47–52.

Scott, K. G. & Carran, D. T. (1989). Identification and referral of handicapped infants. In M. C. Wang, M. C. Reynolds, & H. J. Walberg (Eds.), *Handbook of special education: Research and practice: Vol. 3. Low incidence conditions* (pp. 227–241). Oxford, England: Pergamon Press.

Scott, K., & Masi, W. (1979). The outcome from and utility of registers of risk. In T. Field, A. Sostek, S. Goldberg, & H. Shuman (Eds.), *Infants born at risk* (pp. 485–496). New York: Spectrum Publications.

Sellick, K., & Over, R. (1980). Effects of vestibular stimulation on motor development of cerebral-palsied children. *Developmental Medicine and Child Neurology,* **22**, 476–483.

Shapiro, L., Gordon, R., & Neiditch, C. (1977). Documenting change in young multiply handicapped children in a rehabilitation centre. *Journal of Special Education.* **11**, 243, 257.

Shearer, M., & Shearer, D. (1972). The Portage Project: A model for early childhood education. *Exceptional Children.* **36**, 210–217.

Sheehan, R. & Klein, N. (1989). Infant assessment. In M. C. Wang, M. C. Reynolds, & H. J. Walberg (Eds.), *Handbook of special education: Research and practice: Vol. 3. Low incidence conditions* (pp. 243–258). Oxford, England: Pergamon Press.

Siegal, L., Saigal, S., Rosenbaum, P., Morton, R., Young, A., Berenbaum S., & Stoskopf, B. (1982). Predictions of development in preterm and full-term infants. A model for detecting the at-risk child. *Journal of Pediatric Psychology.* **7**(2), 135–148.

Simeonsson, R., & Huntington, G. (1981). *Correlates of developmental progress in handicapped infants and children.* Unpublished manuscript, The University of North Carolina at Chapel Hill, Carolina Institute for Research on Early Education of the Handicapped, Chapel Hill, NC.

Smith, D., & Simons, F. (1975). Rational diagnostic evaluation of the child with mental deficiency. *American Journal of Diseases of Childhood.* **129**, 1285–1290.

Snyder, S., & Sheehan, R. (1985). Integrating research in early childhood special education: The use of meta-analysis. *Diagnostique.* **9**(1).

Solkoff, N., & Cotton, C. (1975). Contingency awareness in premature infants. *Perceptual and Motor Skills.* **41**, 709–710.

Stedman, D., & Eichorn, D. (1964). A comparison of the growth and development of institutionalized and home-reared mongoloids during infancy and early childhood. *American Journal of Mental Deficiency.* **69**, 391–401.

Utley, B., Duncan, D., Strain, P., & Scanlon, K. (1983). Effects of contingent and noncontingent visual stimulation on visual fixation in multiply handicapped children. *TASH Journal.* **8**, 29–42.

Vadasy, P., Fewell, R., Meyer, D., & Greenberg, M. (1985). Supporting fathers of handicapped young children: Preliminary findings of program effects. *Analysis and Intervention in Developmental Disabilities.* **5**, 125–137.

Watson, J. (1972). Smiling, cooing, and "The Game". *Merrill-Palmer Quarterly.* **18**, 4, 323–340.

White, K. (1984). *An integrative review of early intervention efficacy research.* Unpublished manuscript, University of Utah, Provo.

White, K., & Casto, G. (1985). An integrative review of early intervention efficacy studies with at-risk children: Implications for the handicapped. *Analysis and Intervention in Developmental Disabilities.* **5**, 177–201.

White, K., Mastropieri, M., & Casto, G. (1985). The efficacy of early intervention for handicapped children. An analysis of special education early childhood projects approved by the joint dissemination review panel. *Journal of the Division of Early Childhood.*

Wiedar, D., & Hicks, J. (1970). *Evaluation of an early intervention program for neurologically impaired children and their families.* Jamaica, NY: United Cerebral Palsy of Queens, (ERIC Document Reproduction Service No. ED 050 533.).

Wiener, G. (1968). *Longterm study of prematures: Summary of published findings.* ERIC Report No. ED043389, PS003651, Office of Education, Dept. of HEW, Washington, DC.

Wolery, M. & Dyk, L. (1985). The evaluation of two levels of a center based early intervention project. *Topics in Early Childhood Special Education.* **5**(2), 66–77.

Wright, T., & Nicholson, J. (1973). Physiotherapy for the spastic child: An evolution. *Developmental Medicine and Child Neurology.* **15**, 146–163.

Yu, V., Orgill, A. Bajuk, B., & Astbury, J. (1984). Survival and 2-year outcome of extremely preterm infants. *British Journal of Obstetrics & Gynecology.* **91**, 640–646.

Zausmer, E., Pueschel, S., & Shea, A. (1972). A sensory-motor stimulation program for the young child with Down's Syndrome: Preliminary report. *MCH Exchange.* **11**, 1–4.

Zeitlin, S. (1981). Learning through coping: An effective preschool program. *Journal of the Division of Early Education.* **4**, 53–61.

Epilogue

The preceding chapters of this book have summarized the "state of the art" and the "state of practice" in nine areas of special education and noted discrepancies between the two. Suggestions have been made in each chapter as to how discrepancies might be resolved and where research should be directed to further advance the "state of the art." These suggestions have taken a variety of forms, such as proposals for improved preparation of teachers, policy and regulatory changes, structural changes in school programs, revised priorities for research activities, better communications among researchers and with practitioners, and much more. A large part of the total domain of special education has been covered in this book, omitting only topics such as severely and profoundly handicapped students, speech and some language disorders, and students with physical impairments and chronic health problems.

In this final chapter we offer some impressions, observations, and suggestions that are broader in context than those provided in the earlier chapters. Considering the plethora of knowledge summarized in this book and the state of practice in special education, we believe some significant generalizations and proposals can be advanced. First, we will discuss pressing problems facing today's schools, and in particular special education. Then we will move quickly to positive ground and propose positive solutions to the problems.

From the beginning, our approach to the state of the art and the state of practice has been future-oriented, and this final statement is offered in that spirit. The work of the scholars who contributed to this project should be represented not just passively in a book but in ongoing dialogue—even spirited and challenging dialogue—intended to advance education and related services for exceptional students.

In this chapter, we do not presume to represent all of the 70 scholars who contributed to the three-volume *Handbook* publication; these are our own ideas which grew in the long process of working on this book and the three preceding volumes. The field of special education in the United States is nearing the end of a long journey toward total inclusiveness; all children, even those most difficult and challenging to teach, have clearly established rights to education, and virtually all of them are presently in school. Now that we are past the implementation date of our nation's most important special education policy declarations in Public Law 94-142, it is time for reflection, further development, and change of whatever depth required. We believe there are needs which go beyond incremental change; structural changes are required as well.

We proceed here by listing and discussing several general conclusions, observations, and suggestions. Extended discussions are provided in several general problem areas which we see as having greatest importance. Finally, we present a scenario, including several vignettes, about research and practice in special education for the year 2000. These express, as graphically as possible, some of our hopes and visions for the future.

We begin with observations about research in special education. From there we turn gradually to topics which relate more to the interaction of research and practice.

Lack of Long-Range Studies

Researchers have not done a thorough job in following handicapped students through the school years and into the postschool period. As a result, special educators are very limited in their ability to provide prognoses and future planning for individuals. Because we lack long-range studies, we also lack data-based foundations for curricular changes that would make school programs more functional. In fact, it is likely that the field has recently conducted fewer long-range prospective and retrospective studies of exceptional students than was the case 20 to 30 years ago. That situation needs to be repaired. Hopefully, it will be possible to develop interest in and support for broad and continuing long-range studies of handicapped students. We need to know more about the long-term outcomes of special education.

Lack of Systematic Data On Program Implementation and Outcomes

In general, the implementations of special education programs have not been usefully described and evaluated. The clearest hard data we have show that substantial numbers of children are not learning and behaving well in schools and are therefore referred to special education. Unfortunately, one finds little reliable information on who special education students are, the reason for their placement, and the types of special education programs provided for them. Furthermore, hard evidence on the effects (positive or negative) of alternative programs provided for these students is scarce, at least in the cases of those with milder degrees of "handicap."

It seems likely that in such famous court cases as *Larry P vs. Riles* (1973) in California, it was more the lack of evidence that special classes were helpful for mildly retarded children that caused the conflict than the fact that the tests used in placement processes were faulty. Indeed, if one accepts the dictum that decisions about school placements must be validated (more so than just tests used in placement processes, for example) it becomes clear that placement in a special education program can be justified only when the program has demonstrated merit. But, unfortunately, we do not know who is served well in the various special education programs or whether, in general, programs do much good. The need is for field tests of programs as they *really* operate in schools. Without detail on program implementations and outcomes, there is danger that untested ideas will be rushed into special education classrooms only to be drastically revised or removed a decade later. In an era influenced by the 'least restrictive environment" principle, which we take to mean that children should remain in mainstream classes and schools unless and until there is evidence that a program of some distinct kind offers clear advantages for the child, the need for program evaluation is critical. Both short-range and long-range evaluation studies are needed.

Difficulties Associated with Cohort Changes

It is difficult to build a cumulating knowledge base in special education because of cohort changes. For example, the school-age "pass through" of students handicapped in association with the 1959–65 rubella epidemic occurred in about 1983–84; most rubella babies reached age 18, high school-learning age, in 1983–84. Disabled persons of that group were often multiply handicapped and, as a group, quite different from students of earlier and later periods. Similarly, visual impairments caused by retrolental fibroplasia came to an abrupt downturn in incidence in 1954. The characteristics of blind children born in the late 1940s and early 1950s were remarkably different from those of the late 1950s and early 1960s.

Changes in the definition of mental retardation as reflected, for example, in the classification manual of the American Association of Mental Deficiency in 1973, provide a further important example of cohort change (Grossman, 1973). The changes in characteristics of "mildly mentally retarded" children enrolled in special education programs have been so great in recent decades that most of the pre-1970s literature of mildly retarded students is irrelevant for today's special education teachers and programs.

Clearly, significant time-related cohort changes make it extraordinarily difficult to construct a smoothly cumulative knowledge base. One requirement for improvement is that a broad marker variable system be created and used consistently, so that communications about research findings can be relatively clear, even through periods of significant cohort change.

Incomplete Reporting

Far too many reports of research in special education are incomplete, often omitting clear descriptions of the research populations, the experimental intervention, the control group and evidence of the degree of implementation of the intervention. Again, a marker variable system would be useful to specify the kinds of information which should be required in reporting research. There is also a need for researchers and journal editors to hold tightly to high standards of completeness in research reporting. Only when there is complete reporting is it possible to conduct replications and to synthesize results across studies in valid ways.

Increasing Difficulty and Expense

Research in special education is becoming more difficult and expensive. It is relatively easy to do research on handicapped pupils when they are housed in large numbers in separate schools or institutions. It is more difficult when the pupils are scattered among many schools and classes, which are often hard to reach and which inevitably involve many different contexts in school, home, and community. But it is exactly in the direction of these more scattered and diverse arrangements that special education programs have been moving. In low-incidence areas, such as blindness, it is extraordinarily difficult and expensive to generate a significant population for research projects because of practical problems, such as travel, securing informed consent, and transporting the special equipment that may be required. It is no less important today than in the past to do research and to advance in knowledge about special education, but more resources and greater commitments will be required to do so.

Lack of Coherent Patterns of Research in Low-Incidence Area

We find it particularly disturbing that there is a lack of coherent patterns in research of low-incidence areas of special education. In particular, we speak of the area of vision and to some extent of hearing. Virtually nowhere is there a strong program of research in the areas of blindness and low vision. University staff have made significant contributions in a few places, but the tendency is for faculty to be consumed by training and service functions. Today's research programs of special agencies, such as the Printing House for the Blind, do not loom large as knowledge builders in the field.

The low-incidence areas are not very successful in producing out of their own groups and agencies, people who are prepared and committed to careers as researchers. This contributes to the lack of coherent, programmatic, and deeply penetrating research programs in the field. Much of the research is done by psychologists, sociologists, physicians, and others whose commitments to long-term research programs and to a focus on instructional issues in a special area are often quite limited. It is therefore necessary to draw plans for developing strong, long-term research stations that address needs in low-incidence areas. The research should start at the extreme of low incidence characteristics (such as blindness), then move up the spectrum to other domains.

Although this volume does not cover the area of severe and profound cognitive deficits, it is noteworthy that this area, even though low in incidence rates, has been quite successful in producing significant research and policy studies. It would be helpful to understand why this low-incidence domain has been so uniquely successful in producing its own researchers and research, developing valuable dissemination processes, and transforming research findings into special education practices.

Problems of Generalization and Transfer

There is evidence that exceptional children, such as those labeled emotionally disturbed, often settle down and become more adaptive when they are managed and taught in highly structured environments. However, when such students are returned to ordinary school and community environments, the apparent improvements often do not transfer and survive. In such situations one could judge that some progress has been made, at least for a limited time and place; on the other hand, the program and apparent progress may represent only a delay and distraction from the real and broader issues of adjustment and learning.

Somewhat different kinds of transfer problems have been observed when students with learning problems have been taught perceptual or sensory-motor skills thought to be predispositional to learning basic literacy skills, mainly reading. There are findings on occasion that the direct teaching of the "underlying" or predispositional factors results in some positive learning, only to find later that there is no transfer to reading ability (Arter & Jenkins, 1979). It would be difficult to overestimate the costs of misjudgment in these kinds of approaches to special education programs when they are rushed into practice far ahead of adequate validating research.

The field of special education seems particularly open to theories and practices, even before they are thoroughly tested. There are millions of children whose problems have been diagnosed in terms of cognitive rigidity, angulation difficulties, lack of sensory integration, perceptual problems, auditory sequencing difficulties, or unusual WISC profiles—all of which add up to zero or near zero validity when later tested for instructional relevance. The solution to these problems is a particular responsibility of researchers in the special education community who should call for decent levels of evidence before practices are allowed to enter the field in broad ways.

Effectiveness Principles

It seems very likely that the emerging principles concerning effective schools and effective instruction will have importance in all facets of special education, but they have not yet been applied and tested thoroughly in many programs. Often, there is a kind of narrowness about research in special education, as, for example, Fishgrund noted in his chapter dealing with hearing problems. We believe that research exploiting the "effectiveness" principles in all areas of special education is important for the near future.

Instructional Technology

A somewhat surprising observation concerning the entire review of research summarized in this volume is the infrequent citation of research on the uses of technology. A number of anecdotal references were included, but far fewer research reports than expected. There is obvious use of technology in the field of special education, especially in regard to computers. Perhaps it will take another decade to produce research and evaluative studies in this area.

Unreliable and Invalid Child Classification

Special education programs are organized, in most places, according to narrow categorical delineations. Commonly, for example, local school districts will operate a learning disability program, a separate mild mental retardation program, a behavioral disorders program, and about five other such programs. Teachers are similarly categorized in their preparation, licensing, and employment. The average state issues about eight or nine different kinds of special education teaching certificates or licenses.

At the mild levels (learning disability, mild mental retardation, and behavioral disorders), the classification rates vary greatly in different schools and localities. In addition, the classifications are unreliable and lacking in validity for instructional purposes. Most research in special education is narrowly specific to a given category in spite of all these difficulties; usually the researchers simply accept and report the classifications of children as found in the schools.

The problems of classification also extend to Chapter 1 programs, migrant education services, and remedial programs as operated in many school districts. The characteristics of children in these programs and in special education frequently overlap, but separateness often is forced between programs by state and federal regulations. We have described the results in terms of disjointed incrementalism and proceduralism. The latter term describes the tendency for procedural norms, mostly oriented to managing boundaries and separateness of programs, to become dominant. By the term disjointed incrementalism we refer to the fragmentation of programs that has developed as one program after another was authorized and implemented, often on the assumption that each program would have no interaction with other programs. That assumption has proved to be untrue.

The concern about classification is hardly new. Hobbs, based on findings from his major work in this area (Hobbs, 1975), concluded that the approaches used in the schools to classify and place students in special education programs were "a major barrier to the efficient and effective delivery of services to them and their families" (Hobbs, 1980, p. 274). A National Academy of Sciences panel (Heller et al., 1982) investigated the disproportional placement rates for minority and male children in special education programs. The panel identified the classification problem as being much broader than that of disproportional placement. They suggested that "it is the responsibility of the placement team that labels and places a child in a special program to demonstrate that any differential label used is related to a distinctive prescription for educational practices . . . that lead to improved outcomes" (Heller et al., 1982, p. 94). Judged against that standard, present practices for classifying and placing students in special education are unsatisfactory.

Classification has been particularly troublesome with respect to the category of learning disability. Compared to an increase of 16% for individuals identified in all categories of handicapping conditions between academic years 1976–77 and 1984–85, the increase for students identified as learning disabled was 119% (Keogh, 1988). It has been estimated that more than 80% of normal students could be classified as learning disabled by one or more definitions now in use (Ysseldyke et al., 1983). The widely varying percentages of students classified as learning disabled suggest disparities and anomalies that are difficult to resolve.

Thus, students with identical characteristics may be classified and placed in any one of several special, compensatory, or remedial education programs, depending on the states or school districts in which they reside and on the particular criteria used by school staffs. Often, the greater the numbers of students who are classified, the more money and administrative complexity that are brought into a school.

The multiplicity of classifications and programs may reflect ineffective identification rather than true distinctions in learning ability (Keogh, 1988). But even if true differences among the subgroups of learners could be determined, it is often appropriate to use similar instructional principles and methods to accommodate the variety of student needs (Gerber, 1987). In finding that there is "little empirical justification for categorical labeling that discriminates mildly mentally retarded children from other children with academic difficulties" (Heller et al., 1982, p. 87), the National Academy of Sciences panel went beyond the field of special education. The panel stressed the need for important changes that would improve classification and placement systems for total school systems, not just for special education.

The solution to the classification problems is certain to be difficult in many ways: technically, politically, and economically. A beginning step is to develop and use a marker variable system. This system will ensure that information on research and practice is communicated clearly, especially in regard to the students involved, the instructional programs in which they are served, and the broader context in which activities are conducted. Such a marker variable system will need to go far beyond the simple categorical delineations now used for research and practice in special education.

It will be important for interventions to be tried and tested with children showing a wide range of characteristics. Then, it will be important to determine whether there might be interactions of pupil characteristics and instructional methods/materials. Here we refer mainly to the large numbers of mildly handicapped students plus those in Chapter 1, migrant education, and remedial programs. We do not include deaf and blind pupils, for whom there are obvious accommodations to be made in instructional programs and whose instruction needs to be managed, at least part of the time, by well-prepared specialists. Only through broadly framed studies will it be feasible to determine whether there is well-confirmed evidence in support of sub-classifications that have instructional relevance.

There are many political and economic problems to be faced in connection with revisions of child classification systems. Advocacy groups are organized by categories, as are exceptional children and their teachers. Much money is involved and it is distributed in well-established tracks. It will not be easy to open these operations to change. One way to proceed is to use a "waiver for performance" strategy, which will allow selected school districts to experiment in broad cross-categorical programs; in return, they will be required to furnish data showing pupils outcomes. Such experimentation will require that individual states and the federal government offer supports to avoid financial disincentive in local school districts for trying new approaches. Hopefully, a period of enhanced experimentation and evaluation, along with careful deliberations about policy issues, will provide a basis for a new wave of development in special education. It is certain that further development of special education will involve revisions in the present faulty system of child classification.

Scenario for the Year 2000

As a way of summarizing ideas for solving some of the many problems presented in this chapter, a number of brief vignettes are proposed, comprising a "scenario for the year 2000." These are not so much predictions as they are wishes for projects and programs that might be helpful.

Year 2000 Vignette—Evaluation and Follow-Up Studies

Three regional centers are now serving the nation through follow-up studies of exceptional persons. Each does its work in coordination with other centers. The centers conduct retrospective studies of students enrolled in special education programs during the 1970–90 period, and 20-year prospective follow-up studies of students of school-leaving age are scheduled to begin in the years 2000–05. Each center also provides technical assistance to staff of state education departments and local school districts for improving local program evaluation and follow-up studies. Each center develops and disseminates technical information on the conduct and results of follow-up studies. Biennial conferences will be held beginning in 2002 to focus on outcomes of evaluative and follow-up studies and their policy implications. The centers are funded for an assured period of 20 years.

Year 2000 Vignette—Teams of Educators

Recent statistical reports show that more than 80% of special education teachers now work directly with teams of teachers in various kinds of "regular" instructional environments. Many special educators have helped lead in the restructuring of schools and now serve in roles that are well-integrated into mainstream school operations. "Mainstream" programs are now extremely diverse and different from the one teacher-one class operations of the past. In general, special education teachers provide high-density instruction to students showing the least progress, and they help to modify programs for those who learn most rapidly. They also tend to carry relatively heavy loads in pupil evaluation programs, reporting to and collaborating with parents and managing special studies of children who show special problems. Special education teachers work in full collaboration with other teachers in teams, at elementary, secondary, vocational-technical, and higher education levels.

Year 2000 Vignette—Child Study and Classification

Studies of children with special needs now focus mainly on the necessary modification of instructional programs. Children are not labeled, except in terms of the kinds of instruction and services to be provided. It is common, for example, for selected primary-grade-level children to receive extended and intensive reading instruction. Others receive extended instruction in social and friendship skills. Children with poor vision are taught to read by braille methods. Classification is strictly in terms of the instructional level and methods needed; such classifications may "hold" for only a brief time or throughout the schooling years, depending upon assessment of needs.

Year 2000 Vignette—Research in the Area of Vision

A special center for research in the area of visual impairments among children has been established. The center is a permanent agency, with a staff of six professional researchers and an advisory panel of leading researchers, teachers, and parents. Its mission is to conduct programmatic research and to disseminate findings on methods of teaching braille, mobility, and orientation; improving the use of residual vision; and the uses of technology in improving the instruction of students with limited vision. In addition, the center is authorized to conduct an extramural research program at the level of three full-time researchers per year (plus support staff and expenses) and to engage three full-time research interns at the center each year.

Year 2000 Vignette—Research Reporting

It is now common for research reports in special education to include descriptors and related data in accordance with the new Marker Variable System (MVS). The MVS was developed through research reviews and expert advice to specify the variables most relevant to instruction and learning of exceptional students. Actually, the Marker Variable System for exceptional pupils is only marginally different from an MVS now used for all education. The MVS gives much attention to "situational" variables (descriptions of the school and class situation, the nature of any special intervention involved, the degree and integrity of implementation of the intervention, etc.), to variables relating to persons (students, teachers, classmates, and families), and to "effectiveness" variables identified through research. Editors of research journals in the field now require full adherence to the MVS system before publishing a research report.

Year 2000 Vignette—Monitoring Marginal Pupils

Schools now regularly perform "20/20" analyses or use some comparable procedure to monitor progress of pupils showing most and least progress in school learning. The 20/20 plan involves a review of every student whose rate of progress toward important school learning goals is below the 20th percentile and above the 80th percentile. What are the characteristics of these students? What programs appear to serve them well, and what could be improved? Through such analyses, every child who shows learning problems is identified and studied. The procedure begins not by labeling or classifying the child in traditional special education style, but by identifying students in terms of variables reflecting progress towards important school goals and objectives. Procedures are similar for high-achieving students, on the assumption that they too need adapted school programs to permit them to proceed at high rates in school learning.

Conclusion

The purpose here has been to summarize some of the general problems and issues which emerged from the broad review of special education research and practice summarized in this volume. By focusing on problems, we do not intend to convey the impression that only problems have emerged; there have been successes. Indeed, the story of special education is mainly positive and never more so than in recent decades. Under Public Law 94-142 all handicapped children have been guaranteed a right to free and appropriate education. This is a great moral victory, waiting now for fuller victory on the professional side. We have not yet come to the end of the story. There are many things yet to be investigated, understood, and improved. Indeed, we will never know in any final sense what forms of instruction are most appropriate for each child, and we have not yet penetrated fully the meaning and possibilities associated with the least restrictive environment principle. It is clear that the work of special educators can always be improved and that in some ways instruction will always be faulty. At present, we believe practices are especially faulty in terms of pupil classification and labeling and the highly segregated ways programs are structured. While taking satisfaction in what has been achieved, it is appropriate to note where gaps in knowledge exist and where services are less than optimal, and then move on to still better inquiries and programmatic improvements as readily as possible.

References

Arter, J. A., & Jenkins, J. R. (1979). Differential diagnosis-prescriptive teaching: a critical appraisal. *Review of Educational Research*, **49**, 517–555.

Gerber, M. M. (1987). Application of cognitive-behavioral training methods to teaching basic skills to mildly handicapped elementary school students. In M. C. Wang, M. C. Reynolds, & H. J. Walberg (Eds.), *The handbook of special education: Research and practice: Vol. 1. Learner characteristics and adaptive education* (pp. 167–184). Oxford, England: Pergamon Press.

Grossman, H. J. (Ed.). (1973). *Manual on terminology and classification in mental retardation.* Washington, DC: American Association on Mental Deficiency.

Heller, K. A., Holtzman, W. H. & Messick, S. (Eds.). (1982). *Placing children in special education: A strategy for equity.* Washington, DC: National Academy of Science Press.

Hobbs, N. (1975). *The futures of children.* San Francisco: Jossey Bass.

Hobbs, N. (1980). An ecologically oriented service-based system for the classification of handicapped children. In E. Salzinger, J. Antrobus, & J. Glick (Eds.), *The ecosystem of the "risk" child: Implications for the classification and intervention for disturbed and mentally retarded children* (pp. 271–290). New York: Academic Press.

Keogh, B. K. (1988). Learning disabilities: Diversity in search of order. In M. C. Wang, M. C. Reynolds, & H. J. Walberg (Eds.), *Handbook of special education: Research and practice: Vol. 2. Mildly handicapped conditions* (pp. 225–251). Oxford, England: Pergamon Press.

Larry P v. Riles. (1972). Civil Action N.C.-71-2270, 343 F Supp. 1306 (N.D. Calif.).

Ysseldyke, J., Thurlow, M., Graden, J., Wesson, C., Algozzine, B., & Deno, S. (1983, Spring). Generalization from five years of research on assessment and decision making: The University of Minnesota Institute. *Exceptional Education Quarterly*, **4**, 75–93.

Author Index

Page references refer to the bibliographical notes at the end of each chapter. References in brackets indicate material contained within the text.

Subject Index